THE COMPLEXITIES OF RACE

The Complexities of Race

Identity, Power, and Justice in an Evolving America

Edited by
Charmaine L. Wijeyesinghe

NEW YORK UNIVERSITY PRESS
New York

NEW YORK UNIVERSITY PRESS
New York
www.nyupress.org

© 2021 by New York University
All rights reserved

References to Internet websites (URLs) were accurate at the time of writing. Neither the author nor New York University Press is responsible for URLs that may have expired or changed since the manuscript was prepared.

Library of Congress Cataloging-in-Publication Data
Names: Wijeyesinghe, Charmaine, 1958– editor.
Title: The complexities of race : identity, power, and justice in an evolving America / edited by Charmaine L. Wijeyesinghe.
Description: New York : New York University Press, [2021] | bibliographical references and index.
Identifiers: LCCN 2021009014 | ISBN 9781479801404 (hardback) | ISBN 9781479801411 (paperback) | ISBN 9781479801398 (ebook) | ISBN 9781479801435 (ebook other)
Subjects: LCSH: Race awareness—United States. | Racism—United States. | Race discrimination—United States. | United States—Race relations.
Classification: LCC E184.A1 C5754 2021 | DDC 305.800973—dc23
LC record available at https://lccn.loc.gov/2021009014

New York University Press books are printed on acid-free paper, and their binding materials are chosen for strength and durability. We strive to use environmentally responsible suppliers and materials to the greatest extent possible in publishing our books.

Manufactured in the United States of America

10 9 8 7 6 5 4 3 2 1

Also available as an ebook

*This book is dedicated to Bailey W. Jackson III,
teacher, mentor, colleague, and friend whose work and wisdom
placed me on this path thirty-five years ago and have guided me
ever since*

CONTENTS

Introduction   1
  Charmaine L. Wijeyesinghe

1. The Day George Floyd Died: Change That Goes beyond Police Reform   13
  William E. Cross Jr.

2. Who Gets to Choose? Racial Identity and the Politics of Choice   36
  Marc P. Johnston-Guerrero

3. Naming the Problem: Epistemic Violence, Cognitive Maps, Relationships of Power, and Resistance in National Narratives about Belonging   56
  Nancy López

4. Queer and Trans* People of Color Worldmaking as Subject Formation and Identity Development   83
  Reginald A. Blockett and Kristen A. Renn

5. Race and Power in Transracial and Transnational Adoption: Historical Legacies, Current Issues, and Future Challenges   104
  JaeRan Kim

6. How Did Black Folks Become Indians? What Lived Experiences Say about Belonging, Culture, and Racial Mixture in Native America   126
  Robert Keith Collins

7. Racializing Faith: The Intersections of Racism and (White) Christian Hegemony   148
  Kameelah Mu'Min Rashad and D-L Stewart

8. The Dangers of Being Too Certain: How White Desires for Racial Innocence Hinder Meaningful Racial Justice Work   172
  Zak Foste

9. Islam and Hip Hop in Black America: Oral Tradition as
Critical Liberatory Praxis   192
  Amer F. Ahmed

10. Understanding and Responding to Resistance When
Intersectionality Is Utilized to Address Race, Racism,
and Racial Justice Work   216
  Charmaine L. Wijeyesinghe

11. Embracing the Complexities of Race, Racism, and
Social Justice in Changing Times   240
  Raechele L. Pope, Amy L. Reynolds, and Chazz Robinson

Acknowledgments   267

About the Editor   269

About the Contributors   271

Index   277

Introduction

CHARMAINE L. WIJEYESINGHE

Race and racism provide key but complex lenses through which critical events and issues of any moment can be more fully understood. These lenses have been constructed by generations of policies and practices based on race, power, and inequality, such as miscegenation laws and legislation limiting access to education, employment, and housing. They adapt and change as new issues, causes, and laws emerge. Applying the lenses of race and racism to historical and contemporary events unveils significant and oftentimes troubling areas that call for inquiry, discussion, and action. For example, the public health crisis caused by the COVID-19 pandemic revealed how the interconnections between politics, power, and policies created and supported inequality based on race, geography, and class, and fostered conditions that in part determined who was more likely to contract the virus, receive sufficient and timely care, and in many cases live or die. The notable absence of the words "race" and "racism" in a nearly seven-minute-long speech delivered by President Donald Trump on June 1, 2020, in response to nationwide protests in the wake of the killing of George Floyd by Minneapolis police officers, illustrated how race and racism can be front and center even when they are never named. The proposal of an item designed to ascertain the citizenship status of each resident of the United States by the Trump administration for the 2020 census calls out for the examination of how nationality, citizenship status, race, and racism transcend the level of individual identity and interpersonal interactions, and rise to the level of policies that affect entire groups of people. It is becoming more urgent to examine how the contested subjects of legitimacy, ancestry, identity, and inclusion complicate the experiences of Indigenous communities and people who are Multiracial or transracially and transnationally adopted. For these issues and many more, social media and technology facilitate connections that foster community building, coalitions, and racial justice as well as backlash, resistance, and the maintenance of white supremacy.

In the foundational volume *New Perspectives on Racial Identity Development: A Theoretical and Practical Anthology* (Wijeyesinghe and Jackson 2001, 2, emphasis added), Bailey Jackson and I noted that the "understanding of racial identity development is constantly evolving in response to social dynamics, ongoing research, and the *fluidity* of our understanding of both race and the experiences of racial groups in the United States." Thus, any book centering the topics of race, racism, and their complexities "provides a view of the particular moment in the ever-changing social context related to race and racial identity in the United States." In a sense, *new perspectives* will always be needed because the issues and forces of any period require, create, and feed them. In addition, the meaning and representation of the concepts that these perspectives draw upon, such as race, racial identity, racism, and racial justice, can be captured only momentarily within the changing social, cultural, political, and institutional landscapes of American life.

Several contemporary dynamics both call for and inform the reconsideration of race, racial identity, and racism by scholars, practitioners, and individuals and organizations involved in promoting racial justice. These factors include the increased focus on the interrelationship between social identities (such as race, gender, and ability) and systems of inequality (such as racism, sexism, and ableism) that are influenced by changing contexts (Barker 2016; Harris and Poon 2019); the emergence of intersectionality as a core framework for evaluating identity theories, manifestations of inequality, and strategies addressing social oppression (Collins and Bilge 2016; Jones and Abes 2013; Wijeyesinghe 2019); and the use of critical and poststructural perspectives to interrogate foundational principles of identity development and oppression (Abes, Jones, and Stewart 2019; Jones and Stewart 2016; Torres, Jones, and Renn 2009). In addition, forces beyond academic and theoretical arenas fuel discussions and debates about race, identity, and racism in social, cultural, and political spaces. The very different presidential terms of Barack Obama and Donald Trump, the emergence and increasing impact of the Black Lives Matter movement, the changing racial and ethnic demographics of the United States, the increased use of all types of social media, and many other events and issues are influencing the social, cultural, and political contexts that give meaning to the subjects of race, racial identity, and racism. As these contexts shift, it is essential that topics that draw meaning from race and racism, such as racial identity, racial solidarity, racial backlash, and racial equality, be understood as dynamic, intertwined concepts rather than static, isolated subjects. The complexities of race, racial identity, and racism are in full view through news and social media coverage of pressing topics, events, and policies. These reports, however, do not always center or fully investigate the complicated relationships between race, other social identities, and dimensions of power and privilege embedded within the stories deemed newsworthy. Even so, they create an environment that informs and reflects current values and narratives related to race, racial identity, and racial inequality.

Fluctuating social, cultural, and political dynamics also affect racial justice efforts over time in significant ways. For example, the civil rights movement catalyzed the emergence of racial identity models such as the formative Black identity theories of William E. Cross (1971) and Bailey W. Jackson (1976) and changes in laws pertaining to access to facilities, voting, and education. Such monumental moments and events can result from social activism that spans years or from pivotal moments that, as Cross (1971, 17) once described, "slip by or even shatter" our understanding of self, the conditions of socially oppressed groups, and social systems. Multiple incidents in 2020 provided some of these shattering moments. During that time Americans of all races took to the streets of US cities and towns to protest police brutality and systemic racism in the wake of the killings of George Floyd, Breonna Taylor, Ahmaud Arbery, and other Black and Brown people. These murders and the resulting social activism affected policies (such as police protocols), culture and history (such as the removal of flags and statues related to the Confederacy), and politics (such as the campaign rhetoric of the 2020 presidential election). At the personal level, sequential events or single devastating ones can cause people to consider the roles that race and racism play in their own lives and sense of identity. The *New York Times* (2020) bestseller list posted on June 21, 2020 (reflecting sales for the week ending June 6), noted that the five titles topping the combined print and e-book nonfiction sales were, in descending order, *White Fragility* (DiAngelo

2018), *So You Want to Talk about Race* (Oluo 2019), *How to Be an Antiracist* (Kendi 2019), *Me and White Supremacy* (Saad 2020), and *The New Jim Crow* (Alexander 2012). The top five picture books for children on that list also addressed issues of diversity or race.

It is in these evolving contexts and possibilities for change that the chapters in this volume provide new and detailed snapshots of the diverse and complicated ways that race, racism, racial identity, and racial justice are represented, experienced, and addressed in America. A central premise of the book is that we can gain a fuller analysis of some of the most pressing and contested issues by focusing on the intricate, multileveled roles that race and racism play in modern cultural, social, and political realms. In turn, broader understandings of race and identity are revealed when we examine the context created by these issues. Drawing from historical and contemporary literature, research studies, national surveys, media examples, and narrative or ethnographic sources, the contributors explore modern perspectives, policies, and debates where race and racism are present in significant ways. Chapters are grounded in theoretical, historical, and (where appropriate) legal analysis; however, these areas provide the backdrop for the central investigation of how race and racism inform contemporary and emerging issues and dynamics. Authors use multiple specific examples and accessible language to expand our understanding of questions such as the following:

- How do systemic power and inequality influence how race, racial identity, and racism are portrayed, understood, and addressed in American life?
- In what ways do the experiences of people and groups previously overlooked in discussions of race and identity inform, challenge, and even contradict socially constructed narratives, practices, and policies that often confer community, belonging, and sense of personal identity?
- What are the benefits and drawbacks of applying a more expansive, intersectional perspective to race, identity, racism, and racial justice?
- How does the intentional conflation of race with concepts such as nationality, religion, and culture support multiple forms of systemic oppression?
- How can knowledge (derived from many sources) and social action addressing racial inequality transcend the immediate moment and remain relevant across time and space?

While this book does not center individual identity formation, it expands the understanding of socially constructed identities by adopting a lens of "relational power" (Hancock 2016, 107). Thus, in the chapters that follow, racial identity is considered in the context of interconnected systems of inequality that are embedded in the environments where all social identities are formed and experienced (Collins and Bilge 2016; Wijeyesinghe and Jones 2019). Multiple chapters address the intersections of racism with other systems of oppression, thus advancing the understanding of inequality based on race *and* economic position, sexual orientation, nationality, gender, faith, and other social identities, and the promises and challenges of adopting and implementing an intersectional orientation to race, racism, and racial justice work.

While they investigate diverse topics and draw on an array of sources, the contributors and the chapters share core themes and assumptions:

- Modern dynamics related to race, racial identity, racism, and racial justice are informed by roots that run deep into the past.
- The ways that race, identity, and racism are understood and conceptualized are affected by multiple evolving systems of inequality.
- Race and racism influence culture, politics, policies, and group dynamics even when their presence and impact are unacknowledged, unnamed, discounted, or denied in dominant narratives.
- People of Color, including individuals with other marginalized identities, hold the power to name their experiences, and these experiences yield new, valid, and relevant knowledge about identity, systems of oppression, and the nature of the world.
- Resistance to new knowledge and efforts to address inequality can be used to inform strategies for coalition building and social justice work.

Before turning to a description of the chapters, I offer a brief note about language, form, and usage. In discussing the complexities of race, identity, racism, and racial justice, the contributors were often required to adopt and wrestle with the language, concepts, and structures used in research, theory making, policy, and practices in these areas. Because language and images are complex and contested (Johnston-Guerrero and Wijeyesinghe, 2021), as volume editor I did not request that authors adopt a singular or common way of representing words or subjects. Thus, readers will notice diversity in terminology and grammatical usage and form (such as the use of capital or lowercase letters in words pertaining to racial groups) across chapters. As much as possible, the form and vocabulary that appear in each chapter are reflected in their summaries provided next. Some terms will be familiar and others may feel more novel, mirroring how, at any given moment, language and knowledge both adopt and stretch the boundaries of what is known and used.

Many chapters in this volume highlight contemporary issues related to race, racial identity, racism, and racial justice movements. As noted earlier, these issues arise and draw meaning from centuries of racial inequality in America. In chapter 1, William E. Cross Jr. illustrates how race has been intertwined with class across waves of US history, and how social forces created the conditions that connect the murders of black people by police and the deaths of economically disadvantaged whites caused by alcohol, drugs, and suicide. Citing examples of inequitable educational opportunity, racial violence, residential segregation, and discrimination in programs, the chapter highlights how racial capital resulted in the systematic favoring of white wealth and well-being. However, Cross highlights how even under conditions of severe oppression, black people developed mechanisms that promoted education, community, and artistic expression. After illustrating how white alienation from black people feeds cultural sociopathy and challenges coalitions between economically disenfranchised whites and black and brown people, the author outlines a call for broad-based changes needed to address systematic racial and economic inequalities that are supported by socially constructed conditions.

In chapter 2, Marc P. Johnston-Guerrero engages the topics of racial identity, socially constructed racial categories, and dynamics of power and oppression to explore the question, If race is a choice, who gets to choose? Drawing on the literature from multiple disciplines, the chapter highlights various "rules" related to race, which are then considered in the context of three contemporary topics: the increased presence and impact of Multiracial people and people who can be considered racially ambiguous, the rise in popularity of commercial DNA testing, and the impact of social media on racial identity and connections within and between racial communities. Topics such as passing, colorism, racial fraud and authenticity, and internal choice versus external ascription of racial identity are woven into the chapter. Johnston-Guerrero concludes by offering several recommendations for addressing racial identity and choice in evolving political and social contexts.

Nancy López investigates several complex and interrelated systems that conflate race and nationality in data collection, popular discourse, policies, and social justice efforts in chapter 3. Using examples drawn from autoethnographic accounts, research studies, census documents, and legal opinions, the chapter reveals how the ontological and analytical difference between race and nation are often flattened and used to construct narratives of who belongs and who is considered the "other." Applying critical race theory, intersectionality, and settler colonialism frameworks, López illustrates how attending to nation *and* race unveils the interconnected dynamics of difference, power, inequality, and discrimination in the US body politic. Drawing guidance from United Nations statements on race over several years, the author offers visions for dismantling racism and oppression based on flawed connections between race, ethnicity, citizenship, and belonging.

In chapter 4, Reginald A. Blockett and Kristen A. Renn use interdisciplinary approaches to examine the theoretical and lived realities of queer and trans* people of color (QTPOC). Highlighting the subjects of identity performance, language, and legibility, the chapter reveals the sociocultural experiences that racial, gender, and sexual minorities contend with as they thrive and survive in the current US sociopolitical state. After examining select theories of racial and sexual orientation identity, Blockett and Renn propose the frame of Queer of Color Worldmaking as the basis of understanding QTPOC experiences. Through their analysis, the contributors address pressing questions such as, What would it mean to queer race? In what ways are race and racism constructed by gender and sexuality? How does heteropatriarchy work hand in hand with white supremacy to dictate identity formation for QTPOC? And how might the frame of Queer of Color Worldmaking inform the understanding of identity in the future?

JaeRan Kim explores how power and privilege based on race, gender, economics, and disability shape the narrative of what is "in the best interest of the child" within the intimate sphere of family making through transracial adoption in chapter 5. Context for contemporary issues is provided through an overview of the history of transracial and transnational adoption that includes programs such as the Orphan Trains, Indian boarding schools, and adoption through foster care and their impact on immigrant, Indigenous, Black, and transnationally adopted children. Various ways that communities of color resisted the racism inherent in foster care and adoption systems during each historical era are also discussed. After examining how transracial adoptees navigate and negotiate their identities, Kim offers a framework of transracial adoption justice that centers race, power, and the experiences, needs, and voices of transracial adoptees.

In chapter 6, Robert Keith Collins applies a person-centered ethnographic approach to examine how African cultural change and racial mixture in Native American communities contributed to new definitions of being and belonging and the relationship these definitions share with historical and contemporary race-making practices in the United States. Drawing on life histories and anthropological and historical records, the chapter traces changing racial attitudes among Native Americans toward African populations living among them as citizens and slaves, the relationship between African cultural change and sense of belonging, and manifestations of Native American racism. Collins concludes by highlighting how all of these areas influence historical and future understandings of the dynamics of African and Native American racial mixture and African-Native American self-understanding and experiences of belonging within Native America.

In chapter 7, Kameelah Mu'Min Rashad and D-L Stewart explore the intersection of multiple structures of oppression on the self-perceptions, experiences, and treatment of Religiously Minoritized People of Color (RMPOC). The chapter examines the factors influencing the increased awareness of diverse religious groups, and how racism, colorism, settler colonialism, and Christian hegemony create assumptions and stereotypes based on race, color, and faith. Drawing on narratives, research, and policies, the authors illustrate the personal, cultural, and societal impact of these beliefs, and how they are embedded in policies that discriminate against RMPOC and representations of belonging, kinship, and community. Rashad and Stewart offer strategies for individual RMPOC, their communities, other groups of faith, and the larger society to create change and promote healing.

In chapter 8, Zak Foste draws on the literature; his scholarship, teaching, and experiences with students in service-learning settings; and his personal journey to ground and illuminate the concept of white innocence, defined as the desire by whites to present themselves as morally good and racially enlightened. The chapter examines behaviors and attitudes that reflect white innocence and how it is supported by the racial isolation of white people, the lack of historical connection to centuries of white privilege and supremacy, and the surface-level assessment of diversity-related efforts. After discussing the consequences of white people's investments in innocence for communities of color and coalitions working for racial justice, Foste offers strategies that might challenge and support white people to divest from their desires for goodness and engage in sustained critical reflection about their personal complicity in white supremacy.

In chapter 9, Amer F. Ahmed explores the significant connections and interplay between Islam, Black cultural expression, rap, and Hip Hop. Drawing on the literature, the work and words of historical figures and rap and Hip Hop artists and activists, and the author's own personal and professional narratives, the chapter highlights the infusion of Islamic ideology and knowledge into Hip Hop. Through the frames of public and hidden discourse, Ahmed illuminates how rap and Hip Hop inform and draw meaning from Black Americans' resistance to oppression, as well as other global freedom movements. The chapter applies an intersectional lens to multiple levels of inquiry, and to the subjects of identity, intergroup dynamics, and systemic inequality. Ahmed concludes with recommendations for how Hip Hop can be used in critical, liberatory pedagogy and practice.

Charmaine L. Wijeyesinghe examines the nature and sources of resistance when intersectionality is used in educational programs, coalition building, and social justice work related to race, racial identity, and racism in chapter 10. After reviewing several of intersectionality's tenets, the chapter presents examples of tensions that arise when intersectionality is used to explore individual experiences of race, interconnections between racism and other forms of oppressions, experiences of groups other than Black women, and the content and dynamics of racial justice efforts. Wijeyesinghe then draws on historical and contemporary literature on intersectionality to offer responses to various concerns that often underlie resistance to intersectionality. The chapter concludes with reflections on how intersectionality can be used to understand race, racism, and racial justice even as it is subject to evolving social, political, and cultural dynamics.

In chapter 11, Raechele L. Pope, Amy L. Reynolds, and Chazz Robinson provide tools, strategies, and frameworks for individuals and groups pursuing social justice in challenging and evolving times. Weaving together themes from previous chapters, perspectives from foundational, visionary scholars, frameworks from critical disciplines, and strategies from new social movements, the authors offer both theoretical and practical direction for social justice practitioners. In the chapter, Pope, Reynolds, and Robinson touch on topics such as anti-Blackness, the permanence and impact of racism, racial and social identity development, and forces that support and challenge change efforts. The analysis and insights offered in the chapter can assist people engaged in social activism to understand the assumptions and techniques underlying their movements, as well as individuals considering how, when, and where they may begin their own journey as advocates and allies for racial justice.

The contributors represent a range of voices and perspectives. They include scholars who have studied race, identity, racism, and social justice for decades, as well as emerging researchers and practitioners at the forefront of examining evolving topics related to race, culture, and experiences of naming and belonging. Their exploration of pressing, current, and emerging issues offer the depth, information, and clarity needed to understand many of the questions left unanswered and issues avoided in current discussions of race, identity, and racism, whether those discussions occur in the classroom, in the boardroom, at the dining room table, or throughout the streets of America.

REFERENCES

Abes, Elisa S., Susan R. Jones, and D-L Stewart. 2019. *Rethinking College Student Development Using Critical Frameworks*. Sterling, VA: Stylus.

Alexander, Michelle. 2012. *The New Jim Crow: Mass Incarceration in the Age of Colorblindness*. New York: New Press.

Barker, Lori A., ed. 2016. *Obama on Our Minds: The Impact of Obama on the Psyche of America*. New York: Oxford University Press.

Collins, Patricia Hill, and Sirma Bilge. 2016. *Intersectionality*. Malden: Polity.

Cross, William E., Jr. 1971. "The Negro-to-Black Conversion Experience: Toward a Psychology of Black Liberation." *Black World* 20, no. 9 (July): 13–27.

DiAngelo, Robin. 2018. *White Fragility: Why It's So Hard for White People to Talk about Racism*. Boston: Beacon.

Hancock, Ange-Marie. 2016. *Intersectionality: An Intellectual History*. New York: Oxford University Press.

Harris, Jessica C., and OiYan A. Poon. 2019. "Critical Race Theory: Integrating Race and Racism in College Students' Development." In *Rethinking College Student Development Using Critical Frameworks*, edited by Elisa S. Abes, Susan R. Jones, and D-L Stewart, 17–25. Sterling, VA: Stylus.

Jackson, Bailey W., III. 1976. "The Function of a Theory of Black Identity Development in Achieving Relevance in Education for Black Students." Doctoral dissertation, University of Massachusetts, Amherst.

Johnston-Guerrero, Marc P., and Charmaine L. Wijeyesinghe. 2021. Preface to *Multiracial Experiences in Higher Education: Contesting Knowledge, Honoring Voice, and Innovating Practice*, edited by Marc P. Johnston-Guerrero and Charmaine L. Wijeyesinghe, xxi–xxviii. Sterling, VA: Stylus.

Jones, Susan R., and Elisa S. Abes. 2013. *Identity Development of College Students: Advancing Frameworks for Multiple Dimensions of Identity*. San Francisco: Jossey-Bass.

Jones, Susan R., and D-L Stewart. 2016. "Evolutions in Student Development Theory." In *Critical Perspectives on Student Development Theory: New Directions for Student Services*, number 154, edited by Elisa S. Abes, 17–28. San Francisco: Jossey-Bass.

Kendi, Ibram X. 2019. *How to Be an Antiracist*. New York: One World.

"*New York Times* Best Sellers: Combined Print and E-Book Nonfiction." 2020. *New York Times*, June 21.

Oluo, Ijeoma. 2019. *So You Want to Talk about Race*. New York: Seal.

Saad, Layla. 2020. *Me and White Supremacy: Combat Racism, Change the World, and Become a Good Ancestor*. Naperville: Sourcebooks.

Torres, Vasti, Susan R. Jones, and Kristen A. Renn. 2009. "Identity Development Theories in Student Affairs: Origins, Current Status, and New Approaches." *Journal of College Student Development* 50, no. 6 (November): 577–96.

Wijeyesinghe, Charmaine L. 2019. "Intersectionality and Student Development: Centering Power in the Process." In *Rethinking College Student Development Using*

Critical Frameworks, edited by Elisa S. Abes, Susan R. Jones, and D-L Stewart, 26–34. Sterling, VA: Stylus.

Wijeyesinghe, Charmaine L., and Bailey W. Jackson III, 2001. "Introduction." In *New Perspectives on Racial Identity Development: A Theoretical and Practical Anthology*, edited by Charmaine L. Wijeyesinghe and Bailey W. Jackson III, 1–7. New York: New York University Press.

Wijeyesinghe, Charmaine L., and Susan R. Jones. 2019. "Intersectionality, Identity, and Systems of Power and Inequality." In *Intersectionality and Higher Education: Theory, Research, and Praxis*, 2nd ed, edited by Donald Mitchell, Jakia Marie, and Tiffany L. Steele, 3–14. New York: Peter Lang.

1

The Day George Floyd Died

Change That Goes beyond Police Reform

WILLIAM E. CROSS JR.

Beginning in January 2020, the COVID-19 pandemic spread across the United States in two waves, the first between January and late spring, the second from May until late summer 2020. On May 25, 2020, George Floyd, an African American, was killed during an altercation with police that, after the fact, did not seem to warrant the use of lethal force, as the dispute involved whether a twenty-dollar bill was counterfeit. Floyd's death was recorded on cell phones by bystanders, which when shared on social media, became a flash point for the ongoing Black Lives Matter social movement (BLMsm). The BLMsm seeks to address police brutality as well as a broader concern for the well-being of working-class black/brown men and women. In one narrative (Shiller 2018), the failure to address the massive unemployment and underemployment of black people, the funneling of black people into the prison-industrial complex, and the nonchalance exhibited in police killings of black people are captured by the concept *disposability*. Disposability speaks to social blight produced when deindustrialization results in massive unemployment for which an inadequate social safety net does not protect workers and their families. One can make the case that in the context of BLMsm, disposability has become racialized, as when it is stressed that blacks accounted for 70 percent of the COVID-19–related deaths in the city of Chicago (Farley et al. 2020), a pattern replicated across the nation (Tai et al. 2020). Such a racialized analysis makes invisible the fact that the vast majority of working-class and poor people in the United States are, in fact, white.

As deindustrialization and the disposability of their labor engulfed working-class white communities, the same kind of social blight and family structure deterioration, once thought unique and commonplace to black and brown inner-city communities, overwhelmed once dynamic and healthy white working-class communities (Putnam 2016; Silva 2019). Thus, on the exact same day George Floyd was murdered, scores of mostly white working-class people died from what Anne Case and Angus Deaton (2020) term *deaths of despair*—mortality caused by alcoholism, drug overdose, or suicide. As the COVID-19 pandemic showed, undereducated working-class Americans—regardless of race, gender, or other social identity—are treated as a caste in that they must put together a living from employment that was once the province of people of color and immigrants—that is, jobs paying at or even below the federal minimum wage with no benefits.

This work will explore the connection between racism and classism. The aim is not another tired harangue against capitalism per se, but to point out the need for increased taxation, antitrust regulation, and construction of a social safety net in the tradition of the New Deal and the GI Bill, where health care is considered a human right and displaced workers are supported during economic transitions, dislocations, and disruptions. If the social movement triggered by the murder of George Floyd and others ultimately results solely in police reform, as opposed to more systemic change, the overall quality of life for black people will not change and police killings will probably persist. The BLMsm in conjunction with the COVID-19 pandemic has revealed the interconnectedness of economic forces underpinning the challenges faced by both black and white working-class communities, and thus the complex, historical connections between race and economic position and between racism and classism.

This chapter first offers a context-setting discussion of the treatment of black people from a historical perspective, which sets the stage for the murder of George Floyd, Breonna Taylor, Layleen Polanco, and others at the hands of the police and correctional workers, and then shows how Floyd's murder—positioned alongside deaths of despair of whites—reveals the need for broad-based systemic change that will address disparities based on race, level of education, and economic position.

Emancipation

During slavery, the captive Africans compared the profiles of common white people with those of white elites—the plantation owners—and, at the end of slavery, the once captive Africans started a *social movement* for education (Spencer et al. 2003). They recognized that a fundamental difference separating the elites from commoners was literacy. That is, the ex-slaves exhibited the characteristics of a model minority, long before that term found usage in contemporary parlance. When the demands of ex-slaves were combined with resources and help from those friendly to their cause, what became achievable was incredible. Under Union Army General Nathaniel P. Banks, New Orleans and the state of Louisiana established black schools throughout the state (Du Bois 1935). Under the threat of closure, the ex-slaves produced a thirty-foot-long petition showing the "marks" of ten thousand ex-slaves (Du Bois 1935, 644). The free men and women understood that education led to literacy, which when met with opportunity, resulted in personal and community uplift. Had the black educational thrust been allowed to flower, black people would have institutionalized K-12 education throughout the South. Startling educational success of black youth was evident early on, as recorded in the educational histories of William Pickens (1991) and Lucile Buchanan (McLean 2018), each born to parents who were once slaves, spoke Ebonics, and were illiterate. Pickens progressed from rural schools in the South to the halls of ivy at Yale, where he graduated Phi Beta Kappa in 1904 having mastered multiple European languages. Having fulfilled all the requirements for an undergraduate degree from the University of Colorado in 1918, Lucile Buchanan was not allowed to publicly accept her diploma, nor be pictured in the yearbook. Nevertheless, she excelled.

It is important to stress that the history of slavery shows that the captive Africans were knowledgeable about and responsible for every facet of building, maintaining, and running a plantation. Contrary to historical myth, the concept of family was deeply embedded within the worldview and aspirations of Africans, as they crossed over into freedom (Cross 2021), and likewise they were very familiar with the importance of mother-child attachment and positive early childhood experiences (Cross 2021). Wilma King (2011) reports that on large plantations, blacks established what today would be called daycare or infant-child nurseries. At the end of slavery, blacks as a group exhibited behavior and a mindset of people involved in a social movement for change, which meant, ironically, that they were more, not less, prepared for the responsibilities of citizenship than members of the white working class, a fact that prompted this statement from the sociologist Guy Johnson:

> During the early years of freedom, the Negroes in this country have made remarkable progress. It would probably not be exaggerating to say that in educational and economic attainments the average Negro today is better qualified to discharge the duties of citizenship than were the masses of white men when they were granted the right of full and free manhood suffrage. (Johnson 1933)

Collusion between northern and southern politicians, including the cooperation of President Abraham Lincoln, allowed southern states back into the union, and rather than being imprisoned, the "new" leaders—former plantation owners and their companion elites—were allowed to carry out political realignment. Reconstruction was controlled by the very people who began the war in the first place. The South lost the war, but won the peace, at the expense of the former captive Africans. Rather than employ the former slaves and pay them a reasonable wage, the South reinvented slavery and found ways to make null and void the Fourteenth and Fifteenth Amendments, meant to codify black freedom. By the turn of the nineteenth century, the mass of black people were as poor in 1900 as they had been in 1865 (Logan 1954).

Becoming Urban and Identity Variation

President Woodrow Wilson, who, ironically, is viewed by some as an apostle of peace and international freedom, used his power on the home front to help Jim Crow spread across America. In the South it became common practice to lynch returning black World War I veterans, while they were still in uniform, a practice also recorded after World War II (Gergel 2019). Between 1900 and 1930, the Ku Klux Klan became the extralegal "army" of southern states, given license to butcher black people and, when necessary, to execute pogroms resulting in the mass expulsion of entire black communities, such as the Tulsa Massacre of 1921 in Oklahoma. Blacks responded by migrating in a mass to northern and western parts of the United States. Southern propaganda—depicting blacks as less than human and in need of civilization—was accepted as "fact" and inserted in educational materials for universities and K-12 education. Consequently, black migrants were met with white riots in New York, St. Louis, Chicago, Detroit, and elsewhere, forcing blacks into compressed, spatially segregated ghettos. Homel (2004) found that in Chicago in the 1940s, white immigrants lived in ghettos with twenty thousand humans per square mile, compared to black ghetto compression of ninety thousand humans per square mile.

At the turn of the nineteenth century, a realistic assessment of the everyday life of poor working-class black people saw their status change from enslavement to that of a caste, where the larger society was reticent to allow blacks to make a living through even the lowliest, backbreaking, filthy, dangerous tasks offered by emerging industries. For black maids, work involved constant wariness of the presence and behavior of white men in the household. It was an era when Darwin's "survival of the fittest" trope was translated by the new field of sociology into *social Darwinism*, depicting racial and ethnic groups in a battle for survival and giving birth to the ephemeral science known as eugenics, with its preoccupation for creating hierarchies of social worth through the ranking of racial and ethnic groups. Such was the nadir of nineteenth-century blackness (Logan 1954).

If the travails of slavery found expression in work songs, spirituals, and dance, post-emancipation experiences on chain gangs, the punishing fatigue of tenant farming, and the drudgery of washing and ironing other people's clothes, as well as the magic of intimacy and falling in love, found expression in a new genre—the blues. The blues did not cut corners, and to the ears of the middle class and elite was vulgar, unsophisticated, raw, and perhaps even socially dangerous in its casual acceptance of sexuality (Davis 1998). The lyrics often expressed profound intimacy as a natural fact of life, and while common laborers were drawn to its truth, others felt shame, indignation, and embarrassment. A new technology—the recording of voice and music—played back on a record player priced so that even the poor could afford it, made overnight sensations of nineteenth-century blues singers Charley Patton, Lead Belly, and Blind Lemon Jefferson, among others. The mindset of male performers was encased in hypermasculinity; however, female blues singers in the early 1900s—in particular Ma Rainey, who is considered the Mother of Blues, and Bessie Smith—broached sexual diversity, including homosexuality (Davis 1998; Rabaka 2012).

The blues was poetry, psychology, and theater braided into a single performance and made accessible to blacks in the North and South through LP recordings. Artistic members of the black middle class, having traveled to Africa, the Middle East, France, and, especially, Germany, returned to America as the New Negro—thoroughly intoxicated by the philosophical fusion of enlightenment and romanticism—and ready to forge a Harlem Renaissance. Although they avoided abject assimilationism, a European aesthetic guided most of their artistic productions, be they paintings, music, literature, or drama. Several individuals, including Paul Laurence Dunbar, Zora Neale Hurston, and Langston Hughes, successfully synthesized as foundational to their art a worldview drawn from lower-class black life. In her text on black female blue singers, Angela Davis (1998) uncovered an instance of this conflict that reads like a script from a comedic performance. The record label Black Swan promoted itself as authentically black, yet when the famous and established blues singer Bessie Smith auditioned, "she was rejected because of her grassroots sound" (Davis 1998, 152). The company's board of directors, consisting of prominent members of the black middle class, selected Ethel Waters over Bessie Smith because Waters's "style seemed more compatible with popular white singers of the day" (Davis 1998, 153). This crash of vision and aesthetics anticipated by eighty years the way Hip Hop was first received. Nonetheless, the classic blues and the history of the New Negro and the Harlem Renaissance must be credited in moving sexual diversity from complete invisibility to at least the fringes of any discourse on black identity. It opened the door, ever so slightly, to identity complexity.

Education in the City

Black migration to the North overlapped with the period (circa 1880–1920) of intense immigration to the United States by Eastern European Jews, Irish, Italians, and others. Northern states rushed to expand the education system servicing white immigrants (new schools, increased hiring of teachers, etc.), while the first objective in the schooling for black children was how to erect and maintain underfunded, segregated schools. The historian Michael Homel (2004) found that beginning in 1915, a few years ahead of the 1919 Chicago Race Riot, schools meant to service black students were overwhelmed by the number of students seeking an education, resulting in unfathomable overcrowding. Blacks were provided horrible, unsanitary "temporary" box-like structures instead of new schools, and the most damaging policy, which held back black educational advancement, involved sending black students to school in shifts. For black adolescents this meant being in school for only half the day, resulting in high rates of truancy, an early iteration of the school-to-prison pipeline.

World War II

Ironically, World War II took some pressure off black urban poverty. Going into the war, the US armed forces were still segregated and as the bulk of white men were drafted, the availability of white employees to work in the war munition factories fell short (Kryder 2001). Eventually, black and brown men, along with women of all races, were hired, resulting in an economic respite for scores of black families. Between 1940 and the mid-1950s, the manufacturing sector of the American economy made it possible for many men without a college degree—black, brown, and white—to live a life approximating middle-class existence. While the manufacturing segment of the economy produced the illusion of racial progress among the working class, GIs returning from war in Europe and the Pacific were greeted with a GI Bill that provided support for new business startups; travel to Europe and elsewhere to pursue artistic and creative aspirations; nearly "free" college education; new home purchases with ridiculously low interest rates, and other benefits (Katznelson 2005).

The combination of a college education and a new home meant that white men who entered the war with the status of working class experienced social uplift within one decade following the armistice. Although the word "race" cannot be found in the GI legislation, Ira Katznelson (2005) discovered that all across the United States, the legislation became a program riddled with discrimination. For example, blacks were steered toward "trades" the training for which was not covered by the bill and, at the time, where employment was highly improbable, as unions blocked black membership. Discriminatory practices were particularly rife in southern states. For example, at one point thirteen municipalities in the state of Mississippi approved over three thousand applications for a GI-backed homeownership mortgage, only two of which were approved for black GIs (Katznelson 2005). President Franklin Roosevelt evidenced cowardice and did not intervene, and thus the New Deal and GI Bill evolved into massive affirmative action for whites, resulting in two trends: first, social uplift and explosive growth of the white middle class; and, second, racial isolation and economic and social stagnation for blacks (Perry 2020).

The Wealth Gap

As noted by the historian Walter Johnson (2020), not only do we live in a racial democracy, with special rights for white people, but we practice *racial capitalism*, where the system is rigged to promote white wealth and well-being, while excluding blacks and people of color from sharing in social uplift and social mobility. Over time, the success of racial democracy and racial capitalism has produced and maintained a divide between the well-being and wealth of whites as compared to blacks. For example, between the late 1940s and late 1960s, white wealth increased exponentially based on the phenomenal increasing value of white-owned homes. More recently, between 1992 and 2013, college-educated whites saw their wealth increase by 86 percent, while the wealth of college-educated blacks fell by 55 percent (Kent, Ricketts, and Boshara 2019). The matrix of statistics and facts presented in table 1.1 was gleaned from a profile of white privilege presented in the *New York Times* business section on June 10, 2020.

Each index in table 1.1 took years of accumulated privilege, which explains why *dismantling racism in the present is difficult to nearly impossible*, as one cannot wave a magic wand and change history. From the end of slavery up to the present, whites have been defined as deserving, and black people have been portrayed as undeserving. The countrywide system of *residential apartheid* resulted in spatially encased ghettos and,

Table 1.1. Measures of White Privilege

Category	White/Black Comparison
Pregnancy/birthing problems	Pregnancy complications and infant deaths both higher among blacks.
Median household income	White: $80,000 Black: $36,300
Six-year college graduation rate	White: 64.8% Black: 38.9%
Student loan debt after graduation	White: $20,000+ Black: $40,000+
Wage gap by the dollar	White men: 1.00 dollar Black men: 73 cents Black women: 64 cents
Retirement accounts	White: 60% have at least one such account Black: 34% have at least one account
Inheritance	White: 34% reported receiving Black: 9% reported receiving
Median inheritance	White: $56,000+ Black: $38,000+
Homeownership as of 1960	White: 72% Black: 47.5%
Minimum wage jobs	Blacks hold a high percentage of minimum wage jobs currently at $7.25 an hour, a rate not changed since 2009.
Overall net wealth	White: $171,000 (O'Hanlon 2017) Black: $17,150
Mortality	Data from US government reports, covering 1989–1995 and published in 1999, show non-Hispanic black adults exhibited a rate of mortality 2.3 times that of non-Hispanic whites ages 18 to 44, 1.75 times as high from ages 45 to 64, and 1.23 times as high for ages 65 and above.
Risk of high blood pressure	White: 34.9% Black: 46%
COVID-19 deaths by race	Based on their share of the population, the black mortality rate was twice as large as that for other groups; in some states the rate was three to four times larger.
Rate of incarceration by race	The Sentencing Project (2020) reports that blacks are incarcerated in state prisons at a rate five times that of whites, and in some states 10 times that of whites.
Police shootings	Blacks are 2.5 times more likely to be killed by the police than whites.

at the level of neighborhood, most white and black people do not interact. A 2013 study of the racial compositions of social networks showed whites interacting solely with other whites 75 percent of the time, while the rate for blacks interacting solely with other blacks was 65 percent (Cox, Navarro-Rivera, and Jones 2016). Sam Blair, a lifelong friend and white resident from Portland, Oregon, shared this observation in an email: "What I have always found ironic, is how warmly white America embraces blacks to entertain them with sports. Their skin color matters not at all, so long as you can dunk, hit 3 pointers, hit one out of the park, or average 10 yards each time you're handed the football." Yet the police are assigned the responsibility of keeping black and white communities separate, and the mere spotting of a black person in an otherwise white neighborhood is cause for alarm and action—including the use of deadly force.

Alienation and Dehumanization

In a short chapter such as this, it is difficult to capture the extent to which white society has, from the end of slavery to the present, exhibited nearly absolute levels of alienation and estrangement from black humanity. As a few examples will have to suffice, illustrating the results that this estrangement made possible:

1. The lynching of black men and women between 1875 and 1954, estimated to be over 4,500 (Dray 2003), many instances of which took on a carnival-like atmosphere; white children were often present in a macabre parenting scheme on how to control black people through the use of heinous acts of violence.
2. Medical experiments, the most famous of which was the Tuskegee syphilis study (Brandt 1978), where black men were infected with syphilis in order to study the phases of infection; even after penicillin was discovered as an effective treatment, the men were not informed or treated.
3. In 1949 the US Army Chemical Corps began to field-test aerosolized radiological weapons in Winnipeg, Minneapolis, and St. Louis. In each instance, poor and working-class neighborhoods were sprayed and in St. Louis black neighborhoods were targeted.

In time, black children showed increasing rates of radioactive strontium 90 in their teeth (Johnson 2020).
4. Finally, the chilling look of *nonchalance* on the face of police officer Derek Chauvin as he pressed his knee on the neck of George Floyd for over nine minutes during an arrest, resulting in Floyd's death, replicates to a T the look on the faces of members of lynching parties in photos taken of past lynchings (Dray 2003).

Added together, these events define not individual sociopathy but *cultural sociopathy*, as occurred among Germans during World War II and the United States in the nineteenth-century campaign to exterminate Native communities.

Deindustrialization—Phase One

More recently, capitalism has turned its back on black as well as white people with a high school education or less. Manufacturing is a vanishing part of the American economy and its disappearance is referenced as *deindustrialization*, unfolding in two phases, 1950–1970s and 1990 to the present (Case and Deaton 2020; Cross 2021). The first involved plant closures in urban centers, whose locations made them accessible to black and brown people, providing quality jobs with benefits and even union membership. Their wages helped sustain community life, made the formation of families affordable, and supported small businesses, social organizations, churches, and black arts. In the absence of opportunities for employment in the mainstream economy, black inner-city communities became the site of crime, gangsterism, and drug addiction, repeating history, when in the past working-class Irish, Jewish, and Italian immigrants turned to gangsterism for relief from the ravages of poverty (O'Kane 1992). Rather than focus on root causes, the media, government officials (as in the 1965 Moynihan report), and black and white scholars alike have often attacked the *psychological integrity of black men*, eventually culminating in the passage of draconian crime "prevention" legislation that over time resulted in the school-to-prison pipeline. Again, the office of the president—first President George H. W. Bush, and then Bill Clinton (the so-called soul brother president)—spearheaded legislation said to represent wars on poverty and crime, but ultimately crippling black and brown communities to the degree that they are nearly beyond repair.

Recall, during the nadir of the black experience (circa 1880–1920), when blacks were treated as a caste, the blues narrated every facet of this low point, as exemplified in titles such as "Jailhouse Blues," "Bad Luck Blues," "Blame It on the Blues," "Booze and Blues," "Broken Soul Blues," "Chain Gang Blues," and so forth (Davis 1998). Beginning in the late 1950s, deindustrialization hit black communities, causing *depression-like economic conditions* in practically every isolated black and brown residential community (i.e., ghettos) across the United States. People experienced a malaise and sense of disorientation, while their children hit the streets to squeeze a living from the underbelly of society, causing gang behavior to flourish (Payne 2006). Community leaders sought to mediate gang violence by sponsoring street corner musical events from which sprang Hip Hop, that, like the blues, "documented"—to borrow a phrase from Marvin Gaye—"what's going on." While Hip Hop would flourish, gang violence did not diminish, and figures important to the early evolution of Hip Hop, such as Tupac Shakur and Christopher Smalls (the Notorious B.I.G.), were murdered. Both gang behavior and street life were best explained by social class dynamics or the pathologies of unfettered capitalism, yet important social scientists—black and white—found favor in a culture of poverty trope that essentially blamed black people themselves, as if they controlled the industries that caused their unemployment (Moynihan 1965). It bears repeating that the economic conditions generating black and brown street life replicated how Jewish, Italian, and Irish gangs once used street life and crime to lay the foundation for their track up the ladder toward mainstream acceptance.

Unwittingly, social narratives linking black street life and gang behavior to presumed criminalistic proclivities of black and brown boys and men help feed the image of black males as amoral and even savage (Curry 2017). The mindset of presumptive black male criminality makes every cop—regardless of race—amazingly "prescient," such that spotting a black male brings to mind that he must be up to no good, even in the absence of actual criminal behavior. A "hunch" becomes the basis for applying force, meaning that even ordinary behavior becomes suspect and subject to aggressive police response. It is an expression of cultural or collective sociopathy and once it takes root, as in misogyny, anti-

Semitism, or racism, can last centuries. It led Derrick Bell to argue the case for the permanence of racism (Bell 1993).

Recall that the interface between the blues and the New Negro movement "danced" around themes of sexuality; its initial salute to hypermasculinity and outright misogyny are still evident most recently in the over-the-top collaboration between Tyga, G-Eazy, Tory Lanez, and the porn production company Vixen, where just about every porn actress under contract with Vixen pranced about the singers as they sang lewd lyrics. That said, Hip Hop has become progressive and intersectionally oriented, especially as it and the Black Lives Matters social movement (BLMsm) found common ground. Under the leadership of three black women—Patrisse Cullors, Opal Tometi, and Melina Abdullah—BLMsm has openly courted the participation of black and brown members of the LGBTQX+ communities, and in seeking to protect black and brown males from police harassment, they made Hip Hop culture more receptive to an intersectional worldview and identity complexity. Thus, while the New Negro movement and Harlem Renaissance placed sexuality at the outer edge of their public discourse, sexuality is refreshingly central to Hip Hop. The outpouring of activism following the George Floyd murder has been decidedly intersectional, drawing support from every segment of progressivism, inclusive of participation by the black transgender community, a subgroup subject to the most heinous transgressions by the police and elements within the black community itself (Ransom and Shanahan 2020).

Deindustrialization—Phase Two

The first phase of deindustrialization targeted black and brown workers, and residential segregation created the illusion that something peculiarly "racial" in nature had overtaken black and brown communities. However, starting around 1990, the second phase hit the rural areas of what is now called the Rust Belt, where plant locations were beyond the reach of black and brown people. Thus, the employee rosters were dominated by white people with a high school education or less. The amount of time for these rural white communities to become blighted was incredibly brief. White people found themselves being initiated as new members of the so-called underclass, a label once applied—almost exclusively—to inner-city residents of color. Even though whites were never slaves, the well-being of contemporary working-class whites has dropped to the point that they now share the pain of descendants of slaves living in urban centers (Cross 2021). Historically, not since the Coal Miners' War of 1891 have working-class whites been treated with such disdain by capital. The 1891 conflict started when the Tennessee coal miners' union objected to the owners' use of leased prison labor to break the strike. The owners also controlled most important political voices so that, rather than take a neutral stance, the state militia was pitted against the strikers. In breaking the coal miners' strike, Gatling guns capable of firing two hundred rounds per minute and bombs dropped from planes were used to break the will of the workers (Derickson 1988; Lewis 1987). Today, pink slips have replaced the guns and bombs.

Returning the focus to the present, interviews with white people—men and women—conducted by Jennifer Silva (2019) revealed that the inability to meet the everyday needs of loved ones leads to loss of self-esteem, and converts physiological stress into psychological stress, which makes one vulnerable to accepting various race-based conspiracy theories, with white males even leaning toward fantasies of doing violence to the *perceived* undeserving—racial minority groups, women, and the LGBTQX community. Time and again an interview ended with the vision of Donald Trump as a source of white hope. More so than men's narratives, white women's narratives rejected the social safety net in the belief that suffering is good for the soul. One respondent forged a sense of pride out of her ability to withstand suffering and emerge—theoretically—stronger. These respondents have suffered excruciating poverty, and their mind games ultimately fail to bring relief. In the aftermath of losing well-paying jobs with benefits, poor whites are experiencing a level of nihilism once thought highly improbable. Incredibly, white overdose deaths are 50 percent higher than for blacks, and 167 percent higher than for Hispanics (Berezow 2018).

Instead of finding ways to bring black and white workers and communities together, elites have found a way to convince whites that their pain is caused by "others"—meaning women, black and brown people, and immigrants as well as LGBTQX communities. Case and Deaton (2020) report that working-class white communities disproportionately suffer from deaths of despair—mortality caused by alcoholism, drug overdoses, and suicides. Case and Deaton's analysis of deaths of despair is used to explore their major finding: Any American educated at the level of high school or less—regardless of race, ethnicity, gender, or sexual orientation—is now, and likely will be well into the future, perceived and treated by capital as redundant, that is, not of concern, thus unaccounted for in plans moving forward. Case and Deaton continue by stressing that the economy is "working" primarily for people with a four-year college education, while deindustrialization, globalization, and artificial intelligence have crushed the need and value of the less educated. This helps explain that on the exact same day George Floyd was murdered, scores of working-class whites died deaths of despair. In point of fact, *black disposability and white despair are linked to the same social forces*: personal and societal disruptions caused by unemployment that is exacerbated by the absence of a social safety net designed to prevent working-class people from hitting rock bottom, during dramatic transitions in the political economy.

Social Safety Nets

Interestingly, other rich nations that have also gone through disruptions linked to deindustrialization show deaths of despair statistics radically lower than those recorded in the United States. Why? In large measure because their social safety nets prevent people from becoming desperate and thus overwhelmed by despair (Case and Deaton 2020; Porter 2020). Their social safety nets recognize health care as a human right and include programs providing resources for people that allow them to gain the skills and knowledge needed for jobs in the new economy. As such, they have avoided the pathologies of unfettered, unrestrained, and poorly regulated capitalism. Modern socially conscious and regulated capitalism is driven by other than shareholder profit and seeks to spread wealth and well-being not only among elites, but for commoners as well. Case and Deaton (2020), in addition to Eduardo Porter (2020), conclude that a nation that balances the imperatives of capitalism with the drive to make certain that people at the bottom are able to thrive, results in a more cohesive society that lifts the quality of life for everyone, commoners and elites alike. Working-class people are part and parcel of America's social capital and when treated with material and social respect, their children will seek inclusion, bringing a level of imagination and creativity that will bolster society as a whole and at all levels: education, entrepreneurship, the creative arts, transportation, business and industry, and so on.

As the New Deal and GI Bill demonstrated, a mixed economy is far better than race-based capitalism. So why is the US white working class in so much pain? Because of its own racism and being hung-up on individualism. Jennifer Silva (2020) showed that working-class whites think that they are personally responsible for pulling themselves up by their own bootstraps. Plus, they think that "welfare" is for the undeserving poor, such as people of color. Without union leadership to help them challenge capital, white working-class people elect politicians who have no intention of expanding the US social safety net. For example, had President Trump promoted a massive infrastructure bill rather than tax cuts, he might well have been reelected for three terms! As it is, Americans cannot get past the notion of health care as a human right, let alone envision the expansion of the safety net inclusive of health care. Capital has crushed their value as employees and silenced their imagination on what might be done. They have become zombie-like, without spirit or voice.

On the Same Day

Circling back to the events that began this chapter, on the same day police murdered George Floyd, scores of white working-class men and women died deaths of despair. These two calamities must be addressed simultaneously moving forward. This brings to light why Martin Luther King Jr. became the most dangerous leader in America when he pushed to represent black, brown, and white people through the Poor's People's March on Washington. He was seeking systemic change in America's form of capitalism. Social media's stark, graphic, detailed depiction of Floyd's murder and the infamous look of nonchalance on his killer's face, followed by news reports of the way working-class people—disproportionally people of color—were taking the biggest "hit" from COVID-19, combined to produce a state of being "woke" that reverberated across all fifty states and many international ports of call.

Should the BLM social movement change the mindset of the administration and Congress on the need to modify capitalism—not destroy it—we have a chance. The very rich will have to revisit how wealthy any one person should become, and individual Americans will have to disconnect from notions of who is worthy and who is not. Race is a social construction and illusion, but if enough people believe in it, it becomes reality, and change becomes improbable. Given the importance our society tends to place on racial-ethnic residential separation, it is not clear how we can even come together for a conversation. If and when we do, someone will call us communists for treating each other as human beings. It's the cost one pays for advocating the well-being of working-class people, white, black, or brown, and tying racism to oppression based on social class. In an article in the *New York Times*, Nikita Stewart (2020) asked whether black activists and progressives articulate a change agenda that is readily grasped and thus supported by the general public. During the writing of this work, people are fixated on police reform; the need for broader change is missing.

Substantive Change

George Floyd's murder (the dynamics and power of racism nurturing police brutality) and widespread deaths of despair (the dynamics and power of social class pathologies) reveal that both black and white people with a high school degree or less are the victims of three forms of devastating social forces that enter the body as psychological and physiological stress, producing high blood pressure and other deadly medical conditions:

1. *Deindustrialization.* This is the loss of jobs, wages, and benefits linked to employment. When job loss is experienced by a critical mass of community members, blight corrupts community organizations and various associations—including religious institutions—gutting their capacity to apply salve to social wounds. Otherwise "normal" people are forced to turn to street life for survival, but this defense against nihilism provides only temporary relief, and eventually hopelessness poisons the human spirit, mak-

ing drug addiction, divorce, alcoholism, domestic violence, child sexual abuse, crime, and suicide appear as rational rather than desperate choices.
2. *Porous and inadequate social safety net.* As noted above, Case and Deaton, as well as Porter, showed that other rich nations have curtailed deaths of despair primarily because they regulate capitalism such that the social safety net includes health care and resources (money) for individuals and families in the face of loss of employment. In addition, funds are provided that make it possible for a person to retool their skills and competencies, qualifying the person for the changing economy;
3. *Racism.* The double-edged sword. For blacks, it is the white knee on the neck, choking one's air passageway and causing death; for whites, it is the grand political illusion and scapegoat that prevents them from identifying the real source of their pain and agony: *systemic social class inequities.*

Incessant cases of police brutality have shifted the focus of change—understandably but myopically—toward police reform, leaving questions regarding social class inequalities relatively unaddressed. Here I argue that we must craft more systemic recommendations dealing with employment, health care, education, and prison reform. Failure to stress reparations is intentional, as will be explained below.

From here forward, the definitive statement about the two phases of deindustrialization can be traced to the research by Case and Deaton (2020). However, I independently came to the same conclusion about the phases by examining research on divorce, child abuse, family abuse, out-of-wedlock births, and so forth, as well as drug use and drug overdose rates (Cross 2021). In both my text and this chapter, I began with an eye toward making the case for black reparations. However, in the discovery of "white" pain and its linkage to undereducated whites, I realized that two groups—currently politically estranged from one another—share sources of pain, the origin for which points to the identical causes, meaning deindustrialization and the unemployment and community blight it causes. While I take full responsibility for what I write and advocate here, I am motivated by my interpretation of the writings of James Baldwin and Martin Luther King Jr., who argued that we must love white people—all people—even when the case can be made by others that their historical record of leading the nation is evidence of abject failure. In reading about deaths of despair and the interviews by Jennifer Silva, I perceive and receive the voices of undereducated white and black people fused into a common choir; the suggestions that follow are meant to provide relief to all working-class Americans.

1. *Jobs and a ten-year infrastructure plan.* American culture links meaning in life to steady employment. Rather than a guaranteed income, I recommend the creation of solid well-paying jobs with benefits for which working-class applicants with a high school degree or less qualify. The emphasis should be on construction jobs that do not require protracted additional education or training. Infrastructure should emphasize water purification, wi-fi support in rural America, highway-tunnel-bridge repair and construction, modern sanitation infrastructure, high-speed rail between key cities within each state, and revamping state colleges and K-12 infrastructure needs. These projects should be on a ten-year plan of revitalization.
2. *Health care.* Health care should be treated as a human right with a single payer system paid by the government.
3. *K-12 education.* Given that black, brown, and white working-class persons are employed with ten-year infrastructure projects described above and given health care support, their deeper sense of hope will be anchored by the belief that quality education—both K-12 and higher education—will help their children achieve middle-class social mobility. We must find ways to equalize the funding of education, from one school district versus another, as well as make possible high salaries for teachers and K-12 support staff. Educational support must include universal quality kindergarten, which is especially important for working and single-parent households.
4. *Higher education.* Deaths of despair among whites and survival through street life among black and brown people are prominent issues for anyone with a high school degree or less—regardless of race—while such factors are hardly discernible for those with a four-year college degree—again, regardless of race. Quality K-12 as

the norm must be followed by clearly affordable, if not free, higher education at public institutions. Likewise, private institutions must make Herculean efforts to attract white, black, and brown students whose parents are working-class. Educational institutions servicing Native American and black communities, including historically black colleges and universities, should be infused with support that results in their revitalization.

5. *Education and prisons.* Rethinking social support should focus on prisons for adolescents and young adult prisoners, especially first-time offenders who are not sociopathic or guilty of violent crimes. We can help them reclaim their humanity. The educational and retraining components of prisons should be expanded and refined and include training in mindfulness, as found in European prisons.
6. *Increase minimum wage.* Currently, the federal minimum wage is $7.25 and has not been revised since 2009. This should be raised to $15.00 across three years, with future increases tied to the cost of living index.
7. *Corporate charters.* Pure capitalism is amoral, in that its only—and ironically legal—mission is to produce profits. Capitalism is not required to factor in the public interest when making decisions to pollute, sell products that kill or create addicts, exploit its workers, or move offshore to avoid paying taxes into the system that feeds it. There is a movement toward "G" Corps (Sifonis and Goldberg 1996), which are voluntary so far, but promise to consider overall public welfare in making decisions. Corporate charters, which are granted by the state, should be revoked if the corporation fails to act in the overall interest of society, rather than its own sole motive for profit. Profit is good, but if it's the only consideration, guess who gets messed over? Everyone else.
8. *Monitoring.* Recall that the GI Bill never mentioned race, but nevertheless it became racialized in its administration. Consequently, careful monitoring by an inspector general, who has the authority to take meaningful action, is essential. Monitoring must start at the very beginning and continue to the end of every project.

Even if white elites support the revamping of the safety net, racism and police brutality will continue, because the police are caught between a rock and a hard place. Being wary of black people and people of color, in general, is too much a part of their worldview. Derrick Bell's (1992) conclusion about the permanence of racism is probably accurate. America has made too much of a social investment in the hatred of blacks to ever give it up. However, reconstructing the social safety net can provide much-needed relief to black people in particular, and working-class and poor people in general. Implementation of the revitalization plans described above may ease the pressure on all communities, creating the *social space* within which race and discrimination can be discussed without any of the key actors being distracted by health care, rent, and the education of their children. In effect, expansion of "democratic" capitalism, if achieved, may well facilitate democratic democracy. The street protests are speaking truth to power. Now the question becomes, Will a majority of elites throw their weight and influence behind the revamping of the safety net and reinvestment spread across all fifty states?

REFERENCES

Bell, Derrick. 1993. "The Permanence of Racism." *Southwestern University Law Review* 22: 1103–4.

Berezow, Alex. 2018. "White Overdose Deaths 50% Higher Than Blacks, 167% Higher Than Hispanics." American Council on Science and Health blog, April 5. www.acsh.org.

Brandt, Allan M. 1978. "Racism and Research: The Case of the Tuskegee Syphilis Study." *Hastings Center Report* 8, no. 6 (December): 21–29.

Case, Anne, and Angus Deaton. 2020. *Deaths of Despair and the Future of Capitalism*. Princeton: Princeton University Press.

Cox, Daniel, Juhem Navarro-Rivera, and Robert P. Jones. 2016. *Race, Religion, and Political Affiliation of Americans' Core Social Networks*. Washington, DC: Public Religion Research Institute.

Cross, William E. 2021. *Black Identity Viewed from a Barber's Chair: Nigrescence and Eudaimonia*. Philadelphia: Temple University Press.

Curry, Tommy J. 2017. *The Man-Not: Race, Class, Genre, and the Dilemmas of Black Manhood*. Philadelphia: Temple University Press.

Davis, Angela Y. 1998. *Blues Legacies and Black Feminism: Gertrude Ma Rainey, Bessie Smith, and Billie Holiday*. New York: Pantheon.

Derickson, Alan. 1988. *Workers' Health, Workers' Democracy: The Western Miners' Struggle, 1891–1925*. Ithaca: Cornell University Press.

Dray, Philip. 2003. *At the Hands of Persons Unknown: The Lynching of Black America*. New York: Modern Library.

Du Bois, W. E. B. 1935. *Black Reconstruction: An Essay toward a History of the Part Which Black Folk Played in the Attempt to Reconstruct Democracy in America, 1860–1880*. New York: Harcourt, Brace.

Farley, John H., Jeffrey Hines, Nita K. Lee, Sandra E. Brooks, Navya Nair, Carol L. Brown, Kemi M. Doll, Ellen J. Sullivan, and Eloise Chapman-Davis. 2020. "Promoting Health Equity in the Era of COVID-19." *Gynecologic Oncology* 158, no. 1 (July): 25–31.

Gergel, Richard. 2019. *Unexampled Courage: The Blinding of Sgt. Isaac Woodard and the Awakening of President Harry S. Truman and Judge J. Waties Waring*. New York: Sarah Crichton.

Homel, Michael W. 2004. *Down from Equality: Black Chicagoans and the Public Schools, 1920–41*. Urbana: University of Illinois Press.

Johnson, Guy B. 1933. G. B. Johnson Papers, University of North Carolina, Folder 1252, Proposed Study of Negro Participation in Government and Civic Affairs in the South, dated December 2, 1933.

Johnson, Walter. 2020. *The Broken Heart of America: St. Louis and the Violent History of the United States*. New York: Basic Books.

Katznelson, Ira. 2005. *When Affirmative Action Was White: An Untold History of Racial Inequality in Twentieth-Century America*. New York: Norton.

Kent, Ana, Lowell Ricketts, and Ray Boshara. 2019. "What Wealth Inequality in America Looks Like: Key Facts & Figures." Federal Reserve Bank of St. Louis Open Vault Blog, August 14.

King, Wilma. 2011. *Stolen Childhood: Slave Youth in Nineteenth-Century America*. Bloomington: Indiana University Press.

Kryder, Daniel. 2001. *Divided Arsenal: Race and the American State during World War II*. New York: Cambridge University Press.

Lewis, Ronald L. 1987. *Black Coal Miners in America: Race, Class, and Community Conflict, 1780–1980*. Lexington: University Press of Kentucky.

Logan, Rayford Whittingham. 1954. *The Negro in American Life and Thought: The Nadir, 1877–1901*. New York: Dial.

McLean, Polly E. Bugros. 2018. *Remembering Lucile: A Virginia Family's Rise from Slavery and a Legacy Forged a Mile High*. Boulder: University Press of Colorado.

Moynihan, Daniel Patrick. 1965. *The Negro Family: The Case for National Action*. Report No. 31–33. Washington, DC: US Government Printing Office.

O'Hanlon, Michael E., ed. 2017. *Brookings Big Ideas for America*. Washington, DC: Brookings Institution Press.

O'Kane, James M. 1992. *The Crooked Ladder: Gangsters, Ethnicity, and the American Dream*. New York: Routledge.

Payne, Yasser Arafat. 2006. "'A Gangster and a Gentleman': How Street Life-Oriented, US Born African Men Negotiate Issues of Survival in Relation to Their Masculinity." *Men and Masculinities* 8, no. 3 (January): 288–97.

Perry, Andre M. 2020. *Know Your Price: Valuing Black Lives and Property in America's Black Cities*. Washington, DC: Brookings Institution Press.

Pickens, William. 1991. *The Autobiography of a "New Negro."* Blacks in the Diaspora. Enlarged ed. Bloomington: Indiana University Press.

Porter, Eduardo. 2020. *American Poison: How Racial Hostility Destroyed Our Promise.* New York: Knopf.

Putnam, Robert D. 2016. *Our Kids: The American Dream in Crisis.* New York: Simon and Schuster.

Rabaka, Reiland. 2012. *Hip Hop's Amnesia: From Blues and the Black Women's Club Movement to Rap and the Hip Hop Movement.* New York: Lexington.

Ransom, Jan, and Ed Shanahan. 2020. "17 Guards Face Discipline in Death of Rikers Inmate." *New York Times,* June 29, 31.

Sentencing Project. 2020. "Issues: Racial Disparity." www.sentencingproject.org.

Shiller, Jessica. 2018. "The Disposability of Baltimore's Black Communities: A Participatory Action Research Project on the Impact of School Closings." *Urban Review* 50, no. 1: 23–44.

Sifonis, John G., and Beverly Goldberg. 1996. *Corporations on a Tightrope: Balancing Leadership, Governance, and Technology in an Age of Complexity.* New York: Oxford University Press.

Silva, Jennifer. 2019. *We're Still Here: Pain and Politics in the Heart of America.* New York: Oxford University Press.

Spencer, Margaret Beale, William E. Cross Jr., Vinay Harpalani, and Tyhesha N. Goss. 2003. "Historical and Developmental Perspectives on Black Academic Achievement: Debunking the 'Acting White' Myth and Posing New Directions for Research." In *Surmounting All Odds: Education, Opportunity, and Society in the Millennium,* vol. 1, edited by Carol Camp Yeakey and Ronald D. Henderson, 273–304. Greenwich, CT: Information Age.

Stewart, Nikita. 2020. "Black Activists Welcome White Allies, But Wonder If They'll Stay." *New York Times,* June 27, 1.

Tai, Don Bambino Geno, Aditya Shah, Chyke A. Doubeni, Irene G. Sia, and Mark L. Wieland. 2020. "The Disproportionate Impact of COVID-19 on Racial and Ethnic Minorities in the United States." *Clinical Infectious Diseases* 72, no. 4: 703–6.

2

Who Gets to Choose?

Racial Identity and the Politics of Choice

MARC P. JOHNSTON-GUERRERO

The ability to choose one's racial identity has been a central theme in literature and theory related to multiracial people. Indeed, it is one of the "rights" in Maria Root's (1996) groundbreaking "Bill of Rights for Racially Mixed People" and is at the center of Charmaine Wijeyesinghe's (2001) foundational Factor Model of Multiracial Identity (FMMI). Many people of mixed heritage have taken this sense of agency to heart, choosing to racially identify differently across time and depending on the situation. Renn (2004) named this a "situational" pattern of mixed-race identity and found it to be prevalent among the young mixed-race college student participants in her path-paving, multi-institutional study. Aligning with the social science consensus and common phrasing that "race is a social construct," those who identify situationally, and therefore by choice, support the notion that race is fluid, malleable, and influenced by context.

Yet some people who exercise this right to choose their race—perhaps even situationally—are often judged as inauthentic at best, or as committing "ethnic fraud" at worst. Ethnic fraud has been conceptualized in relation to Native communities by noted Indigenous scholar Sandy Grande (2004, 108) as "the practice of claiming an Indian identity based on the recent discovery of real or imagined residuals of Indian blood in one's distant ancestry" and is particularly problematic when "such claims are opportunistically used to cash in on scholarships, set-aside programs, and other affirmative actions intended to correct centuries of unequal treatment." Questioning of fraudulent identity claims was highlighted by the media in two prominent cases: Rachel Dolezal, a former NAACP chapter president and Africana studies instructor who claimed to be Black; and Andrea Smith, a Native studies professor whose claims to Cherokee ancestry have been refuted repeatedly. More recently, two additional white scholars made headlines for their deceptive passing as Black: Jessica Krug, a former history professor at George Washington University, and CV Vitolo-Haddad, a PhD candidate at the University of Wisconsin. Unlike the individuals in these recent cases, who admitted to being impostors, Dolezal and Smith have held strong to their identity claims. For example, both women reportedly used DNA ancestry testing as a way to try to "prove" their rights to identify as Black or Native, respectively. The backlash to their identity claims made it apparent that there is no consensus on the rules of racial identification and that public perceptions of race, identity, and choice are complex.

In these high-profile cases of contested racial identity choices and many others that may not make it on the news, it becomes clear that there are rules of race that must be followed and that not everyone equally gets to choose their race. But what are these rules and how do we learn them? In this chapter, I engage issues of racial identity and the politics of choice, guided by the question, If race is a choice, who gets to choose?

The focus on race and choice in this chapter is not meant to erase heterogeneity and multiple identities within populations or the intersections of multiple systems of oppression spotlighting those identities. Instead, I employ the strategy Rachel Luft (2009, 101) named "strategic singularity" to focus on one dimension of differential power in order to advance larger efforts toward social justice. I aim to highlight the politics associated with choosing one's race, which is ultimately constrained by the categories provided by institutions that may or may not align with the naming practices preferred by communities and individuals themselves. Thus, the chapter addresses aspects of racial choice that transcend the experiences of individuals toward revealing how larger social forces related to power and privilege (e.g., racism, classism) influence the discussion of race as a choice and who gets to choose.

The Rules of Race: What Dictates How We (Know How to) Racially Identify

Throughout our lifetime—from birth to death certificates—we are faced with questions about racial identity, namely, "Who are you (racially)?"

While for some, this question could be answered simply, without much deliberation or any change across their lifespan. For many others, simple answers won't suffice, or their answers change repeatedly over time or depending on the situation. For example, many white individuals' exposure to racial identity questions mainly occurs when they have to fill out forms, since as the US norm, they are rarely asked about their background or racial identity. Here power (in being seen as the norm) influences a very basic level of individual life. Yet how do we know how to answer the race question? For this chapter, I borrow the language of "the rules of race" from sociologist Anthony Ocampo's (2016, 10) work documenting the racial ambiguity (both internally conceptualized and externally imposed) of many Filipino Americans who must navigate being categorized as either Asian (e.g., given the US Census Bureau classification) or Latino (e.g., given the legacy of Spanish colonization). Filipino Americans may at times assume the role of chameleons, playing in to people's rules about who counts as particular races, often in order to break those rules. Racial ambiguity can be used in ways to gain acceptance and belonging even if it goes against supposed rules.

As opposed to guidelines or criteria, *rules* signal that they are strict and should not be broken. For instance, the "one-drop rule," which in essence made anyone with a recognizable Black ancestor racially Black, was encoded into undeniably racist laws. Breaking this rule could result in dire consequences, from loss of community to imprisonment and even death (Davis 1991; Hobbs 2014). While the question of current adherence to the "one-drop rule" or other so-called laws of hypodescent (taking the identity of the lowest group within the US racial hierarchy) is up for debate (e.g., Khanna 2010; Bratter 2010), I use this example not to equate current-day racial rule-breaking with the life-or-death choices associated with racial passing for Black Americans during and after slavery, or to apply it to any and all racial groups, but to provide a rationale for our present rules of race and evidence that, yes, these rules can and do change over time.

We have different rules of race; that is clear. But what are these rules? Are they individually decided or universally applied to everyone? Are there caveats to individual or larger rules? Do they differ by group in terms of application or adherence? How are rules of race related to racism? These questions are posed here to get the reader thinking about what rules they have for how to racially identify others—and themselves. No matter how we answer those questions, my argument is that the rules aren't applied consistently. But more importantly, they aren't necessarily made transparent, thus continuing to mask racist power dynamics associated with the politics of choice. Yet underpinning these rules guiding racial identity choices are how we understand and frame race.

Framing Race to Understand Choice

How we define "race" relates to the extent we believe that it can be freely chosen. Race is often an amorphous concept, one that john a powell likened to gravity, stating, "Race is a little like gravity. We're all affected by it, but we don't really understand it" (Grossman n.d., para. 2). We tend to "do race" in a number of ways that are often difficult to articulate, but we know race when we see it (Moya and Markus 2010). But what is race? Here, I highlight various meanings of race that have been described and distinguished in the literature. Perhaps most compelling for theory development around racial identity is Kerry Ann Rockquemore, David Brunsma, and Daniel Delgado's (2009) argument that researchers must differentiate between (a) racial category, (b) racial identity, and (c) racial identification. A person might choose a particular racial category in a given situation for any number of reasons (most likely based on the constrained categorical choices offered), which may or may not align with their own understanding of their racial identity (how they name themselves racially). These two choices may or may not align with how others identify the individual racially (external identification). In theorizing that race should not be thought of in an all-encompassing metric, my colleagues and I (Johnston et al. 2014) further differentiated these varied meaning of race, using racial ascription (as opposed to identification, given the potential confusion with self-identification) to more adequately capture the external placement of racial identities onto others.

While this move to break down race in more nuanced ways seemed innovative, we were actually continuing a longer conversation about racial identity. For instance, Wijeyesinghe (2001) differentiated between several different racial concepts related to identity, including (a) racial ancestry, (b) chosen racial identity, (c) ascribed racial group membership, and (d) chosen racial group membership. Centering the "chosen" aspects of race that Wijeyesinghe offered, we can make an important distinction between individual identity choices and group membership choices, one that I believe tends to get lost in more recent discourse or debates on racial identity.

These various meanings of race and identity interact with our conceptualizations of race (Johnston-Guerrero 2016; Morning 2009), which then feed related beliefs about race, how we decide what race we are (or others are), and perhaps how fluid or malleable race can be. Based on in-depth interviews with a diverse group of college students on how they made meaning of race, I developed six classifications of beliefs about race that reflect underlying conceptualizations about what race is, how it works, or why it matters:

1. race as embodiment—how bodies get marked as belonging to certain races
2. race as power—how historical and contemporary forms of power and oppression (i.e., racism) create and maintain races
3. race as culture—how traditions, customs, or values are connected to racial groups
4. race as ancestry—how lineage or heritage inform racial grouping
5. race as concept—how one's mind creates race as something conceptual/ideological
6. race as identity—how individuals or groups claim race as an important identifier (Johnston-Guerrero 2016)

These meanings and conceptions constrain our thinking about racial "choices" yet are often unnamed. For instance, if our main way of approaching race is through biology and/or ancestry, we may privilege heritage/lineage (or perhaps DNA ancestry tests, though the next section will highlight limitations of these tests) over individuals' claims about who they are. An example would be if Rachel Dolezal's DNA ancestry results documented a substantial amount of "Sub-Saharan African" ancestry, those people privileging race as ancestry might be more willing to give her a pass. Their racial conceptualizations allow the choice to be made given evidence that meets criteria according to some unwritten rules of race—namely, that race is encoded in ancestry.

The conceptual influences outlined above interact in situations where readability (or legibility) is ambiguous or questioned. The various factors in Wijeyesinghe's (2001) FMMI are important influences on one's choice of racial identity, but are also entry points by which a person's chosen race could be questioned, potentially if any factor is out of alignment with socially acceptable rules of racial identity (as can often be the case for multiracial people). For example, misalignment could occur when one's racial ancestry does not match one's phenotype or physical appearance. Multiple frames influence how race is defined (by individuals and society/culture).

Three Contemporary Influences on Dynamics of Race and Racial Identity Choices

Many contemporary issues complicate the rules of race. In this section I center on three that I believe need more attention within the larger landscape of race and identity research. These influences are the increasing (a) presence of multiracial populations and racially fluid individuals, (b) popularity of DNA ancestry testing, and (c) pervasiveness of social media.

Increasing Presence of Multiracial and Racially Ambiguous Individuals

Focusing on mixed-heritage individuals and others who don't fit monoracially normative "rules of race," such as Filipino Americans (Ocampo 2016), transracial adoptees (Ashlee 2019), and even some "contested white" populations (e.g., Southwest Asian, Middle Eastern, and North African) (Mohajeri 2018), might help us to understand broad questions of racial identity and the politics of choice. By centering racially ambiguous and mixed-race identities as they relate to both research and popular culture, this section highlights influences on the politics of racial choices constrained by structural constraints and power dynamics.

There is no question that multiracial people—those individuals identifying with more than one racial group—are making their presence known. Instead of providing estimates of the growth of the populations, which can be critiqued for falling back into traps associated with racial essentialism (Osei-Kofi 2012), many have argued that the presence is not only due to growth in numbers of people, but in the changing contexts allowing for these identities to be fully embraced (Parker et al. 2015). This is especially true for Black Americans, who may be feeling the lessening grip of the one-drop rule, or perhaps white Americans letting go of white supremacist legacies of erasing their Black ancestors. Indeed, the US Census Bureau data between the years 2000 and 2010 demonstrated that the growth in all Americans identifying with "two or more races" increased from about 6.8 million to 9.0 million (Jones and Bullock 2012). Yet Nicholas Jones and Jungmiwha Bullock (2012, 1) also documented that "people who reported White as well as Black or African American . . . grew by over one million people, increasing by 134 percent." While this may be surprising, it is important to note that more Americans changed their racial identification choices on the census between 2000 and 2010 (approximately 9.8 million) than people who identified with two or more races in 2010 (Liebler et al. 2017). More attention is needed to understand this apparent racial fluidity that gets overlooked in how race is utilized in research and operationalized in popular discourse. Yet these numbers provide evidence that the growing number of multiracial Americans is likely not due solely to increases in births from interracial unions, but to the changing contexts that allow those who might have identified monoracially in 2000 to claim all of their racial backgrounds in 2010.

This changing context is highlighted by multiracial Americans who have spoken out about their racial identity *choices*. Two prominent examples are former President Barack Obama and the Duchess of Sussex Meghan Markle. Though much has been written about Obama and his racial identity (e.g., Hollinger 2014; Tesler and Sears 2010), more research is likely needed to understand the impact and legacy of his racial identification choices (e.g., Williams et al. 2014). Markle's race is an area of inquiry ripe for attention, especially given her popularity after joining (and then exiting) the British royal family.

Recounting some of her experiences related to her racial identity, Markle (as cited in Johnston-Guerrero and Ford 2020) famously shared a childhood experience in struggling to fill out the "race question" on a school form:

> There I was (my curly hair, my freckled face, my pale skin, my mixed race) looking down at these boxes, not wanting to mess up, but not knowing what to do. You could only choose one, but that would be to choose one parent over the other—and one half of myself over the other. My teacher told me to check the box for Caucasian. "Because that's how you look, Meghan." . . . When I went home that night, I told my dad what had happened. He said the words that have always stayed with me: "If that happens again, you draw your own box."

Markle's experience being forced to choose is a common theme in the literature on multiracial identity (Renn 2004; Wijeyesinghe 2001). Yet this vignette provides a clear example of how one develops one's rules of race, influenced by teachers' rules and parents' rules, which may actually conflict (Johnston-Guerrero and Ford 2020). Given Markle's fame, her individual racial identity choice and rationale have likely influenced how others view race.

A further example of changing context is the prime-time ABC network TV show *Mixed-ish* (2019), a prequel spin-off of the sitcom *Black-ish*, which has purposefully spotlighted multiracial identities and interracial relationships. The show surrounds the early family and school life of the *Black-ish* matriarch Rainbow "Bow" Johnson, played by Tracee Ellis Ross (another prominent biracial American, given her famous mother, singer Diana Ross), growing up in the 1980s. With its premier on September 24, 2019, the show mixed comedy with the real struggles surrounding interracial marriages and raising biracial children who have to navigate the Black-white binary so prevalent in school and even enforced by Bow's monoracial family members. Adding to the show's centering of the mixed experience is the use of the song "In the Mix" by mixed-identified superstar Mariah Carey as the show's theme song. As of this writing, the show completed its first season (twenty-two episodes) and is in the middle of its second season. One interesting note is that the show has been framed differently to perhaps reach various audiences. For instance, the brief synopsis on the show's IMDb.com web page does not mention mixed identity or navigating race at all. Instead, it states that the show "Follows Bow's parents, Paul and Alicia, who are forced to move from a hippie commune to the suburbs to better provide for their family after the dissolution of their cult."

In higher education specifically, there are increasing numbers of multiracial students entering US higher education (Johnston-Guerrero and Renn 2016). While individuals face questions about their racial identity on forms throughout childhood (like the Meghan Markle example above), the racial designations they choose on college applications may be the most prominent situation in which this choice has material consequences. The high-stakes nature of college applications (Renn 2004) lends itself to being an often stressful and anxiety-producing experience. And when there are misconceptions about affirmative action and how race may be used in holistic admissions reviews, students may find themselves participating in what political essayist Chauncey DeVega (2011, para. 10) called "the race hustle," with increasing suspicions of attempts to game and manipulate the college admissions process. For instance, in a *New York Times* story highlighting multiracial college students, Susan Saulny and Jacques Steinberg (2011, para. 8) argued that "the number of applicants who identify themselves as multiracial has mushroomed, adding another layer of anxiety, soul- (and family-tree-) searching and even gamesmanship to the process."

It is true that many mixed-heritage college students find themselves identifying differently depending on context and at least partially informed by ancestry (Johnston et al. 2014; Renn 2004). Yet should these choices and outcomes be viewed with suspicion? No matter what your answer is now, I want to point out that the ramifications of such identification choices extend beyond individuals to the realm of institutional diversity and related efforts. For instance, multiracial students can get exploited to assert different racial claims, including arguments during the 2013 US Supreme Court affirmative action case *Fisher v. University of Texas*, where Justices Roberts and Scalia used mixed-race students to question the legitimacy of all self-identification choices for tracking student diversity. Again, we see how racist power on multiple levels and from various directions impacts and constrains racial identity options outside of just individual choice.

When individuals are being questioned about the authenticity or validity of their racial identity choices, they may turn back to their rules of race and follow them. For many mixed-heritage college students, who may be seeking out specific answers to questions surrounding their racial identity, genetics has become a source of information to lend legitimacy to their choices (Daniel and Haddow 2010).

Increasing Popularity of DNA Ancestry Testing

There continues to be much debate about the relationship between race and biology and, specifically, genetics (Morning 2014). Some might suggest that the atrocities associated with the pseudoscientific eugenics movement and scientific racism are solely rooted in the past and have been debunked due to the evolving social and scientific consensus that race is a social construct. However, recent evidence confirms that both popular and college student perceptions of race and genetics continue to perpetuate ideas that races have underlying essences that are largely determined by biology (e.g., Dar-Nimrod and Heine 2011; Morning 2014).

In the case of college students, perhaps their beliefs are influenced by encounters with DNA testing on college campuses. For example, in February 2011 researchers at Cornell University launched a "Genetic Ancestry Project" where a random sample of two hundred undergraduates received DNA testing to learn about "their ancestors' human origins and migrations" (Ramanujan 2011, para. 3). Similarly, the "DNA Discussion Project" at West Chester University in Pennsylvania uses DNA ancestry testing to engage the campus in discussions of diversity (see Foeman 2012). Although project organizers claim that the testing encourages understanding of the social construction of race, others suggest that these DNA tests can actually reinforce college students' thinking of racial categories as biological given the technological results with racialized percentages for ancestry (e.g., "9 percent West African") (Harmon 2007). Indeed, a news story on the DNA Discussion Project highlighted one twenty-year-old white student's reaction to his DNA results that indicated "60 percent Southeast Asian" and that he "filled out a recent survey that asked for ethnicity, and he checked Asian for the first time" (Holmes 2013, para. 1).

This explicit racialization of ancestry is likely due to the potential markets the businesses behind the testing see as growth opportunities.

As the direct-to-consumer DNA ancestry testing companies find niche markets, they may be targeting particularly vulnerable populations. These include individuals who may not have access to family histories for any number of reasons, but in particular adoptees and descendants of enslaved Africans are two populations that companies may see as lucrative markets. I don't use this language of markets to downplay the real sense of connection that can come with these tests for individuals seeking answers to questions about their identity. I use it to remind readers that there are likely dangers in entrusting such personal information as our genomic code with for-profit companies that have other intentions than to help us find "genetic cousins" or feel affinity with current-day peoples and places based on ancient migrations.

It is important to note that the same companies promoting the ability to find one's lost heritage are also providing tests for white supremacists who try to assert their white/European "purity." A *New York Times* story highlights examples of white nationalists using DNA ancestry testing to try to "prove" the extent of their European-ness (Murphy 2019). At the heart of these efforts is their belief that "racial purity" actually exists in some biological sense despite a long history of debunking race as biological (American Anthropological Association 1998; Montagu 1964). Moreover, when the test results come back counter to their intended goals (e.g., a white supremacist having African ancestry), they often rationalize the results away by questioning the legitimacy of the tests in order to "repair" their identity (Panofsky and Donovan 2019). Here the power allowing some to differentially utilize evidence to support their racial identity claims is clearly associated with racism and the legacy of white supremacy.

No matter what DNA ancestry tests might say, or whether or not someone is "surprised" by the results, what one does with the results is the most intriguing area for further inquiry. For instance, my colleague Amanda Tachine served as the director of Native American student affairs at the University of Arizona. She shared with me examples of presumably white college students approaching her and her staff with a printout of DNA ancestry test results indicating a small percentage of "Native American" ancestry. The students would then ask, "What can I get for being Native American?" The tests are a flawed tool that one might use to confirm one's already established conceptions of race.

However, individuals from all backgrounds are increasingly sharing their DNA test results and reactions on social media.

Increasing Pervasiveness of Social Media

Sharing DNA testing results through social media is just one case of the increasing usage and utility of social media for racial identity expression and racial group connection. Individuals are increasingly contributing to what might be categorized as a potential genre of "reveals" of DNA ancestry test results made through social media platforms like YouTube. What is it about sharing these results that people find necessary, provocative, or intriguing? Perhaps sharing results is most interesting when they do not necessarily align with popular rules of race, or when individuals claim that they didn't need to pay someone to tell them what they already know. In any case, the social aspects of revealing one's DNA ancestry virtually builds upon more educational or reality entertainment such as popular TV shows like the Henry Louis Gates-hosted *Finding Your Roots* on PBS and TLC's *Who Do You Think You Are?* Yet the increase in prominence of these kinds of "reveals" is also likely due to the nature and ubiquity of social media as a whole.

There has been an influx of social media and expansion of social connections into digital and online environments (Baym 2015), which creates potential opportunities for beneficial exploration of racial identity online as well as manifestations of cyber-racism (Daniels 2009; Bliuc et al. 2018). Ana-Maria Bliuc et al. (2018, 76) defined cyber-racism as "any form of communication via electronic or digital media by groups or individuals which seeks to denigrate or discriminate against individuals (by denying equal rights, freedom and opportunities) or groups because of their race or ethnicity." Understanding this definition is important, as social media offer multiple opportunities for individuals to assert their claimed racial identities, yet with much potential for others to question, deny, or erase those choices.

Social media—also often referred to as social networking sites (SNS)—serve as public or semipublic displays of connection across multiple social groups through computer-mediated communication (boyd and Ellison 2007). Most social media collapse different types of social context (e.g., coworker, family, friend, acquaintance) into one common context for all social connections, in which all "friends" or connections see the same content a user posts to their profile (though users can also curate content for targeted audiences depending on the outlet). This collapse of social contexts in social media has implications for individuals sharing information with an actual audience that may be different from the imagined or intended audience (Marwick and boyd 2011). For instance, sharing one's identity reflections (e.g., after receiving DNA ancestry results) with family and close friends through Facebook feels different from a more public announcement through Twitter or YouTube. Yet, in any case, the online environment collapses social contexts, and individual users may lose control over how other users share their information and then how even more unintended audiences might post negative or damaging reactions. Such might have been the case for Rachel Dolezal, when social media reactions, largely through Twitter and the trending hashtag #AskRachel, mocked her belief in racial identity being solely based on one's looks and, thus, asked her to explain African American upbringing and cultural practices (Rosenbaum 2017).

Social media have literally become part of college students' everyday lives (Rowan-Kenyon and Alemán 2016; Gin et al. 2017), playing a vital role in how they connect with their peers and engage on campus (Junco 2014). Yet, despite the ubiquity of social media and their potential for connections and community building, users also have the potential to become increasingly siloed. As Manuel Castells (2001) argues, social media produce an increasingly limited experience of the world because individuals are able to filter out experiences or perspectives that conflict with their own. This filtering was famously illustrated around the 2016 US presidential election as Hillary Clinton supporters were truly shocked when Donald Trump won. Many people speculated that the contentious nature of the political race, particularly in relation to identity-related aggressions, led social media users to narrow their friend groups and, in essence, create a filter bubble or echo chamber of the world viewed through similarly minded individuals (Grimes 2017). What happens when these bubbles are increasingly segregated by race? How might this segregation limit opportunities to view race as a choice, or interrogate the rules underlying racial identification? Or within these segregated bubbles, might someone be able to intentionally curate their network to align with their chosen racial identity, offering some level of protection from identity policing?

The potential of curating one's social media to align with a chosen racial identity has both positive and negative manifestations. One positive aspect has been the ability to develop and create online and virtual communities. On Facebook, more groups and pages are forming around different identities that may disrupt the rules of race (e.g., specific communities like the Garifuna; see Oro 2019). A compelling example is the recent and ongoing push for multiethnic Latin* populations (see Salinas 2020) to be accurately counted on the US census. Organizing through Facebook (Latinas and Latinos of Mixed Ancestry [LOMA]), leaders such as Thomas Lopez, director of LOMA, have been advocating for census changes that would allow for the Hispanic ethnicity question to act more like the race question, in being able to "Mark one or more." Though LOMA is a project of the nonprofit Multiracial Americans of Southern California (MASC), much of its community building and organizing has occurred online, likely recognizing MASC's regional mission and need to expand its reach further. As institutions, communities, and individuals themselves are influenced by the far-reaching and systemic categories on the census, social media may be mitigating some of this influence when the census categories are deemed to not work for smaller communities with unique histories of racialization (López, this volume).

More negative consequences of social media curation include increasing issues of "digital blackface" through the use of Black emojis/GIFs/memes as well as white Instagram influencers posing as Black (also known as "blackfishing") (Jackson 2018) or even white Twitter users, like University of New Hampshire professor Craig Chapman, taking on Black identities (termed "identity tourism") (Nakamura 1995; Newton 2020). These examples take the Rachel Dolezal case to another level—perhaps some of those participating in digital blackface might even have felt emboldened by Dolezal's example. Lauren Jackson (2018, para. 7) highlighted the prominent example of Swedish model Emma Hallberg, who uses makeup, tanning, and hairstyles to flirt with Blackness, "though it is only incidental that Hallberg's presumed biraciality would render her black according to racial codes on American soil." Even if one denies that they are claiming to be "Black," their choices in how they represent themselves are clearly racialized. And they are using popular "rules" of race to increase their capital associated with racialized looks to garner further influence. Here, racist power differentials allow white people the ability to play with the rules of race for personal and professional gain. By curating both looks and likely other forms of cultural material, social media offer individuals more flexibility in choosing how to represent and build community around their racial identity, yet others may take advantage and exploit such opportunities.

Recommendations for Moving Forward

So how do we move forward with considering the politics of choice related to racial identity in ever-changing contexts? Here I highlight three specific recommendations and lines of inquiry that I believe can be broadly applied not just to "research and practice" but to our unending conversations and work around racial justice.

Naming the Rules

Name the rules you're following: What are your rules of race? Where did they come from? Are they widespread/common or narrowly tailored? Do you always follow them? How are they informed by social forces based on power and privilege and maintenance of the status quo? These types of questions are important for understanding the foundation for your answers to the question, "Who gets to choose?" and how we all have been socialized in various ways to answer that question from particular standpoints. Scholars of racism and racial identity broadly, and higher education scholars in particular, must explore further the perceptions of students, the general public, and educators about both racial identification choices and how to make sense of changing dynamics of identification when utilizing data, especially in light of affirmative action policies.

Rethinking Rules and Their Intersections

Think with and across intersections: How do our rules potentially look different when we consider different identities within racial groups? Are our rules for women the same for men or Trans and nonbinary people? Highlighting these potential differences might allow for interrupting rules of race and static notions of choice by exploring identity choices across other axes of difference (and their intersections with different interconnected systems of oppression). This question of "who gets to choose?" may be generative when we consider and compare various dimensions of identity/difference, especially since some identities are viewed as more controllable (and therefore might allow for more choice) than other identities viewed as more immutable. Further, what are the consequences of these choices and how might they look different across different intersections? This inquiry may be helpful for disrupting current discourse around "choosing" identity toward what might be more appropriately considered "affirming" or "aligning" with one's identity. When we consider how identities evolve over time, changing or fluid identifications could be better understood as realignments rather than choices.

Reenvisioning the Future

Consider and envision the future: As we move to the future, what ultimately do we hope for when it comes to race and choice? Do we want to see a world where everyone gets to always freely choose their racial identities? What constraints do you feel need to stay in place and why? I pose these questions not to come to some naïve "we'll all be one race someday" vision, but to help us understand the larger goals of this work and area of inquiry. Questions of race and choice must be connecting to larger efforts to dismantle racism, racial hierarchies, and white supremacist legacies that connect material and symbolic resources to the racial-naming practices of groups and individuals. As outlined in many examples throughout this chapter, racial choices are political, and not all choices serve social justice. Many, in fact, seem to mirror the dominant group's adaptation to the changing cultural and political landscapes that allow for claims to adopt benefits fought for by those groups who have historically been, and continue to be, targeted by racism.

REFERENCES

American Anthropological Association. 1998. "Statement on 'Race.'" *American Anthropologist* 100, no. 3: 712–13.

Ashlee, Aeriel A. 2019. "Neither, nor, Both, Between: Understanding Transracial Asian American Adoptees' Racialized Experiences in College Using Border Theory." Dissertation, Miami University. etd.ohiolink.edu.

Baym, Nancy K. 2015. *Personal Connections in the Digital Age*. 2nd ed. Malden: Polity.

Bliuc, Ana-Maria, Nicholas Faulkner, Andrew Jakubowicz, and Craig McGarty. 2018. "Online Networks of Racial Hate: A Systematic Review of 10 Years of Research on Cyber-Racism." *Computers in Human Behavior* 87 (October): 75–86. https://doi.org/10.1016/j.chb.2018.05.026.

boyd, danah m., and Nicole B. Ellison. 2007. "Social Network Sites: Definition, History, and Scholarship." *Journal of Computer-Mediated Communication* 13, no. 1 (October): 210–30. https://doi.org/10.1111/j.1083-6101.2007.00393.x.

Bratter, Jennifer. 2010. "The One Drop Rule through a Multiracial Lens: Examining the Role of Race and Class in the Racial Classification of the Children of Partially Black Parents." In *Multiracial Americans and Social Class: The Influence of Social Class on Racial Identity*, edited by Kathleen O. Korgen, 184–205. New York: Routledge.

Castells, Manuel. 2001. *The Internet Galaxy: Reflections on the Internet, Business, and Society*. New York: Oxford University Press.

Daniel, G. Reginald, and G. L. Haddow. 2010. "All Mixed Up: A New Racial Commonsense in Global Perspective." In *Color Struck: Essays on Race and Ethnicity in Global Perspective*, edited by J. O. Adekunle and Hettie V. Williams, 311–48. Lanham, MD: University Press of America.

Daniels, Jessie. 2009. *Cyber Racism: White Supremacy Online and the New Attack on Civil Rights*. Lanham, MD: Rowman and Littlefield.

Dar-Nimrod, Ilan, and Steven J. Heine. 2011. "Genetic Essentialism: On the Deceptive Determinism of DNA." *Psychological Bulletin* 137, no. 5 (September): 800–18. https://doi.org/10.1037/a0021860.

Davis, Floyd James. 1991. *Who Is Black? One Nation's Definition*. State College: Pennsylvania State University Press.

DeVega, Chauncey. 2011. "Doing the Race Hustle: How 'Mixed Race' Students Game the College Admissions Process." *Alternet*, June 15. www.chaunceydevega.com.

Foeman, Anita K. 2012. "An Intercultural Project Exploring the Relationship among DNA Ancestry Profiles, Family Narrative, and the Social Construction of Race." *Journal of Negro Education* 81, no. 4 (Fall): 307–18.

Gin, Kevin J., Ana M. Martínez-Alemán, Heather T. Rowan-Kenyon, and Derek Hottell. 2017. "Racialized Aggressions and Social Media on Campus." *Journal of College Student Development* 58, no. 2 (March): 159–74.

Grande, Sandy. 2004. *Red Pedagogy: Native American Social and Political Thought*. Lanham, MD: Rowman and Littlefield.

Grimes, David Robert. 2017. "Echo Chambers Are Dangerous—We Must Try to Break Free of Our Online Bubbles." *Guardian*, December 4. www.theguardian.com.

Grossman, Sara. n.d. "Race and Interconnectedness." Othering and Belonging Institute blog. https://belonging.berkeley.edu.

Harmon, Amy. 2007. "In DNA Era, New Worries about Prejudice." *New York Times*, November 11. www.nytimes.com.
Hobbs, Allyson. 2014. *A Chosen Exile: A History of Racial Passing in American Life*. Cambridge: Harvard University Press.
Hollinger, David A. 2014. "Obama, the Instability of Color Lines, and the Promise of a Postethnic Future." In *Race and the Obama Phenomenon*, edited by G. Reginald Daniel and Hettie V. Williams, 167–74. Jackson: University Press of Mississippi.
Holmes, Kristin E. 2013. "DNA Project Surprises, Enlightens Pa. Students." *Reporter*, May 13. www.thereporteronline.com.
Jackson, Lauren Michele. 2018. "Women 'Blackfishing' on Instagram Aren't Exactly Trying to Be Black. They're Doing Something More Insidious." *Slate*, November 29. https://slate.com.
Johnston, Marc P., C. Casey Ozaki, Jane Elizabeth Pizzolato, and Prema Chaudhari. 2014. "Which Box(es) Do I Check? Investigating College Students' Meanings behind Racial Identification." *Journal of Student Affairs Research and Practice* 51, no. 1 (February): 56–68. https://doi.org/10.1515/jsarp-2014-0005.
Johnston-Guerrero, Marc P. 2016. "The Meanings of Race Matter: College Students Learning about Race in a Not-So-Postracial Era." *American Educational Research Journal* 53, no. 4 (April): 819–49. https://doi.org/10.3102/0002831216651144.
Johnston-Guerrero, Marc P., and Karly Ford. 2020. "'Draw Your Own Box?': Further Complicating Racial Data for Multiracial/Two or More Races College Students." In *Measuring Race: Why Disaggregating Data Matters for Addressing Educational Inequality*, edited by Robert T. Teranishi, Bach Mai Dolly Nguyen, Edward R. Curammeng, Cynthia M. Alcantar, and James A. Banks. New York: Teachers College Press.
Johnston-Guerrero, Marc P., and Kristen A. Renn. 2016. "Multiracial Americans in College." In *Race Policy and Multiracial Americans*, edited by Kathleen O. Korgen, 139–54. Bristol: Policy Press.
Jones, Nicholas A., and Jungmiwha Bullock. 2012. "The Two or More Races Population: 2010." 2010 Census Briefs C2010BR-13. September. Washington, DC: US Census Bureau.
Junco, Reynol. 2014. *Engaging Students through Social Media: Evidence-Based Practices for Use in Student Affairs*. San Francisco: Wiley.
Khanna, Nikki. 2010. "'If You're Half Black, You're Just Black': Reflected Appraisals and the Persistence of the One-Drop Rule." *Sociological Quarterly* 51, no. 1 (January): 96–121. https://doi.org/10.1111/j.1533-8525.2009.01162.x.
Liebler, Carolyn A., Sonya R. Porter, Leticia E. Fernandez, James M. Noon, and Sharon R. Ennis. 2017. "America's Churning Races: Race and Ethnicity Response Changes between Census 2000 and the 2010 Census." *Demography* 54, no. 1 (February): 259–84. https://doi.org/10.1007/s13524-016-0544-0.
Luft, Rachel E. 2009. "Intersectionality and the Risk of Flattening Difference: Gender and Race Logics, and the Strategic Use of Antiracist Singularity." In *The Intersectional Approach: Transforming the Academy through Race, Class, and Gender*, edited

by Kathleen Guidroz and Michele Tracy Berger, 100–117. Chapel Hill: University of North Carolina Press.

Marwick, Alice E., and danah boyd. 2011. "I Tweet Honestly, I Tweet Passionately: Twitter Users, Context Collapse, and the Imagined Audience." *New Media & Society* 13, no. 1 (January): 114–33. https://doi.org/10.1177/1461444810365313.

Mixed-Ish. 2019. Comedy. Khalabo Ink Society, Artists First, Cinema Gypsy Productions.

Mohajeri, Orkideh. 2018. "Constructions at the Borders of Whiteness: The Discursive Framing of Contested White Students at a Predominantly White Institution of Higher Education." Dissertation, University of Minnesota.

Montagu, Ashley. 1964. *Man's Most Dangerous Myth: The Fallacy of Race*. 4th ed. Cleveland: World Publishing.

Morning, Ann. 2009. "Toward a Sociology of Racial Conceptualization for the 21st Century." *Social Forces* 87, no. 3 (March): 1167–92. https://doi.org/10.1353/sof.0.0169.

———. 2014. "And You Thought We Had Moved beyond All That: Biological Race Returns to the Social Sciences." *Ethnic and Racial Studies* 37, no. 10 (August): 1676–85. https://doi.org/10.1080/01419870.2014.931992.

Moya, Paula M. L., and Hazel Rose Markus. 2010. "Doing Race: An Introduction." In *Doing Race: 21 Essays for the 21st Century*, edited by Hazel Rose Markus and Paula M. L. Moya, 1–101. New York: Norton.

Murphy, Heather. 2019. "How White Nationalists See What They Want to See in DNA Tests." *New York Times*, July 12. www.nytimes.com.

Nakamura, Lisa. 1995. "Race in/for Cyberspace: Identity Tourism and Racial Passing on the Internet." *Works and Days: Essays in the Socio-Historical Dimensions of Literature and the Arts* 25–26 (Fall 1995–Winter 1996): 181–93.

Newton, Kamilah. 2020. "White Male Professor Caught Posing as Black Woman on Twitter Is Just the Latest in a Bizarre Trend: 'Identity Tourism.'" *Yahoo!Life*, October 16. www.yahoo.com.

Ocampo, Anthony Christian. 2016. *The Latinos of Asia: How Filipino Americans Break the Rules of Race*. Palo Alto: Stanford University Press.

Oro, Paul Joseph López. 2019. "Digitizing Ancestral Memory: Garifuna Settlement Day in the Americas and in Cyberspace." In *Indigenous Interfaces: Spaces, Technology, and Social Networks in Mexico and Central America*, edited by Jennifer Gómez Menjívar, Gloria Elizabeth Chacón, and Arturo Arias, 165–79. Tucson: University of Arizona Press.

Osei-Kofi, Nana. 2012. "Identity, Fluidity, and Groupism: The Construction of Multiraciality in Education Discourse." *Review of Education, Pedagogy, and Cultural Studies* 34, no. 5 (November): 245–57. https://doi.org/10.1080/10714413.2012.732782.

Panofsky, Aaron, and Joan Donovan. 2019. "Genetic Ancestry Testing among White Nationalists: From Identity Repair to Citizen Science." *Social Studies of Science* 49, no. 5 (July): 653–81. https://doi.org/10.1177/0306312719861434.

Parker, Kim, Juliana Menasce Horowitz, Rich Morin, and Mark Hugo Lopez. 2015. "Multiracial in America: Proud, Diverse and Growing in Numbers." Pew Research Center, July 11. www.pewsocialtrends.org.

Ramanujan, K. 2011. "200 Students Offer Cheek Samples for Cornell's Genetic Ancestry Project." *Cornell Chronicle Online*, February 2. www.news.cornell.edu.

Renn, Kristen A. 2004. *Mixed Race Students in College: The Ecology of Race, Identity, and Community on Campus*. Albany: State University of New York Press.

Rockquemore, Kerry Ann, David L. Brunsma, and Daniel J. Delgado. 2009. "Racing to Theory or Retheorizing Race? Understanding the Struggle to Build a Multiracial Identity Theory." *Journal of Social Issues* 65, no. 1 (January): 13–34. https://doi.org/10.1111/j.1540-4560.2008.01585.x.

Root, Maria P. P. 1996. "A Bill of Rights for Racially Mixed People." In *The Multiracial Experience: Racial Borders as the New Frontier*, edited by Maria P. P. Root, 3–14. Thousand Oaks, CA: Sage.

Rosenbaum, Judith E. 2017. *Constructing Digital Cultures: Tweets, Trends, Race, and Gender*. Lanham, MD: Lexington.

Rowan-Kenyon, Heather T., and Ana M. Martínez Alemán. 2016. *Social Media in Higher Education: ASHE Higher Education Report*, vol. 42, no. 5. Hoboken, NJ: Wiley.

Salinas, Cristobal. 2020. "The Complexity of the 'x' in Latinx: How Latinx/a/o Students Relate to, Identify with, and Understand the Term Latinx." *Journal of Hispanic Higher Education* 19, no 2 (January): 149–68. https://doi.org/10.1177/1538192719900382.

Saulny, Susan, and Jacques Steinberg. 2011. "On College Forms, a Question of Race, or Races, Can Perplex." *New York Times*, June 13. www.nytimes.com.

Tesler, Michael, and David O. Sears. 2010. *Obama's Race: The 2008 Election and the Dream of a Post-Racial America*. Chicago: University of Chicago Press.

Wijeyesinghe, Charmaine L. 2001. "Racial Identity in Multiracial People: An Alternative Paradigm." In *New Perspectives on Racial Identity Development: A Theoretical and Practical Anthology*, edited by Charmaine L. Wijeyesinghe and Bailey W. Jackson III, 129–52. New York: New York University Press.

Williams, Javonda, Kathleen A. Bolland, Lisa Hooper, Wesley Church, Sara Tomek, and John Bolland. 2014. "Say It Loud: The Obama Effect and Racial/Ethnic Identification of Adolescents." *Journal of Human Behavior in the Social Environment* 24, no. 7 (October): 858–68. https://doi.org/10.1080/10911359.2014.909343.

3

Naming the Problem

Epistemic Violence, Cognitive Maps, Relationships of Power, and Resistance in National Narratives about Belonging

NANCY LÓPEZ

> Because race and nation have been mutually constructing categories, nationalism and racism are also linked.
> —Patricia Hill Collins (2006, 17)

US racial categories explicitly or implicitly conflate and homogenize race, nation, nation-state, nationalism, and national identity. As a scholar, sociologist, and intellectual activist, I have explored and experienced the complex connections between race, nationality, naming, and belonging and I have come to the conclusion that there are myriad reasons why we should not link nationalities to race. Decoupling race, origin, and nation enables us to better understand racial oppression and the forces of racism, and reveals who benefits when we use race, origin, and nation interchangeably. Attending to the ontological status or theories of reality and the relationship between our institutionalized and internalized narratives about nation and race provides a greater understanding of the dynamics of difference, power, inequality, discrimination, and resistance in the United States as well as global power dynamics and contestations about belonging.

While I have studied the complicated and troubled relationships between race and nation, I have also experienced manifestations of them across my lifetime, including years well before my academic engagement with these issues. In this chapter I draw on these experiences, the lived experiences of other people, several disciplinary lenses, and research to unveil the complex connections between race and nation, and how these ties support the policies and consequences of naming and belonging in the US body politic. My analysis is grounded in tenets of critical race theory and intersectionality, lenses that are necessary to better understand the historic and contemporary relationships between race and nation, naming, and belonging and the impact of these constructs on systemic inequities and access to opportunity structures (Bell 2008; Mills 1997; Bonilla-Silva 2009; Collins and Bilge 2016; Crenshaw 1989; Crenshaw 1995; Hancock 2016; Collins 2019). While several domains, past and present, could be used as avenues of investigation, in this chapter I explore the relationship between race and nation in two settings: (1) policies and practices in higher education; and (2) the politics and consequences of how race, ethnicity, nationality, and citizenship are addressed in the US census.

Autoethnographic Moments: Sharing Critical Reflections on the Boundaries of Race and Belonging

The conflation of race, nationality, and citizenship affects people every day, across time and space. Autoethnographic explorations provide fertile ground for bringing the relationships between these concepts to light, and to direct the actions necessary to create change (Martinez-Cola 2020). In this section, I share four stories, some my own and some that recount the experiences of others.

What Does an American Look Like, Anyway?

In 1986, the summer before my senior year in a de facto segregated large New York public high school, I had the privilege of participating in a summer program called the High School Peace Corps Awareness Program, which involved living with a host family in Costa Rica. When my host mother, a white, middle-class Costa Rican woman, opened the door, she appeared surprised to see me and blurted out in Spanish, "Oh, I thought we were getting an American girl." Apparently, a Black Latinx US-born Dominican woman was not a "real" American. Smiling, I countered in Spanish, "I am an American girl. Americans come in all colors." Although this episode took place over thirty-five years ago, it resonates with anti-Blackness in Latinx communities across the globe as well as the immigration debates about who "belongs" as an authentic representative of the US national family today (Flores and Jiménez Román 2010; Collins 2006).

Reflecting on the Difference between Social Location and Emotional Attachments to Identity

In 1990 I participated in a college summer study abroad experience in the birthplace of my immigrant parents, the Dominican Republic. As a dominicana college student born and raised in New York City and majoring in Latin American and Caribbean studies, I was thrilled to meet Pedro Mir, national poet laureate at the Universidad Autónoma de Santo Domingo. Curious about our backgrounds, Pedro Mir asked all students to introduce themselves. When it was my turn, I spoke in my first language, the cibaeño Dominican Spanish that I learned from my parents, who never had the privilege of schooling beyond the second grade: "Soy dominicana nacida y criada en Nueva York." (I am a Dominican woman, born and raised in New York City.) Seemingly amused, Pedro Mir chuckled, "Usted no es dominicana, señorita. Usted es estadounidense." (You aren't Dominican, young lady. You are a US citizen.)

On the surface, Pedro Mir's comment points out an inconvenient truth. My US citizenship by birthright did mean that I occupied a social location distinct from and more privileged than that of my extended family living in the Dominican Republic who could not just travel across borders. At the same time, his words also shone a light on what Collins (2019) and Yuval-Davis (2011) describe as the importance of distinguishing among distinct domains of belonging such as social location in systems of privilege/oppression (e.g., citizenship), emotional attachment to an affinity group based on ethnic identity (e.g., cultural sense of belonging), and political and ethical commitments (e.g., reflection and action that advance human rights and flexible solidarity with oppressed communities) that can help us better understand the complexities of belonging.

Using Public Accommodations While Black and Perpetual Second-Class Citizenship

Living in Boston during my first tenure-track job at a public university furthered my understanding of the conflation of nation and race, particularly as it plays out through the parallel experiences of African Americans and Black Latinxs in the United States of not belonging due to structural and ontological anti-Blackness (Mills 1997; Dancy, Edwards, and Davis 2018). In 1999, late one evening while riding the T (Boston's public transportation subway system), I noticed a middle-aged white woman glaring at me and a Black young man wearing headphones sitting across from me on the train. Just as she exited, she turned to me and yelled, "You better behave yourself because they are building a prison for you colored folks!"

This woman's outburst on the Boston T was a stark reminder of the long and sordid legacy of anti-Blackness that has characterized the second-class citizenship of anyone racialized as Black (no matter what ethnic or citizenship status) in the United States as the anticitizen who is outside the imaginary "American" family (Collins 2006; Ray et al. 2017). The previous story revealed that, ironically, in the Dominican Republic—the birthplace of both of my immigrant parents—I didn't belong. And yet, in the United States—my birthplace—I also didn't belong. As a Black woman in the United States I am part of "the collective Black," and therefore the antithesis of the "ideal" citizen, and a person who needed surveillance, containment, and discipline in order to stay in my place (Bonilla-Silva 2009).

Presumed Non-Citizen: Dark-Skinned Children of Immigrants

Contemporary debates about immigration and belonging echo tropes about who is and is not entitled to all the rights of citizenship, regardless of whether one is born in the United States or not. While conducting research for my book *Hopeful Girls, Troubled Boys: Race and Gender Disparities in Urban Education* (2003), I heard countless stories from US-born second-generation Caribbean young adults living in New York City, all the children of immigrants from the Dominican Republic, Haiti, and the Anglophone West Indies, about the limits of belonging in the US family for those who don't "look American." Each person had painful stories of exclusion from the national family, despite their US birthright citizenship. For example, Peter, one of the young men I interviewed, was technically mixed race. His mother, a Black immigrant woman, was born in the Dominican Republic and his father was a white Italian immigrant. When Peter went looking for a job, he encountered the limits of his citizenship. As he recounted,

> I will never forget. I went to the Department of Labor and there was a white man that was helping me. And he looked at me and really quickly asked me, "Can I see your green card? Can I see your green card!" And I looked at him and I said, "I was born in the United States." And then he didn't apologize or anything and I didn't like that. (López 2003, 142)

While it is true that Peter was technically mixed race, his discrimination was not based on his mixed-race status (Hernandez 2018). It is also important to note that had Peter been racialized as a white Italian or a light-skinned white Latinx man, he may have been presumed to be more "American."

Epistemic Violence and Exclusion from National Belonging

I tell these stories to highlight the dangerous and enduring consequences of the conflation of race and nationality and the implications this reality has for the dynamics of belonging. The idea that whiteness is synonymous with Americanness and is defined by the exclusion of racial "others" constitutes what Ruth Frankenberg (1993, 16) called "epistemic violence," or the ideas that justified colonial domination by excluding racial "others." As the stories illustrate, in the national and international imagination, racially stigmatized, visible minorities are automatically seen as outside US nationhood because hegemonic notions of US citizenship are coupled with being racialized as white, not only in the United States but also across the globe (Frankenberg 1993; Haney López 1997; Okazawa-Rey 2017; Yuval-Davis 2011).

The dynamics of belonging and exclusion for visible minorities remains commonplace among many second-generation (US-born) children of Dominican, Haitian, and Anglophone Caribbean immigrants in New York City; they are repeatedly reminded that they are not "real" Americans when they apply for work, attend school, go shopping, or simply walk down the streets of New York City (López 2003). A study in Texas by Julie Dowling (2014) documents that the conflation of nationality and race has become so commonplace that some Mexican Americans who are brown-skinned, visible minorities have internalized dominant images and practices that arise from this mixing and merging of concepts. Even though they report incidents of racism based on what they look like, when asked about race, many mark "white" on the US census and in other administrative data collection. When asked why they did this, participants in the study replied, "I'm white 'cause I'm an American, right?" (Dowling 2014, 23). Sue (2014) found a similar phenomenon among dark-skinned and Black Mexicans in Veracruz, Mexico. She argued that by embracing the vision of a mixed-race nation free of racism (e.g., land of the cosmic race), participants were able to avoid directly confronting and acknowledging their lived experiences with racism and what she called "race-color prejudice and discrimination" (26). Before moving from personal reflections to critical analysis, I provide an activity where readers can explore how some of the issues raised thus far may be relevant to their own lives and stories.

What's Your Street Race? An Invitation to Lifelong Critical Reflexivity

In the activity offered here, readers are invited to reflect on a series of questions. These questions underlie several areas that I have researched and written about (López 2003, 2018; Vargas et al. 2019). I encourage readers to pause and use writing, drawing, or other artistic methods to capture their thoughts.

- What is your street race (e.g., what race would strangers assume you were based on what you look like)?
- How often do you think about your race? How often do you think about your nationality? Your citizenship?
- How often do you think about other people's race? How often do you think about other people's nationality? Their citizenship?
- How often do you think about racism and white supremacy as happening at multiple levels, from internalized forms of racism to personally mediated forms of racism to the institutionalized, structural, and systemic forms of racism and white supremacy?

- How often do you think about solutions to racism and white supremacy? Do these solutions take into account the topics of nationality and citizenship?

The objective of this exercise is to invite everyone to engage in lifelong critical reflexivity about race, nation, and belonging in their own lives and how these areas play out in the lives of other people, and to examine how lived experiences and relationships of power shape the reality of identity.

Intersectionality, Settler Colonialism, and Critical Race Theory for Truth Telling and Empowerment

Before we delve deeper into understanding how we cultivate a vibrant and healthy participatory democracy around race, nation, and citizenship, it is important to clarify our conceptual, ontological, epistemological, and theoretical underpinnings. The conceptual underpinnings of intersectional knowledge projects, settler colonialism, and critical race theory are invaluable resources for unpacking the dynamics of race, nation, inequality, contestation, and resistance vis-à-vis belonging (Tuck and Yang 2012; Glenn 2015; Collins [1999] 2009; Yuval-Davis 2011). First, Nira Yuval-Davis (2011) offers us powerful tools for conceptualizing the difference between social location, social belonging, and political values, and these tools are useful for understanding the dynamics of belonging. The arenas of belonging can be measured in three distinct ways: (1) intersecting social locations, such as race, gender, class, and nationality in systems of oppression and resistance; (2) identity narratives and emotional attachments to social groups; and (3) political and ethical values used to assess belonging and where boundaries should be drawn. Yuval-Davis (2011) stresses that while these distinct domains of belonging may be related and overlapping, they are not interchangeable. Figure 3.1 depicts a visual I created to represent Yuval-Davis's (2011) conceptualizations of belonging. Because intersectional ontologies and theories of belonging are anchored in the concepts of simultaneity and relationality, they are prerequisites for revealing the fault lines and possibilities related to belonging, nation, race, and racism. Simultaneity

INTERSECTING SOCIAL LOCATION IN GRIDS OF POWER	IDENTIFICATIONS & EMOTIONAL ATTACHMENTS	ETHICAL & POLITICAL VALUES
For example, tribal status, race/street, gender, ethnicity, class origin, current socioeconomic status, sexuality, disability, immigration status, citizenship status, age, parental status, etc.	For example, the individual and collective narratives people tell themselves about who they are and who others are.	For example, ideological commitments and values differ among people from the same families, social locations, identifications, and emotional attachments.

Figure 3.1. Representation of Yuval Davis's (2011) conceptualizations of belonging. ©Nancy López, 2019. Used with permission.

captures the understanding that one can't stop being a woman because one is racialized as Black—both social statuses are happening at the same time. Relationality implies that these social statuses (e.g., Black woman) are socially constructed and only understood when placed in a sociohistorical context and defined in relation to another social location such as white woman.

Perhaps what is most encouraging is that intersectional ontologies also create the possibilities for engaging in what Hancock (2011) calls deep political solidarity that creates the possibility for transformative, ethical solidarity (Wijeyesinghe, this volume). Patricia Hill Collins (2019) explains that intersectional flexible solidarity represents critical awareness of being rooted in one's identity, experience, and political ethical commitments at the same time that one is able to engage in flexibility and shift to understand and empathize with those who are different. Herein lie the seeds for pursuing human rights and dismantling structural violence that allows for the dehumanization of entire categories of people.

Settler colonialism refers to the ongoing social structure that seeks to displace and overtake Indigenous lands via genocide, anti-Blackness, assimilation, and ongoing dynamics of oppression that normalize masculine whiteness, heterosexism, patriarchy, gendered racism, racialized capitalism as the epitome of citizenship, and belonging (Glenn 2009, 2015; Gómez 2007; Dancy, Edwards, and Davis 2018; Robinson 2000). For example, during the COVID-19 pandemic the Navajo Nation experienced high rates of infection, indeed the highest per capita—even higher than New York City, the epicenter of the crisis. When I attended a Zoom conference, the presenter, regardless of intent, implied that the high rates of COVID-19 infections may be due to intergenerational families. During the question-and-answer segment, I posed a question to the state representative who presented the data on the problem of the disproportionate impact of COVID-19 on the Navajo Nation. I said that we need to think about the elephant in the room: the root causes of the epidemic in the Navajo Nation and the marginalized communities in New Mexico—settler colonialism, structural racism, and other structural inequities. There are plenty of intergenerational families that live without high rates of infection when they have adequate housing, water, and health services. I ended by explaining that these comments were made in the spirit of finding solutions to the fundamental causes and not meant as a personal attack on the presenter. The presenter thanked me for my remarks and said that going forward he would be more careful in how he described the cause of the disparity for the Navajo Nation. My hope was that by taking a different perspective we can begin to change the conversation and view intergenerational families as assets, rather than liabilities, in protecting communities that have survived centuries of violence due to settler colonialism, structural racism, and racial capitalism.

After the conference, I received unsolicited emails from individuals who were in attendance at the meeting thanking me for raising these issues. The inequities experienced by the Navajo Nation are due to structural conditions caused by settler colonialism, including lack of access to running water and inadequate medical facilities (Associated Press 2020a). At the same time that state agencies engaged in narratives that implicitly framed intergenerational families and "cultural practices" as the drivers of the disparity, acts of personally mediated racism and hate crimes were being visited on anyone who was assumed to "look Navajo" (Associated Press 2020b). We must always engage in critical reflection about our narratives that can include color-blind racism. Cultural racism and color-blind frames are anchored in deficit narratives that blame Indigenous nations and families for historic and contemporary oppression. Power-evasive selective memories contribute to historical amnesia replete with active devaluation of the funds of knowledge and cultural wealth of Indigenous families, communities, and nations (Tuck 2009).

Critical race theory (CRT) is another lens that illuminates properties of the state in which race, nation, citizenship, and belonging are named and ordered (Crenshaw 2019; Mills 1997; Bell 2008). CRT unveils how the state, far from being neutral, "is a tool created, maintained, and used by whites to advance their collective racial interests" and how it contributes to the reproduction of white supremacy (Bracey 2015, 558). In the case of Indigenous nations, TribalCrit is another powerful tool for unveiling the interworkings of settler colonial structural violence (Brayboy 2005). The fight over the Dakota Access Pipeline showcased the limits of belonging. In this situation and related legal case, members of the Sioux Nation who lived on the Standing Rock Indian Reservation in North Dakota and their allies from other Indigenous nations and other locations protested the building of the Dakota Access oil pipeline. The pipeline, which traversed four states, jeopardized the main water source for the reservation, and its construction would damage sacred sites protected under tribal treaty. The protesters were criminalized for their actions (Sherwood 2019). The truth telling that took place during the resistance movement of sovereign Indigenous nations speaks of the long historical fight for decolonization and the struggle to protect Mother Earth. One strategic changing of the conversation was the rearticulation of protesters as "water protectors" who were present to honor and ensure the sustainability of life for generations to come and to protect human rights. As Tuck and Yang (2012) remind us, decolonization requires fundamental changes in power relations as well as careful attention to our language in describing ongoing structural violence through settler colonialism and other injustices.

A final example that illuminates the limits of belonging, nation, and race was the election of Barack Obama as the forty-fourth president of the United States. The first Black president, he was the son of a

Black Kenyan immigrant man and a white woman from Kansas, and many people, including the future forty-fifth president of the United States, questioned Obama's legitimacy as president, alleging that he was not born in the United States and demanding to see his birth certificate. However, what if Barack Obama had been the US-born son of a white Kenyan immigrant and a white US-born woman from Kansas? Would there have been questions about his citizenship, belonging, and legitimacy as the forty-fourth president of the United States? The forty-fifth president also insisted that President Obama release his college transcripts, implying that Obama was unqualified to attend a highly competitive and prestigious university, at the same time he barred his own alma mater from ever doing so. This episode points to another arena where battles about belonging, race, and nation are waged—higher education.

Who Belongs in Higher Education? Neoliberal Logics and Hegemonic Narratives of Belonging in Public Universities and Elite Private Universities

Narratives of race, nation, and belonging are visible in debates about who should have access to higher education. Recent Supreme Court rulings have chipped away at the legitimacy of programs for ameliorating structural inequities in higher education. In 2014 the US Supreme Court buttressed states' right to hold referendums to outlaw race-sensitive (but not gender-sensitive) affirmative action in higher education. For example, the *Grutter v. Bollinger* (2003) case upheld the University of Michigan Law School's race-sensitive holistic admissions process; however, the justices' majority opinion minimizes the reality of structural racism by saying that they expect that there will be no need for these types of program in twenty-five years.

In spite of this ruling, other cases have been filed against race-sensitive affirmative action programs. On October 1, 2019, a federal judge rejected the case alleging that Harvard University discriminated against Asian Americans; however, this case may eventually make it to the Supreme Court. It is important to underscore that all of these cases are anchored in explicit and implicit anti-Blackness. The hegemonic narrative is that unqualified and undeserving racial and ethnic minorities (e.g., Black as well as Latinx students) are being admitted to elite universities and that more so-called meritorious whites and Asians are being denied. While these cases are often used to restrict access to elite private and public institutions, these hegemonic narratives also trickle down to non-elite public universities across the country.

At a faculty governance meeting at a large public university in the US Southwest, I spoke against the proposal to limit the state-funded universal opportunity scholarship to students with high scores in standardized college entrance exams. I queried a white male administrator about whether there had been an equity analysis of the impact of this policy on historically underrepresented communities. Dodging my question, he defended the policy by arguing that it will actually help students because it would still allow them to attend a community college for the first two years. He continued by asking me whether I would want unprepared students to come to the university, incur debt, and fail. In other words, so-called unprepared students simply didn't "belong" in the four-year research university. Instead, their bodies "belonged" at substantially lower-resourced "junior" colleges.

Color-evasive and power-evasive discourses of exclusion masquerading as excellence are mired in settler colonialism and anti-Blackness (Dancy, Edwards, and Davis 2018; Wacquant 2001). For example, high-level academic affairs appointments remain in the hands of white settlers, while programs dedicated to centering the lives of Indigenous, Latinx, and Africana studies remain grossly underfunded and marginalized. Doctoral degrees granted to underrepresented racial and ethnic minority students are also not representative of the demographics of the state, and the tenure stream of faculty remains predominantly white.

The institutional discourses against race-sensitive programs in higher education and the attempts to raise standardized test scores for admissions serve to create a symbolic taint on racial and ethnic minorities, specifically Black and Latinx/Brown youth, as undeserving and outside to the boundaries of higher education (Wacquant 2001). Because they are uniformly framed as unqualified and illegitimate members of the national family, Black and Latinx youth are subjected to ongoing stigma (Ray et al. 2017). These narratives also serve to undermine efforts to provide what Ruth Zambrana (2019) has called "equity lifts" for historically underserved racial and ethnic minority students.

The latest iteration of color-blind racism at the national level is a proposal by the College Board. Administrators of the Scholastic Aptitude Test (SAT) argue that we should identify "at risk or disadvantaged students" who take standardized test scores through the use of ZIP codes as a proxy for disadvantage. This seemingly well-intentioned universal approach to cultivating equity in college admissions is ill advised on at least two grounds. First, ZIP code is not an indicator of family wealth, power, and social networks. Whether in an urban or a rural area, two families in the same ZIP code may have very different life chances based on family wealth profiles. And second, even if ZIP code correlated neatly with income, power, and wealth, the empirical evidence on race-gender-class shows that class is not a proxy for systemic race or gender inequality in wealth (Darity et al. 2018). It is also not a proxy for racialized and gendered inequalities in higher education.

In a study I conducted with colleagues (López et al. 2017), we used nine years of institutional data from a large public university in the Southwest to uncover inequities in six-year graduation rates. We found major and statistically significant gaps in graduations that traditionally remain unseen in most reporting of graduation rates in higher education that rely on reporting outcomes by class alone, gender alone, or race alone. Our results show why income is not a proxy for race or gender gaps in education (see table 3.1). We chose to limit the sample to first-time, first-year students who graduated from a high school in the state. Our analytical sample included over 6,400 students. We sought to examine the odds of graduating within six years. The results are organized from the group that experienced the highest disparity to the group that experienced no disparities in the odds of graduating from a large public university when compared to our reference group, high-income white women. It is important to understand that even if a group has the same odds of graduating, we should never assume that they have the same lived experiences.

If we look just at the low-income groups, the group with the highest disparity was Native American low-income men, who were 45 percent less likely to graduate than high-income white women (reference group). In comparison, low-income white women were only 14 percent less likely to graduate than high-income white women. Low-income Hispanic men (24%) and Hispanic low-income women (23%) were also

Table 3.1. Multilevel Logistic Estimates of Probability of Six-Year Undergraduate Graduation by Race, Class, and Gender, 2000–2008

Variables	Marginal Effects
White, high-income women	(reference group)
American Indian, low-income men	-.45***
American Indian, low-income women	-.40***
American Indian, high-income men	-.37***
Black, high-income men	-.32**
White, low-income men	-.29***
Hispanic, low-income men	-.24***
Black, high-income women	-.23***
Hispanic, low-income women	-.23***
Black, low-income men	-.22***
Asian, low-income men	-.22***
Asian, high-income men	-.21***
Black, low-income women	-.19***
Hispanic, high-income men	-.17***
White, low-income women	-.14***
White, high-income men	-.14***
Asian, low-income women	-.14***
American Indian, high-income women	-.09*
Hispanic, high-income women	-.03
Asian, high-income women	.00

p<.1, * p<.05, ** p<.01, *** p<.001
Note: This reconstituted table has not been previously published, but it references study findings in López et al. 2017.

less likely to graduate than high-income white women. Low-income Black men (22%) and low-income Black women (19%) were also less likely to graduate than high-income white women.

These results illustrate why an intentional focus on race-gender-class social locations and inequalities in college graduation can be important for rectifying injustices in the opportunity structures. Yet the funding formula for institutions of higher education in the state department of higher education assumes that PELL status (federal financial aid) is a proxy for "at-risk" populations. To be sure, institutions that make improvement in the graduation of PELL-qualified students are rewarded with extra resources, in spite of the fact that this color-evasive and gender-evasive approach does not address the complex configurations of inequality and structural intersectional inequities in college graduation.

Indicators of class (e.g., PELL status, income, etc.) are not a proxy for identifying "at-risk students." If our goal is eliminating race-gender gaps in opportunity and achievement, using PELL eligibility (or income measures, parental educational attainment/class origin measures) alone is not enough for reducing inequality in higher education. We need to include measures of structural disadvantage by examining race, gender, and income as simultaneous social statuses in our analysis of social inequalities. We must focus on solutions. Table 3.2 illustrates the type of studies and policy priorities that are necessary for transforming the status quo and advancing equity in higher education.

We invite everyone to consider using a critical race intersectional analysis that considers the simultaneity of complex inequalities in a given context for examining inequality and belonging in higher education outcomes. This would mean that we would embrace a new gold standard of intersectional data when looking at graduation. The new standard would interrogate race-gender-class gaps in a given sociohistorical context.

Federal Data Collection and Narratives about Nation, Race, and Belonging

The complex and confused relationships between nation, race, and belonging are very visible when we engage in a critical race and intersectional analysis of the politics of race and ethnic data collection in the US census. These politics underlie questions that often emerge after the results of the decennial census are released, such as: Is the United States post-racial? Why did the 2020 census ask about race and origins in one question? Who benefits when race, national origin, ethnicity, and ancestry are conflated in one question? The following discussion, which uses materials drawn from the 2020 census, was written during the 2020 census enumeration, and published in this volume immediately after the completion of it. In some instances, I use myself as an example of a person completing the questionnaire. To complete the item as shown in figure 3.2, I would mark "Yes, another Hispanic, Latino, or Spanish origin" and write in "Dominican." The text of the very next item, the

Table 3.2. How We Can Improve the Definition of "at-Risk" Students in Higher Education Funding Formulas

Current Practice & Assumption	Dominant Narrative	Tradeoffs	Transition	Projected Outcomes	Stress Test
Use of PELL status is the best way to identify and serve at-risk students	"PELL-eligible students graduate at lower rates than others. Since many racial and ethnic minority students are PELL eligible, this is a neutral way of achieving equity."	(1) We will never have income data for everyone; only 42% of students at a large public university in the Southwest fill out the FAFSA (2) PELL eligibility is not a proxy for racialized intergenerational wealth gaps	Not needed; this is the current practice	Institutions that demonstrate improvements in graduation for PELL-eligible students receive additional funding	Historic and contemporary inequalities in graduation by race-gender-class remain unseen and inactionable under so-called "color-blind" approaches

ALTERNATIVE #1: USE OF RACE-GENDER-CLASS (E.G., PELL STATUS) SOCIAL LOCATIONS FOR IDENTIFYING AT-PROMISE STUDENTS

Alternative Assumption	Alternative Narrative	Tradeoffs	Transition	Projected Outcomes	Stress Test
Use of race-gender-class as simultaneous social locations is necessary for identifying at-promise students	"Using PELL eligibility alone is not enough. We need to include race, gender, and income as simultaneous social locations and units of analysis for interrogating inequalities and cultivating solutions for at-promise students."	(1) Some institutions of higher education do not have the technical capacity to do analysis of complex and simultaneous race-gender-class inequalities, so they must build analytical capacity in their respective state-level departments of higher education (2) See tradeoff #1 & #2 above	Centralize all institutional data analysis in their respective state-level departments of higher education	Institutions that demonstrate improvements in reducing complex and simultaneous race-gender-class inequalities in six-year graduation will receive additional funds	Pilot this analysis at the research-intensive (R1) institutions for three years; then scale up to include other institutions in the state; evaluate value added for policy making and practice

Table 3.2. (cont.)

ALTERNATIVE #2: USE OF RACE-GENDER-CLASS (E.G., FIRST-GENERATION COLLEGE / NO PARENT OR GUARDIAN EARNED 4-YR COLLEGE DEGREE) SOCIAL LOCATIONS FOR IDENTIFYING AT-PROMISE STUDENTS IN A GIVEN INSTITUTION

Alternative Assumption	Alternative Narrative	Tradeoffs	Transition	Projected Outcomes	Stress Test
Use of race-gender-class as simultaneous social locations is necessary for identifying at-promise students	"This university is a leader in race-gender-class equity based analysis and policy making. Our funding formula reflects our values and seeks to reward institutions that reduce complex and simultaneous inequalities for at-promise students."	See tradeoffs #1 and #2 above	Collect parental educational attainment data on all college applications	Institutions that demonstrate improvements in reducing complex and simultaneous race-gender-class inequalities in six-year graduation will be rewarded	Pilot this analysis at the research-intensive (R1) institutions for three years; then scale up to include other institutions in the state; evaluate value added for policy making and practice

question pertaining to race, is replicated in figure 3.3. The race question illustrates the illogical nature of the categories and the orientation toward origins and race in the census. Origins are automatically linked to a given race box. I notice that with the exception of Native American, not a single Latino origin is listed under the white or Black race. But more importantly, the census question about race contributes to the falsehood that a national origin "belongs" to a given race box. If I follow this logic, I wonder where US census designers would place a person who is South African. Would they place that person in the white box? Why not in the Black box? Aren't there South Africans who are racialized as Asian? Following this line of questioning, where should they place people of Canadian origins? Would the census designers include Canadian as an example of "origin" in the white box? Aren't there Canadians who are racialized as Black or Asian? What about people in Canadian First Nations?

The logic of linking a particular nationality or origin to a given race box is simply sloppy social science. Would census designers construct a survey asking about gender and sexuality in one question? What about income and occupation? Disability and age? I have to believe

> NOTE: Please answer BOTH Question 8 about Hispanic origin and Question 9 about race. For this census, Hispanic origins are not races.

8. Is Person 1 of Hispanic, Latino, or Spanish origin?

   ☐ No, not of Hispanic, Latino, or Spanish origin

   ☐ Yes, Mexican, Mexican Am., Chicano

   ☐ Yes, Puerto Rican

   ☐ Yes, Cuban

   ☐ Yes, another Hispanic, Latino, or Spanish origin – Print, for example, Salvadoran, Dominican, Colombian, Guatemalan, Spaniard, Ecuadorian, etc.

   _____

Figure 3.2. Text preceding and within Hispanic origin question in 2020 US census.

9. What is Person 1's race?

Mark ☑ one or more boxes AND print origins.

   ☐ White—Print, for example, German, Irish, English, Italian, Lebanese, Egyptian, etc.

   _____

   ☐ Black or African Am.—Print, for example, African American, Jamaican, Haitian, Nigerian, Ethiopian, Somali, etc.

   _____

   ☐ American Indian or Alaskan Native—Print name or enrolled or principal tribe(s), for example, Navajo Nation, Blackfeet Tribe, Mayan, Aztec, Native Village of Barrow Inupiat Traditional Government, Nome Eskimo Community, etc.

   _____

☐ Chinese	☐ Vietnamese	☐ Native Hawaiian
☐ Filipino	☐ Korean	☐ Samoan
☐ Asian Indian	☐ Japanese	☐ Chamorro
☐ Other Asian—Print, for example, Pakistani, Cambodian, Hmong, etc.		☐ Other Pacific Islander—Print, for example, Tongan, Fijian, Marshallese, etc.

   _____

   ☐ Some other race—Print race or origin

   _____

Figure 3.3. Text from race question in 2020 US census.

that census designers have had an introductory social science statistics class in which they learned that asking about two analytically distinct concepts—race and origins—requires different questions. And yet this is precisely what the Census Bureau designers did for the 2020 census.

Census designers argued that the reason they chose to include a space for entering "origins" under each race box in the 2020 census was to provide everyone, not just Hispanics, an opportunity to recognize their unique ethnic origins, thereby ensuring "equitable" treatment of all groups. If Hispanics have their own origin box, why shouldn't everyone else also be able to indicate their origins? Census designers also stipulate that the origins they listed under each race box are simply the "official" origins listed in the 1997 guidelines from the US Office of Management and Budget (OMB). An inconvenient truth, seldom invoked by census designers, is that the OMB guidelines stipulate that Hispanic origin groups can be of any race. Why would this OMB dictum be an exception for Hispanic origin groups alone? Wouldn't the reverse apply? Could European origin groups, African continent origin group, Native American origin groups, or Asian origin groups be of any race? The reasoning of census designers in stipulating the boundaries of race, origin, and ancestry groups bears no resemblance to logic, but it does make sense if we consider the backdrop of *color-blind racism* and what Eduardo Bonilla-Silva (2009) has called the *minimization of racism frame*, whereby the ongoing ravages of racism prevail in housing, employment, and voting. It also fuels anti-Blackness and dilutes our ability to track inequities experienced by Black Latinx people (Hernández 2018; Telles 2014).

The census designers also neglect to mention that the American Community Survey (ACS), which is an annual survey administered to 1 percent of the population, already includes a separate question for ancestry as analytically distinct from Hispanic origin and race. If origins are such an important data point, why wasn't the separate ancestry question from the ACS included in the 2020 census questionnaire? If the ACS also includes a citizenship question, why did the Trump administration's Department of Justice argue that it needed to include a citizenship question in the 2020 census for civil rights enforcement? In the national imagination, the count for political redistricting and resources should not include "non-citizens," regardless of whether they are documented or undocumented. It is important to underscore that since the majority of so-called "non-citizens" are visible racial and ethnic minorities coming from Latin America and Asia, in the national imagination these individuals are again not part of the "national family."

Another threat posed to the integrity of our data collection systems for civil rights enforcement became visible to me while watching a 2020 webinar on the Census Academy website. Census designers explained that if an individual fills out the census and indicates that they were not of Hispanic origin and then mark their race as Black on the 2020 census, and also wrote "Egyptian" on the line below the Black box, that individual would automatically be recorded as indicating that they are mixed race (e.g., both Black and white). The reasoning given by the census designers is that according to the OMB guidelines, the national origin of Egyptian corresponds to the "White" race box. In short, another cost of the conflation of race and national origin is the further dilution of our ability to discern the color line and the monitoring of the status of civil rights outcomes in housing, voting, employment, education, law enforcement, and health.

Recommendations

Where do we go from here? What should the testing for the 2030 census look like? What type of research protocol do we need? How can we center the color line and social inequalities faced by racially stigmatized visible minorities—those most likely to suffer injustice and punitive discrimination while voting, seeking employment, health care, and other civil rights at the local, community, organizational, state, national, and global levels? There is a solution to this conundrum. First, questions about race and ethnicity, national origin, and ancestry should be decoupled. The unpleasant truth is that race and origin are different analytical concepts that should never be linked. Separate questions are needed for tribal status, race, or what I call "street race," as a social status that is distinct from origin or ancestry.

Second, looking ahead to the 2030 census, if we embrace the premise that census data must focus on civil rights, the litmus test for future research to improve data collection must include minimal criteria for ethical and rigorous scientific research on inequality and policy-relevant solutions. Among the questions that should be asked are:

1. Do the proposed methods and question formats include social outcomes of interest to the civil rights community, such as our progress in addressing the color line and social inequalities in fair housing, implications for voting redistricting, and other civil rights outcomes?
2. Will these data help us better serve vulnerable communities, especially visible minorities that fall to the bottom of the color line?
3. Are Black Latinx scholars who focus on social inequalities at the decision-making table when the research protocol is created and implemented?

Any talk about testing a citizenship question for the decennial census should be interpreted as a racist racial project in the form of a blatant move to depress the numbers of racial and ethnic minorities from an immigrant background that are counted in the census (Gómez 2020). Instilling fear and contributing to undercounts for voting redistricting and the distribution of resources for the most vulnerable are not only unconstitutional—they are unethical and immoral.

Third, we must commit to creating clarity about the use of the data for studying social inequality. Over a century ago, sociologist W. E. B. Du Bois proclaimed that the problem of the twentieth century is the problem of the color line (Du Bois 2008). To continue measuring our progress toward eliminating discrimination along the color line, we must protect our data infrastructure for civil rights enforcement. This means working with congressional representatives to introduce legislation that protects the integrity of our federal, state, and local data infrastructure. It is troubling that none of the testing that took place for the 2020 census included a single social outcome such as voting redistricting or residential segregation. We cannot let this happen again. The next time that census designers want to flatten the difference between race and national origin, we must engage in counternarratives and ask, Is the United States post-racial? Who benefits from color-evasive and power-evasive data? Other options to resist include filing a case with the US Government Office of Accountability (GOA) to underscore that government resources are being wasted when testing questionnaire formats exclude the preponderance of social science research evidence. We saw an embrace of evidence-based research for proactively dealing with the

COVID-19 pandemic. We should expect no less for decisions around racial and ethnic data collection that is of major importance for advancing civil rights and justice.

Relatedly, public outreach and messaging that educate the general public about the use of these data for civil rights enforcement and policy making are paramount. This will require that we clarify the difference between race/color or "street race," and ethnicity or ancestry as an ethical imperative. These concepts are not the same, and the difference between them matters for serving vulnerable, underrepresented, and oppressed communities. Regardless of intention, color- and power-evasive racism transpire when we ignore or minimize ongoing structures of institutional racism (Frankenberg 1993; Bonilla-Silva 2009; Crenshaw 2019).

Finally, we must imagine the emancipatory possibilities of decoupling race, nation, and belonging and cultivating intersectional "flexible solidarity" or "building coalitions among distinctive projects" (Collins 2019, 219). This may mean that we develop deep understanding of our own social location, sense of belonging, and political values at the same time that we develop intersectional-flexible solidarity or the ability to understand and pivot the center to comprehend and empathize with those who are different from ourselves (Collins 2019). These actions may provide the basis for coalition politics among Indigenous, Black, Latinx, Asian, Middle Eastern, and other communities subjected to historic and contemporary forms of injustice, oppression, exclusion, and dehumanization.

Conclusions: Imagining Political Landscapes of Belonging: Revisiting the United Nations Statements on Race

As the discussion presented in this chapter has indicated, decoupling race, origin, and nation can help us understand and combat racial oppression and the forces of racism. As practitioners, policy makers, researchers, and activists continue to wrestle with the complexities of these issues and the questions raised in this chapter, the United Nations (UN) statements on race issued in the aftermath of World War II and issued periodically thereafter (Doniger 1950; UNESCO 1969; United Nations 2001, 2014) may help us imagine a way forward. This is particularly true in current times, when we see a resurgence of white supremacy on a global scale that harkens back to the impetus for the UN 1950 statements that were echoed after World War II:

> Many national, religious, geographic, linguistic, or cultural groups have, in such loose usage, been called "race," when obviously Americans are not a race, nor are Englishmen, nor Frenchmen, nor any other national origin groups. (UNESCO 1969, 31)

Over a decade later, a 1964 UN statement only tangentially addresses this point: "There is no national, religious, geographic, linguistic or cultural group which constitutes a race ipso facto" (UNESCO 1969, 47); however, the 1967 UN statement planted the seeds for transformative institutional change. It claimed that schools should ensure that the "curricula contain scientific understandings about race and human unity." The 1967 UN Statement on Race and Race Prejudice also urged that special attention be paid to training of teachers. Specifically, it underscored the importance of self-reflexivity or ongoing attention to the extent to which teachers have internalized racist messages. The 1967 statement even stipulated that where there have been historic oppressions, corrective measures should be taken. Below is a representative excerpt of this statement that still resonates today:

> The schools should ensure that their curricula contain scientific understandings about race and human unity, and that invidious distinctions about peoples are not made in texts and classrooms. . . . In view of the importance of teachers in any educational programme, special attention should be given to their training. Teachers should be made conscious of the degree to which they reflect the prejudices, which may be current in their society. They should be encouraged to avoid these prejudices. (UNESCO 1969, 53)

These UN statements point to promising possibilities for moving toward a beloved community anchored in the principles of belonging. For example, they lead us to imagine a world where teachers would commit to culturally responsive teaching, always engaging in self-criticism and examining their commitment to marginalized communities. This could pave the way for dismantling systems of oppression.

Looking ahead, I am left to wonder whether future generations of my family members will face similar comments about what "Americans" look like as I did in the 1980s. Will my great-great-grandchildren seeking to understand their familial history encounter boundaries of belonging when visiting the Dominican Republic? What will my great-great-grandchildren experience when using public transportation in the cities of the future? In order to create change for the generations to come, we have to ask the questions, What if all teacher education programs across the globe heeded UN guidelines in their certification programs? What if all of our educational institutions and media outlets created counternarratives of belonging that decoupled race, citizenship, and belonging? What if all census data collection across the globe made sure that the differences between race, nation, and origin were not conflated in institutional narratives, national data collection, and popular discourse? What we do today in terms of national and global data collection, distribution of resources, and national and global narratives of belonging will shape the experiences and opportunities and contours of belonging for generations to come.

REFERENCES
Associated Press. 2020a. "Number of Coronavirus Cases Rises 17% on Navajo Reservation." April 11.
———. 2020b. "Page Man Arrested for Urging Killings of Navajo over Coronavirus." Fox 10, Phoenix, Arizona, April 7.
Bell, Derek. 2008. *And We Are Not Saved: The Elusive Quest for Racial Justice*. New York: Basic Books.
Bonilla-Silva, Eduardo. 2009. *Racism without Racists: Color-Blind Racism and the Persistence of Racial Inequality in the United States*. 2nd ed. Lanham, MD: Rowman and Littlefield.
Bracey, Glenn E. 2015. "Toward a Critical Race Theory of State." *Critical Sociology* 41, no. 3 (Fall): 553–72.
Brayboy, Bryan M. J. 2005. "Toward a Tribal Critical Race Theory in Education." *Urban Review* 37, no. 5: 425–46.
Collins, Patricia Hill. (1990) 2009. *Black Feminist Thought*. Reprint, New York: Routledge.
———. 2006. *From Black Power to Hip Hop: Racism, Nationalism and Feminism*. Philadelphia: Temple University Press.
———. 2019. *Intersectionality as Critical Social Theory*. Durham: Duke University Press.
Collins, Patricia Hill, and Sirma Bilge. 2016. *Intersectionality*. Hoboken, NJ: Wiley.

Crenshaw, Kimberlé. 1989. "Demarginalizing the Intersection of Race and Sex: A Black Feminist Critique of Antidiscrimination Doctrine, Feminist Theory and Antiracist Politics." *University of Chicago Legal Forum*, issue 1, article 8: 139–67.

———. 1995. "Mapping the Margins: Intersectionality, Identity Politics, and Violence against Women of Color." In *Critical Race Theory: The Key Writings That Formed the Movement*, edited by Kimberlè Crenshaw, Neil Gotanda, Gary Peller, and Kendall Thomas, 357–83. New York: New Press.

———. 2019. *Seeing Race Again: Countering Colorblindness across the Disciplines*. Berkeley: University of California Press.

Dancy, Elon T. J., II, Kirsten T. Edwards, and James Earl Davis. 2018. "Historically White Universities and Plantation Politics: Anti-Blackness and Higher Education in the Black Lives Matter Era." *Urban Education* 53, no. 2 (February): 176–95.

Darity, William, Jr., Darrick Hamilton, Mark Paul, Alan Aja, Anne Price, Antonio Moore, and Caterina Chiopris. 2018. "What We Get Wrong about Closing the Racial Wealth Gap." Samuel DuBois Cook Center on Social Equity and Insight Center for Community Economic Development. https://socialequity.duke.edu.

Doniger, Simon. 1950. "UNESCO Statement on Race." *Pastoral Psychology* 1, no. 9 (December): 9–12.

Dowling, Julie A. 2014. *Mexican Americans and the Question of Race*. Austin: University of Texas Press.

Du Bois, W. E. B. 2008. *The Souls of Black Folk*. New York: Oxford University Press.

Flores, Juan, and Miriam Jiménez Román. 2010. *The Afro-Latin@ Reader: History and Culture in the United States*. Durham: Duke University Press.

Frankenberg, Ruth. 1993. *White Women, Race Matters: The Social Construction of Whiteness*. Minneapolis: University of Minnesota Press.

Glenn, Evelyn Nakano. 2009. *Unequal Freedom: How Race and Gender Shaped American Citizenship and Labor*. Cambridge: Harvard University Press.

———. 2015. "Settler Colonialism as Structure: A Framework for Comparative Studies of US Race and Gender Formation." *Sociology of Race and Ethnicity* 1, no. 1 (January): 52–72.

Gómez, Laura. 2007. *Manifest Destinies: The Making of the Mexican American Race*. New York: New York University Press.

———. 2020. *Inventing Latinos: A New Story of American Racism*. New York: New Press.

Hancock, Ange-Marie. 2011. *Solidarity Politics for Millennials: A Guide to Ending the Oppression Olympics*. New York: Springer.

———. 2016. *Intersectionality: An Intellectual History*. Oxford: Oxford University Press.

Haney López, Ian. 1997. *White by Law: The Legal Construction of Race*. New York: New York University Press.

Hernández, Tanya Katerí. 2018. *Multiracials and Civil Rights: Mixed Race Stories of Discrimination*. New York: New York University Press.

López, Nancy. 2003. *Hopeful Girls, Troubled Boys: Race and Gender Disparities in Urban Education*. New York: Routledge.

———. 2018. "The US Census Bureau Keeps Confusing Race and Ethnicity." *Conversation*, February 28.

López, Nancy, Edward Vargas, Melina Juarez, Lisa Cacari-Stone, and Sonia Bettez. 2017. "What's Your 'Street Race'? Leveraging Multidimensional Measures of Race and Intersectionality for Examining Physical and Mental Health Status among Latinxs." *Sociology of Race and Ethnicity* 4, no. 1: 49–66.

Martinez-Cola, Marisela. 2020. "Collectors, Nightlights, and Allies, Oh My! White Mentors in the Academy." *Understanding and Dismantling Privilege* 10, 1: 25–57.

Mills, Charles W. 1997. *The Racial Contract*. Ithaca: Cornell University Press.

Okazawa-Rey, Margo. 2017. "A 'Nation-ized' Intersectional Analysis: The Politics of Transnational Campus Unity." In *Enacting Intersectionality in Student Affairs: New Directions for Student Services*, number 157, edited by Charmaine L. Wijeyesinghe, 81–90. San Francisco: Jossey-Bass.

Ray, Victor E., Antonio Randolph, Megan Underhill, and David Luke. 2017. "Critical Race Theory, Afro-Pessimism, and Racial Progress Narratives." *Sociology of Race and Ethnicity* 3, no. 2: 147–58.

Robinson, Cedric J. 2000. *Black Marxism: The Making of the Black Radical Tradition*. 2nd ed. Chapel Hill: University of North Carolina Press.

Rodríguez, Clara, Grigoris Agreros, and Michael Miyawaki. 2012. "Does Race and National Origins Influence the Hourly Wages That Latino Males Receive." In *Invisible No More: Understanding the Disenfranchisement of Latino Men and Boys*, edited by Pedro Noguera, Aída Hurtado, and Edward Fergus, 207–17. New York: Routledge.

Sherwood, Yvonne. 2019. "The Political Binds of Oil versus Tribes." *Open Rivers: Rethinking Water, Place and Community* 13 (Spring): 48–69.

Sue, Cristina. 2014. *Land of Cosmic Race: Race Mixture, Racism and Blackness in Mexico*. Oxford: Oxford University Press.

Telles, Edward, and the Project on Ethnicity and Race in Latin America (PERLA). 2014. *Pigmentocracies: Ethnicity, Race and Color in Latin America*. Chapel Hill: University of North Carolina Press.

Tuck, Eve. 2009. "Suspending damage: A letter to communities." *Harvard Educational Review* 79, no. 3: 409-28.

Tuck, Eve, and K. Wayne Yang. 2012. "Decolonization Is Not a Metaphor." *Decolonization: Indigeneity, Education and Society* 1, no. 1: 1–40.

UNESCO. 1969. *Four Statements on the Race Question*. Including 1950, 1951, 1964, and 1967 statements. Paris: United Nations Educational, Scientific and Cultural Organization (UNESCO).

United Nations. 2001. World Conference against Racism, Racial Discrimination, Xenophobia and Related Intolerance, Durban, South Africa.

———. 2014. OHCHR's Recommended Principles and Guidelines on Human Rights at International Borders.

Vargas, Edward, Nancy López, Lisa Cacari-Stone, and Melina Juarez. 2019. "Critical 'Street Race' Praxis: Advancing the Measurement of Racial Discrimination among

Diverse Latinx Communities in the US." *Critical Public Health.* https://doi.org/10.10 80/09581596.2019.1695040.

Wacquant, Loïc. 2001. "Deadly Symbiosis: When Ghetto and Prison Meet and Mesh." *Punishment and Society* 3, no. 1 (January): 95–133.

Yuval-Davis, Nira. 2011. *The Politics of Belonging: Intersectional Contestations.* Thousand Oaks, CA: Sage.

Zambrana, Ruth. 2019. "Intersectionality: Theory and Method." Presentation at the Intersectional Qualitative Research Methods Institute for Advanced Doctoral Students (IQRMI-ADS), University of Texas-Austin. Latino Research Initiative, five-day course, June.

4

Queer and Trans* People of Color Worldmaking as Subject Formation and Identity Development

REGINALD A. BLOCKETT AND KRISTEN A. RENN

> Queers of color and other minoritarians have been denied a world.
> —José E. Muñoz (1999, 200)

Queer and trans* people of color (QTPOC) have experienced historical, cultural, social, political, and economic erasure in the US state since the onset of their identity formation. In *Queering the Color Line: Race and the Invention of Homosexuality in American Culture*, Siobhan B. Somerville explored the lineage of scientific racism and the creation of the homosexual subject. She found that the rise of empiricism in the nineteenth century allowed science and scientists to justify the demarcation of sexual and racial minorities. Used politically, science has propagated the notion that people of color are physiologically different from white people. Eugenics, as Somerville (2000, 30) explained, became "a political and scientific response to the growth of a population beginning to challenge the dominance of white political interests." When the increased representation of people of color and immigrants threatened whiteness, the notion of "white racial suicide" was proliferated as the rationale for racial hierarchy and division in the United States (Blee 2019). From lay citizens to President Theodore Roosevelt, the nation-state upheld white supremacy by way of biological and supposedly empirical evidence.

Concurrently, sexologists and white sexuality scholars drew on the same logics as the eugenics movement to rationalize the marginalization of nonheterosexual people. In the early twentieth century, medical doctor William Robinson (1914, 550–51) wrote the highly publicized article "My Views on Homosexuality," in which he stated that homosexuality was "a sad, deplorable, pathological phenomenon. Every sexual deviation or disorder which has for its result an inability to perpetuate the race is *ipso facto* pathologic, *ipso facto* an abnormality, and this is preeminently true of homosexuality." Similarly, other eugenicists supported the notion that homosexuality inherently threatened white racial dominance and therefore ought to be eradicated. Science and society began to coalesce under these racist and homophobic ideologies, effectively laying the building blocks for justified demarcation of QTPOC within the US state and beyond. This lineage underlines how separatism has always been a factor in the subject formation and identity development of QTPOC. The dominant ideologies propagated by early eugenicists have positioned QTPOC as the opposition to normalcy—threatening whiteness, straightness, gender conformity, and other formations of US nationalism. Jasbir Puar (2018) theorized queer of color separatism, coining the term *homonationalism* to describe the adhering of queerness to the normalizing politics of the US state. Whereas people of color and queer people often face criticism for "self-segregating" (Tatum 2017), in reality they are already set apart from the majority through racism, genderism, and heterosexism; homonationalism reframes queer of color separatism in this context as a strategic approach to survival under white supremacist capitalism.

In this chapter, we draw on this political history to situate the need for agentic models and political agendas espoused from and for QTPOC. First, we briefly describe some past and current perspectives on identity development of QTPOC. Then we shift our lens to understand how QTPOC come to know their identities by way of worldmaking practices aimed at reclamation and liberation. Finally, we end this chapter by discussing how worldmaking offers a new approach to understanding identification and identity development.

Using transdisciplinary works, the chapter begins to answer the following questions: (1) What would it mean to queer race? (2) In what ways are race and racism constructed by gender and sexuality (and vice versa)? (3) How does the construct of race *require* heterosexual sexual activity (presumed or otherwise)—and what does this mean for the perpetuation of cisgender heteronormativity (i.e., heterocisnormativity), white supremacy, and other dominant power structures? (4) What has all this meant for "racial uplift" and other political agendas like respectability politics or the politics of passing? and (5) How does the production of heteropatriarchy work hand in hand with white supremacy to dictate identity formation, specifically for LGBTQ people of color? The interrelations of sexualities, genders, race, and racism run throughout the discussion as cocreative identities, forces, and social systems.

Throughout this chapter we use varying terms for racial, gender, and sexual orientation identities. When referring to an author's work, we attempt to use the original terms they used even if the term is no longer in wide use. For example, *homosexual* is no longer preferred for gay men and lesbians, though some authors from the 1970s used it in contemporary context and there are reasons that authors might still use it to refer to the term from the past. We also recognize that in historical and contemporary contexts not all people in a given identity category shared or share the same terminology. We use the term heterocisnormativity to indicate the ideology of compulsory heterosexuality and compulsory cisgender identity.

QTPOC Intersectional Identity Models: Past and Present

Existing models of identity development are limited in the ways that they can describe the intersectional identities of QTPOC. Historically, developmental theories about racial identity and sexual orientation identity emerged separately from studies mainly in psychology, sociology, and social psychology (Torres, Jones, and Renn 2009). Ecological framings put these identities into the same developmental landscape, and models of multiple or intersecting identities provide additional insight into QTPOC identity development. In this section we provide an overview of these theories as a background to understanding the Queer of Color Worldmaking perspective we introduce subsequently.

Single-Category Models: Racial Identity Development and Sexual Orientation Identity Development

Beginning in the 1970s, theorists began to propose models of racial identity development and sexual orientation identity development. These models focused on the experience of people minoritized by racial and sexual orientation identities. They moved away from pathologizing people of color and LGB people and thus were important additions to the literature on human development.

Early models of racial identity development were stage-based, focused on individual racial groups, and oriented to identity exploration and commitment (Renn 2012). Typical examples moved an individual person of color from identification with white culture through dissonance, resistance and immersion, and introspection to synergy (Atkinson, Morten, and Sue 1979; Cross 1971; Jackson 1976). These models provided a breakthrough in understanding healthy identity development in racially minoritized people at a time when existing models of overall identity development paid little attention to the specificities of living in a racist society.

Racial identity development models for people of color proposed that individuals moved from a lack of awareness of racial identity through a series of stages, prompted forward by increasing awareness of race and racism coupled with personal awareness of how to address them. A desire to disengage from white values, norms, and sometimes people emerged alongside an affinity for identifying with one's racial heritage. A greater understanding of self resulted from connection to positive images and role models within the group, and turning away from images provided and perpetuated by the dominant society. Engagement with other people who shared experiences under racial oppression further advanced positive racial identification. The final stages of these models were marked by skills and willingness to see racism as one system of oppression that influenced lives, and the ability to build coalitions with other racially minoritized people and, perhaps, people minoritized along other domains of identity, such as gender, disability, and sexual orientation.

Early models of minoritized sexual orientations also followed a stage-model approach to an end point of identity synthesis or integration. Until 1973 the American Psychological Association classified "homosexuality" as a mental illness (Drescher 2015), so the emergence of models of healthy minoritized sexual orientation identities represented a substantial advancement in the literature. The best known of the early stage models is that of Vivienne Cass (1979), who framed homosexual identity development within interpersonal congruency theory. Cass proposed stages that moved the individual out of an assumed state of heterosexual identity through six stages she identified as Identity Confusion, Comparison, Tolerance, Acceptance, Pride, and Synthesis. Similar to the early racial identity stage models, Cass's model relied on the interaction of self and other in a cycle of increasing exploration and pride in homosexual identity, as well as separation from dominant heterosexual assumptions. If an individual did not foreclose or stall at some point on this pathway, they could reach a point where they are "able to integrate [their] homosexual identity with all other aspects of self. Instead of being seen as *the* identity, it is now seen as being merely one aspect of self" (Cass 1979, 223). Although called "Identity Synthesis," this final stage still held gay or lesbian identity as "one aspect" of many, not in a way that synthesized sexual orientation with another identity, such as race; the synthesis occurred across identities, not as an interaction or combination of sexuality and race.

Anthony D'Augelli (1994) offered another model that advanced the field by moving away from a series of stages toward a set of processes that did not need to occur in a particular order, and foreclosure in one did not necessarily mean an end to identity development. The first process is "existing heterosexuality" and represents a key moment for LGB people being raised in a heteronormative society. After that process is accomplished, individuals may vary in the order and extent to which they engage with processes relating to joining an LGB community, having an intimate relationship, and taking up activism on behalf of LGB people. Like Cass, D'Augelli did not address intersecting identities of race and sexual orientation.

Ecological Approaches

Ecological approaches to understanding identity development offer ways to think about the mutual coconstruction of sexual orientation, gender, and racial identities. Although most do include aspects of the wider social context in a macrosystem or similar concept, ecological models have often been used to consider individual development in ways that appear value-neutral or power-neutral. Ecological models do not typically name systemic oppressions like racism and leave to the interpretation of the reader the roles of privilege and oppression in how identity is developed, experienced, and named. Two examples point to the affordances and limitations of ecological models in understanding QTPOC identity development.

In the first example, three approaches to understanding multiracial identity development and its contexts are explicitly ecological: Maria Root (1990, 1999), Charmaine Wijeyesinghe (2001, 2012), and Kristen Renn (2003, 2004). In these models, a multiracial person's racial identity forms in the context of proximal contexts such as family and school, through daily interactions with others. Larger social contexts also play a role, with factors such as media representation, public policy, and societal views about race, ethnicity, and nationality, expanding and/or constraining identity possibilities. An ecological framing of racial identity allows for individual agency and recognizes interdependence of individuals in social contexts, an approach that holds possibilities for understanding the individual and contextual elements of QTPOC identity development.

In the second example, two approaches to understanding sexual orientation and/or gender identity show how ecological models may inform a theory of QTPOC identity development. Michael Woodford, Jessica Joslin, and Kristen Renn (2016) presented a theoretical model for LGBTQ identity development in college students, taking into account precollege environment (family, school, personal views on gender and sexual orientation) and the college environment (academic and social contexts). They embedded this model within local, state, and national environments of attitudes, climate, and public policy, pointing to the ways that the developmental ecosystem could influence LGBTQ identity pathways. Frank Dillon, Roger Worthington, and Bonnie Moradi (2011) likewise pointed to critical environmental and personal factors in the development of sexual orientation identities. Importantly, they presented a "universal" model that applies across all sexual orientations. By including biopsychosocial aspects, they linked inherently individual characteristics, behaviors, and attitudes to social processes and contexts. Like the ecological models of multiracial identity development, these two models of sexual orientation identity development rely on interactions between person and environment.

Models of Multidimensional and Intersecting Identities

Framing QTPOC identity development would seem to be an ideal application of models that account for multiple dimensions of identity and/or that take an intersectional approach to identity. In fact, Elisa Abes, Susan Jones, and Marylu McEwen's (2007) Reconceptualized Model of Multiple Dimensions of Identity (RMMDI) presents a useful framework for understanding how an individual's development of cognitive complexity contributes to their ability to filter external messages about various identities they hold. The RMMDI provides a way to understand how one's racial, gender, and sexual orientation identities may come to be more self-defined than externally imposed, as the meaning-making filter between an individual and external messages become more refined. Though it accounts for the simultaneous presence and interaction of multiple dimensions of identity, it does not deal directly with the kinds of intersections of meaning-making about one's queer-trans*-person-of-color identity or the ways that QTPOC identities evolve over time. A cisgender man who grew up gay and Black in Atlanta, for example, might experience and express his gayness, Blackness, masculinity, and gay-Black-masculinity differently when attending college in a different region of the United States, then in a new way when taking a job as a teacher on the Texas-Mexico border, and again differently when partnering with someone of a different racial identity and raising children in a mixed-heritage home. The salience of various aspects of identity and the ways that local cultures interpret identities could influence the intersecting experiences of race, gender, and sexual orientation.

In taking up intersectionality as a way to analyze multiple dimensions of identity, Jones and Abes (2013) applied due caution to avoid what Patricia Hill Collins (2009, 136) described as a "turning inward" that "reflects the shift within American society away from social structural analyses of social problems" to a focus on "individual identity narratives." In the Intersectional Model of Multiple Dimensions of Identity (IMMDI) they propose that key aspects of intersectionality, including sociocultural structures of privilege and oppression, shape an individual's meaning-making filter. This influence is both indirect, as when an individual is not cognitively aware of how privilege and oppression have operated on them to shape their thinking, and direct, as when the individual has learned about social structures, racism, and cisheterosexism. The IMMDI suggests, though does not elucidate, that QTPOC identity development entails the mutual construction of racial, gender, and sexual orientation privileges and oppression and the individual's awareness of this mutual construction.

Opportunity for a New Approach to Understanding QTPOC Identity Development

To date, ecological models have been applied in silos, as the earlier stage models of identity development were: Here is racial identity development, here is sexual orientation and gender-identity development. Models of multiple identities (MMDI, RMMDI, IMMDI) bridge the silos, but do not take up the ways that white supremacy and heterocisnormativity work together as central forces in the United States; these forces shape racial, gender, and sexual orientation identities *and* the ways that they mutually act to create possibilities for QTPOC identities and identity development. A multidimensional, ecological approach encompassing individual agency, interactions in the environment, and an overarching context of social attitudes and public policy embedded in white supremacy could form the basis of a QTPOC identity development model.

Toward Queer of Color Worldmaking

Worldmaking refers to the epistemological, discursive, and performative politics that QTPOC employ as they destabilize compulsory heterosexual and white racial homogeneous spaces and locations and create anti-oppressive, sexually heterogeneous counterpublics (Berlant and Warner 1998). These counterpublics act as public spheres that are parallel to and resist the norming power of oppressive forces. José Muñoz's (1999, 195) theory of disidentifications is central to understanding the labor that queers of color perform as they create new politics, possibilities, and futures. These phenomena of creating counterpublics and disidentifying with compulsory heterosexism and white supremacy, which Muñoz referred to as queer worldmaking, "are oppositional ideologies that function as critiques of oppressive regimes of 'truth' that subjugate minoritarian people."

Worldmaking involves the deployment of new cultural forms to resist prevailing ideologies and expectations typically rooted in empiricism and normativity (Duran, Blockett, and Nicolazzo 2020). In her ethnography of dance culture in New York as a response to the HIV/AIDS epidemic, Fiona Buckland (2002, 4) described queer worldmaking as "a production in the moment of space of creative, expressive, and transformative possibilities." While this concept has been employed ethnographically to understand cultural practices and phenomena, worldmaking has yet to be realized for its use in understanding queer of color identity development and subject formations.

Lauren Berlant and Michael Warner (1998, 558) suggested that queer culture, in and of itself, was a worldmaking project, characterized by the "space of entrances, exits, unsystemized lines of acquaintance, projected horizons, typifying examples, alternate routes, blockages, incommensurate geographies." Worldmaking involves dissecting portions of broader society and reworking them to produce a more sensible, more just, more practical, and less rigid experience that is not rooted in an elusive quest for hegemony and uniformity. Muñoz (1999) viewed worldmaking as a deconstruction of dominant paradigms and worldviews by undermining gender and sexual practices undergirded by heteropatriarchal hegemony and as a complete abandonment of racialized heterosexual performances that center straightness, whiteness, and cisnormativity.

Muñoz called this worldmaking process for queers of color *disidentification*—the extent to which racial, gender, and sexual minoritized persons disengage from dominant cultures and construct their own culture. Jourian (2017, 247) mobilized Muñoz's work to illustrate the ways trans* men defy gender norms. Jourian explained, "To disidentify is an agentic political act of resistance that creates new truths rather than either adopting the dominant reality or opposing it entirely." As such, disidentification takes up performativity as a politics with potential to produce new and countercultural formations. Muñoz (1999, 146) posited that the act of disidentification works to create counterpublics, which he defined as "communities and relational chains of resistance that contest the dominant public sphere." Ballroom culture, as depicted on the FX network television show *Pose*, is one example of queer worldmaking that highlights disidentification. Cultural workers produce counterpublics through a varied and dynamic gender system, kinship networks that extend beyond biological expectations, and performances that reflect actual survival strategies. The outcome is a queer of color cultural phenomenon that dismantles hegemonic systems of gender identity and expression, while also creating space for queer and trans* communities to thrive.

Reginald Blockett (2018) employed queer of color analysis to interpret data from a multiyear critical ethnographic study of Black queer men in college. He designed his study to understand the dynamic ways that this sexual culture created lifeworlds within predominantly white and largely heterocisnormative campus contexts. Blockett observed his study participants' sensemaking of their fluid identities as gender nonconforming and/or genderqueer Black men. They described experiences of dislodging hegemonic and, at times, destructive masculinities that mapped themselves onto Black male bodies and both straight and queer Black men. Blockett witnessed as participants reworked their relationship with masculinity, explaining that "the project of queer worldmaking required a collapsing of and complete detachment from heteromasculinity, particularly hegemonic and destructive masculinity" (Blockett 2018, 117). For example, one study participant, Angel, who identified as femme and gender nonconforming, described how he found it necessary to disidentify with heteromasculinity, which he viewed as penetrative and dominating. Angel stated, "I'm trying to accommodate, right, so everybody has the space to talk and to do whatever, right? Because I'm not particularly interested in being super-duper masculine. That's not at all what I'm interested in" (Blockett 2018, 116–17). This reworking of masculinity has been confirmed in other studies exploring the diverse masculinities of Black men and boys, such as Lance McCready's (2010) study on Black gender nonconforming youths in dance programs and Lori Patton's (2014) study of gender nonconforming Black men at historically Black colleges and universities. Unlike conventional ways of coming to know identity formation and development, the ways of worldmaking for QTPOC rely on individual and collective agency to disrupt normative constructions of gender, sexuality, and race. Edward Brockenbrough (2015) offered that deploying intellectual agency for queers of color allowed them to disidentify with dominant ideologies and logics intended to control their bodies and minds. In the following sections, we examine literature that highlights the cultural politics QTPOC must contend with as they respond to oppressive regimens and practices intended to marginalize their identities.

QTPOC Sexual Politics and Racialized Heteropatriarchy

Rejecting the notion that Black people are a monolithic group, Collins (2005) urged readers to consider the sexual, racial/ethnic, and gender differences that are constantly being augmented and constructed, oftentimes by members outside the Black community. Collins posited three key differences in what she called "the new racism": (1) a global economy that disproportionately disenfranchises people of African descent, (2) transnational racism existing without governmental policy support, and (3) the manipulation of ideas through mass media. Looking at the actions that were set in place during chattel slavery, Collins argued that dehumanizing practices such as rape, negative imagery, and lynching are all part of the creation of a regressive Black sexual politics. Collins offered some methods for developing a progressive Black sexual politics, stating, "The antidote to a gender-specific racial oppression that advances controlling images of deviant Black sexuality does not lie in embracing a conservative politics of respectability that mimics the beliefs of those responsible for the sexually repressive culture in the first place" (Collins 2005, 51). Marlon Riggs (1991) and Cathy Cohen (2005) named controlling images, such as the punk, sissy, faggot, bull dagger, or Snap! queen, as demeaning and reductive to Black queer people.

These negative images and their lineages to chattel slavery have an enduring impact on Black sexual minorities today. The totalizing impact has condensed and deprived Black sexuality of the cultural history that enriches and affirms Black livelihood. For example, while emasculating practices employed during slavery, like buck breaking—which included sodomizing male slaves—have been eradicated, violence and assault are still common practices to reprimand those deemed socially, morally, and reproductively illegitimate. Stacey Patton (2012) argued that rather than being hostile toward and afraid of Black sexuality, society must free itself from fears that impede all forms of sexual diversity. Taken together, these conceptualizations enhance an understanding of progressive Black sexual politics that embraces both hetero- and nonheterosexual subjectivities. Collins's chapter on mapping racism and heterosexism speaks specifically to Black LGBTQ people and their prolonged existence and suffering as an underclass within an already oppressed population. She also drew on the HIV/AIDS epidemic as a key site to expose national discourses of Black and Brown LGBTQ people as incubators of disease. Collins's literary contribution is refreshing and rearticulates an understanding of Black queer men's subject formation in the context of the United States.

Several scholars have argued that the HIV/AIDs epidemic led to further deterioration of Black sexual politics broadly, and Black and Brown antiracist projects specifically. Darren Hutchinson (1999, 57) explained, "Despite the devastation of AIDS within communities of color, anti-racist political organizations have largely ignored this issue, due to homophobia, heteronormativity and a false 'belief' that the issues presented by AIDS lie outside the scope of 'traditional' anti-racist politics." This sort of fragmenting within Black and Brown antiracist organizing and coalition building across communities of color is precisely how homophobia and heterosexism are racialized by dominant power structures (Carruthers 2018). Understanding how HIV/AIDs is taken up as solely a Black queer issue dislodges antiracist projects from their potential to advocate for a progressive Black sexual politics. Therefore, the eradication of HIV and other sexually transmitted infections creates boundaries that explicitly fracture communities of color and their ability to transform public health discourses.

Cohen's (1999) provocative book *The Boundaries of Blackness: AIDS and the Breakdown of Black Politics* analyzed how the epidemic has created fault lines of differences within the Black community. She exposed precarious efforts made within Black political agendas to ignore the AIDS epidemic, which has disproportionately affected African Americans and Latinos, and particularly Black and Brown gay, bisexual, and queer men (Centers for Disease Control and Prevention 2010). Cohen pointed to fear of the unknown, Black respectability politics, and state-endorsed policies and practices as sites where the endemic effects of Black heteropatriarchy circumvents any redress for QTPOC surviving the HIV/AIDS epidemic. The totalizing consequence after years of disregard for Black and Brown queer life equates to the current state of affairs, where the CDC estimates that one in two Black gay and bisexual men and one in four Latino men will be infected with HIV in their lifetime (Centers for Disease Control and Prevention 2016). This evidence suggests that Black queer men in the United States are devalued by the political agendas of broader queer communities and within their Black racial communities. Lives are at stake, and the nation-state appears to be a part of the problem.

Andrea Smith (2006, 2010) proposed a framework for women of color and people of color organizing and coalition building, and described the three pillars of white supremacy that advance heteropatriarchy:

1. Slavery/capitalism—resting on the idea that Black people are inherently enslavable, advanced by logics of capitalism and ownership;
2. Genocide/colonialism—the idea that indigenous people must disappear and nonindigenous white people are justified in controlling land, spirituality, resources, and culture in an effort to preserve the nation-state; and
3. Orientalism/war—centers on the use of unending militia, both domestic and abroad, to impose superior civilization on the exotic other.

Using these pillars as tools of exploitation, the state strategically colonizes cultures, communities, and other nation-states through capitalism and political power. Smith concluded by suggesting that "heteropatriarchy is the building block of the US empire," and furthermore "the building block of the nation-state form of governance" (2006, 71). The production of heteropatriarchy as a state formation to law and order is exactly the sort of legitimized violence that Chandan Reddy (2011) posited when exploring lawmaking and queer of color experiences in the United States. En masse, the state creates a peculiar environment for QTPOC, who must exist at the paradox of racial, gendered, and sexual manipulations that deteriorate their possibilities for noble livelihoods.

Sexual Language and QTPOC Legibility

Scholars in the fields of linguistics, literacy studies, sexuality studies broadly, and Black queer studies particularly have long explored the embodiment and cultural production of sexual language within sexual cultures. In their text titled *Speaking in Queer Tongues: Globalization and Gay Language*, William Leap and Tom Boellstorff (2004, 12–13) contend with the politics of sexual cultures and sexual languages as a worldmaking phenomenon constructed by queer communities to navigate broader structures of power and inequality. They explained:

> If there are sexual cultures then there must be sexual languages, that is, modes of describing, expressing, and interrogating the ideologies and practices relevant to the sexual culture(s) to which speakers of that language belong and modes of communication through which they constitute agreement and disagreement.

This framework of sexual language centers on transnational sexual and political economies that create systems where queer people rework forms of "intersubjective meaning" that "attends to the linguistic and cultural knowledge that underlies and enables those textual and discursive practices" (Leap and Boellstorff 2004, 13). In other words, sexual cultures produce sexual language by reconstituting what might be considered proper and therefore normative modes of communication to resist and "talk back" (hooks 1989) to dominant discursive power structures.

Patrick Johnson (2004, 251) offered a perspective on the uniqueness and collaborative nature of Black gay language as a mechanism to resist monolithic understandings of Blackness and gayness. He explained, "Ultimately, black gay language or black gay vernacular is a hybrid discourse that relies solely on neither gay English nor black vernacular but draws from each and functions in relation to its users' specific contexts, needs, desires, and social and political purposes." In this line of thought, Black queer vernacular can be understood as a liberatory cultural practice embodied and performed by Black queers and other QTPOC to (re)claim, recognize, and express language through nonheteronormative ways of thinking and being.

Multiple studies show that QTPOC employ sexual language, such as Black queer vernacular, to dismantle racialized heteronormativity. In her study of Black queer youth in a peer-support group, Mollie Blackburn (2005, 90) and her study participants termed this language "gaybonics," which they used as a "Borderland Discourse to elicit pleasure and to subvert oppression." Blackburn's participants deployed gaybonics as an intimate language used among predominantly Black and Brown queer communities. She explained, however, that gaybonics "is also about constructing borders within this community as practice for subverting homophobia," or "the salt that's to come" (Blackburn 2005, 101) outside this community. Blackburn's study elucidates the worldmaking possibilities of gaybonics to subvert homophobia, heterosexism, and perhaps racism. We further discuss the delimitations of Black queer vernacular in the following subsection, but first describe the importance of considering the pleasures involved in sharing a unique language in the process of worldmaking and identification.

Black queer vernacular is a key mode of identifying queer subjectivities. Johnson (2004) delineated Black queer vernacular from other forms of sexual language not only for its political and sociocultural assemblages, but also for its role in membership recognition—that is, the ability to discern those who are members of the LGBTQ community, specifically the QTPOC community, versus those who are not. Common terms and phrases like "reading, throwing shade, spilling tea, and kiki" have lineages in queer and trans* communities of color, specifically through ballroom drag culture. Hearing these terms being used in casual language might be an indicator that the space is affirming queer culture and queer lifeworlds. As QTPOC stake a claim in the creation and meaning-making of such terms, they embody and perform sexual language that is recognizable to others with queer subjectivities. As a sexual language, the production and performance of Black queer vernacular becomes a legibility marker, mapped onto Black and Brown queer and trans* people by way of their immersion within the sexual culture.

This is not to say that everyone who uses or performs Black queer vernacular should be read as having a queer or nonheterosexual identity. In fact, terms and phrases that are typically associated with Black queer language have often become a part of mainstream culture, just as voguing (a dance style) crossed from queer of color communities into mainstream pop culture in the 1980s. The idea that terms like *shade*, *reading*, *kiki*, or *slay*, for example, have become a part of mainstream culture might suggest that Black queer language is not so subverted and subcultural after all; it is a sexual language with roots in Black and Brown queer spaces and has been taken up by nonqueer and even non-Black communities.

While queer vernacular is engaged as both an intimate pleasure and legibility marker used among Black and Brown queers, it also serves as a way of responding to dominant power structures. bell hooks (1989,

9) theorized that "talking back" was a revolutionary politic that Black women deployed to reject silencing inherent in patriarchal capitalist societies, like that of the United States. She explained, "It is that act of speech, of 'talking back,' that is no mere gesture of empty words, that is the expression of our movement from object to subject—the liberated voice." This liberatory voice embedded in the act of "talking back" is exactly a consequence of Black queer vernacular and often deployed similarly to the liberatory strategies that hooks illuminated. Queer vernacular and other worldmaking cultural productions demonstrate the labor, resistance, and new technologies being taken up by queer and trans* communities of color as they fashion anti-oppressive worlds and counterpublics.

QTPOC worldmaking offers a new way to think about identity development for Black and Brown queer and trans* people. QTPOC worldmaking stands in contrast to stage models of race, sexual orientation, and gender identity that gesture toward intersections and contexts of white supremacy and heterocisnormativity even as they reinforce respectability politics through end points that emphasize integration of identity over identity pride. Worldmaking extends models of multidimensional identity development and ecological perspectives to center new identities through counterpublics, shared language, and talking back.

Conclusion

Consciously shifting from single-category models of racial and sexual orientation identity development into the intersectional, ecological mindsets inherent in QTPOC worldmaking opens possibilities for new ways to think about identities and identity development. Taking at its core the ways that race and racism construct gender and sexuality, and the ways that gender and sexuality construct race and racism, QTPOC worldmaking opts in to a new space of counterpublics that embraces a hopeful conception of self and community, personal and group identities. QTPOC worldmaking opts out of the heterocisnormativity required to maintain the historical and contemporary reality that white supremacy depends upon policing Black, Brown, *and* white bodies and desires.

The implications of taking seriously the possibilities presented by QTPOC worldmaking as identification and identity development are many. For queer and trans* people of color, it could be valuable to know about and enact worldmaking strategies, such as creating and maintaining social and intellectual counterpublics. As educators, we advocate teaching about QTPOC worldmaking as an identity development process; minoritized youth and college students repeatedly report that having access to language, ideas, stories, and models of identity development provides ways to think about themselves (Linley, Renn, and Woodford 2018). Instructors in K-12 and postsecondary education can talk with students in age-appropriate ways about intersecting identities and social contexts that attempt to shape individuals' identity development and identifications; staff who work in social service settings (e.g., church, scouting, or community centers) and in extracurricular settings on college campuses (e.g., student activities, LGBT resource centers, ethnic and racial cultural centers) can talk with youth and students about creating counterspaces through media, arts, and political action.

An ecological perspective that acknowledges that individuals, and QTPOC specifically in this case, can actively change the environment or opt out of existing systems and create their own provides a framework for thinking and talking about how worldmaking might occur and the value in attempting it. When QTPOC worldmaking is taken seriously, it opens identity possibilities for queer and trans* people of color that also provide a model for other communities. The concept of worldmaking emerged from the lives of QTPOC, and certainly that history must always be acknowledged if and when people of other identities take up a similar approach. With that caveat in mind, it is exciting to think about the possibilities for hope and light that QTPOC worldmaking provides.

REFERENCES

Abes, Elisa S., Susan R. Jones, and Marylu K. McEwen. 2007. "Reconceptualizing the Model of Multiple Dimensions of Identity: The Role of Meaning-Making Capacity in the Construction of Multiple Identities." *Journal of College Student Development* 48, no. 1 (January–February): 1–22. doi: 10.1353/csd.2007.0000.

Atkinson, Donald R., George Morten, and Derald W. Sue. 1979. *Counseling American Minorities: A Cross-Cultural Perspective*. Dubuque, IA: W. C. Brown and Benchmarks.

Berlant, Lauren, and Michael Warner. 1998. "Sex in Public." *Critical Inquiry* 24, no. 2 (Winter): 547–66.

Blackburn, Mollie V. 2005. "Agency in Borderland Discourses: Examining Language Use in a Community Center with Black Queer Youth." *Teachers College Record* 107, no. 1 (January): 89–113. doi: 10.1111/j.1467-9620.2005.00458.x.

Blee, Kathleen. 2019. "Doing Violence, Making Race: Lynching and White Racial Group Formation in the US South, 1882–1930." *Ethnic and Racial Studies* 42, no. 8 (June): 1360–62. doi: 10.1080/01419870.2018.1525499.

Blockett, Reginald A. 2018. "Thinking with Queer of Color Critique: A Multidimensional Approach to Analyzing and Interpreting Data." In *Critical Theory and Qualitative Data Analysis in Education*, edited by Rachelle Winkle-Wagner, Jamila Lee-Johnson, and Ashley N. Gaskew, 127–40. New York: Routledge.

Brockenbrough, Edward. 2015. "Queer of Color Agency in Educational Contexts: Analytic Frameworks from a Queer of Color Critique." *Educational Studies* 51, no. 1 (January): 28–44. doi:10.1057/978-1-137-55425-3_28.

Buckland, Fiona. 2002. *Impossible Dance: Club Culture and Queer World-Making*. Middletown, CT: Wesleyan University Press.

Carruthers, Charlene. 2018. *Unapologetic: A Black, Queer, and Feminist Mandate for Radical Movements*. Boston: Beacon.

Cass, Vivienne C. 1979. "Homosexual Identity Formation: A Theoretical Model." *Journal of Homosexuality* 4, no. 3 (Spring): 219–35.

Centers for Disease Control and Prevention. 2010. "The Role of STD Prevention and Treatment in HIV Prevention." www.cdc.gov.

———. 2016. "Half of Black Gay Men and a Quarter of Latino Gay Men Projected to Be Diagnosed within Their Lifetime." www.cdc.gov/.

Cohen, Cathy J. 1999. *The Boundaries of Blackness: AIDS and the Breakdown of Black Politics*. Chicago: University of Chicago Press.

———. 2005. "Punks, Bulldaggers, and Welfare Queens: The Real Radical Potential of Queer Politics?" In *Black Queer Studies: A Critical Anthology*, edited by E. Patrick Johnson and Mae G. Henderson, 22–51. Durham: Duke University Press.

Collins, Patricia Hill. 2005. *Black Sexual Politics: African Americans, Gender, and the New Racism*. New York: Routledge.

———. 2009. "Foreword: Emerging Intersections—Building Knowledge and Transforming Institutions." In *Emerging Intersections: Race, Class, and Gender in Theory, Policy, and Practice*, edited by Bonnie Thornton Dill and Ruth Enid Zambrana, vii-xiii. New Brunswick: Rutgers University Press.

Cross, William E., Jr. 1971. "The Negro-to-Black Conversion Experience: Towards a Psychology of Black Liberation." *Black World* 20, no. 9 (July): 13–27.

D'Augelli, Anthony R. 1994. "Identity Development and Sexual Orientation: Toward a Model of Lesbian, Gay, and Bisexual Development." In *Human Diversity: Perspectives on People in Context*, edited by Edison J. Trickett, Roderick J. Watts, and Dina Birman, 312–33. San Francisco: Jossey-Bass.

Dillon, Frank R., Roger L. Worthington, and Bonnie Moradi. 2011. "Sexual Identity as a Universal Process." In *Handbook of Identity Theory and Research*, edited by Seth J. Schwartz, Koen Luyckx, and Vivian L. Vignoles, 649–70. New York: Springer.

Drescher, Jack. 2015. "Out of DSM: Depathologizing Homosexuality." *Behavioral Sciences* 5, no. 4 (December): 565–75. doi: 10.3390/bs5040565.

Duran, Antonio, Reginald A. Blockett, and Z. Nicolazzo. 2020. "An Interdisciplinary Return to Queer and Trans* Studies in Higher Education: Implications for Research and Practice." In *Higher Education: Handbook of Theory and Research*, vol. 35, edited by Laura W. Perna, 111–73. New York: Springer. doi: 10.1007/978-3-030-11743-6_9-1.

hooks, bell. 1989. *Talking Back: Thinking Feminist, Thinking Black*. Boston: South End.

Hutchinson, Darren Lenard. 1999. "Ignoring the Sexualization of Race: Heteronormativity, Critical Race Theory and Anti-Racist Politics." *Buffalo Law Review* 47, no. 1: 1–117.

Jackson, Bailey W., III. 1976. "Black Identity Development." In *Urban, Social, and Educational Issues*, edited by Leonard H. Golubchick and Barry Persk, 158–64. Dubuque, IA: Kendall/Hunt.

Johnson, Patrick E. 2004. "Mother Knows Best: Black Gay Vernacular and Transgressive Domestic Space." In *Speaking in Queer Tongues: Globalization and Gay Language*, edited by William L. Leap and Tom Boellstorff, 251–79. Urbana: University of Illinois Press.

Jones, Susan R., and Elisa S. Abes. 2013. *Identity Development of College Students: Advancing Frameworks for Multiple Dimensions of Identity*. San Francisco: Jossey-Bass.

Jourian, T. J. 2017. "Trans* Forming College Masculinities: Carving Out Trans* Masculine Pathways through the Threshold of Dominance." *International Journal of Qualitative Studies in Education* 30, no. 3: 245–65. doi: 10.1080/09518398.2016.1257752.

Leap, William, and Tom Boellstorff. 2004. *Speaking in Queer Tongues: Globalization and Gay Language*. Urbana: University of Illinois Press.

Linley, Jodi L., Kristen A. Renn, and Michael R. Woodford. 2018. "Examining the Academic Microsystems of LGBTQ STEM Majors." *Journal of Women and Minorities in Science and Engineering* 24, no. 1: 1–16. doi: 10.1615/JWomenMinorScienEng.2017018833.

McCready, Lance T. 2010. "Black Queer Bodies, Afrocentric Reform and Masculine Anxiety." *International Journal of Critical Pedagogy* 3, no. 1: 52–67.

Muñoz, José E. 1999. *Disidentifications: Queers of Color and the Performance of Politics*. Minneapolis: University of Minnesota Press.

Patton, Lori D. 2014. "Preserving Respectability or Blatant Disrespect? A Critical Discourse Analysis of the Morehouse Appropriate Attire Policy and Implications for Intersectional Approaches to Examining Campus Policies." *International Journal of Qualitative Studies in Education* 27, no. 6: 724–46. doi: 10.1080/09518398.2014.901576.

Patton, Stacey. 2012. "Who's Afraid of Black Sexuality?" *Chronicle of Higher Education*, December 3. www.chronicle.com.

Puar, Jasbir K. 2018. *Terrorist Assemblages: Homonationalism in Queer Times*. Durham: Duke University Press.

Reddy, Chandan. 2011. *Freedom with Violence: Race, Sexuality, and the US State*. Durham: Duke University Press.

Renn, Kristen A. 2003. "Understanding the Identities of Mixed-Race College Students through a Developmental Ecology Lens." *Journal of College Student Development* 44, no. 3 (May–June): 383–403. doi: 10.1353/csd.2003.0032.

———. 2004. *Mixed Race Students in College: The Ecology of Race, Identity, and Community on Campus*. Albany: State University of New York Press.

———. 2012. "Creating and Re-Creating Race: The Emergence of Racial Identity as a Critical Element in Psychological, Sociological, and Ecological Perspectives on Human Development." In *New Perspectives on Racial Identity Development: Integrating Emerging Frameworks*, 2nd ed., edited by Charmaine L. Wijeyesinghe and Bailey W. Jackson III, 11–32. New York: New York University Press.

Riggs, Marlon T. 1991. "Black Macho Revisited: Reflections of a Snap! Queen." *Black American Literature Forum* 25, no. 2 (Summer): 389–94.

Robinson, William J. 1914. "My Views on Homosexuality." *American Journal of Urology*, no. 10: 550–52.

Root, Maria P. 1990. "Resolving 'Other' Status: Identity Development of Biracial Individuals." *Women & Therapy* 9, nos. 1–2: 185–205.

———. 1999. "The Biracial Baby Boom: Understanding Ecological Constructions of Racial Identity in the 21st Century." In *Racial and Ethnic Identity in School Practices*, edited by Rosa Hernandez Sheets and Etta R. Hollins, 77–100. Mahwah, NJ: Erlbaum.

Smith, Andrea. 2006. "Heteropatriarchy and the Three Pillars of White Supremacy: Rethinking Women of Color Organizing." In *Color of Violence: The INCITE! Anthology*, edited by INCITE! Women of Color Against Violence, 67–73. Durham: Duke University Press. doi: 10.1215/9780822373445.

———. 2010. "Queer Theory and Native Studies: The Heteronormativity of Settler Colonialism." *GLQ: A Journal of Lesbian and Gay Studies* 16, nos. 1–2: 41–68.

Somerville, Siobhan B. 2000. *Queering the Color Line: Race and the Invention of Homosexuality in American Culture*. Durham: Duke University Press.

Tatum, Beverly Daniel. 2017. *Why Are All the Black Kids Sitting Together in the Cafeteria? And Other Conversations about Race*. New York: Basic Books.

Torres, V., Susan R. Jones, and Kristen A. Renn. 2009. "Identity Development Theories in Student Affairs: Origins, Current Status, and New Approaches." *Journal of College Student Development* 50, no. 6 (November–December): 577–96. doi: 10.1353/csd.0.0102.

Wijeyesinghe, Charmaine L. 2001. "Racial Identity in Multiracial People: An Alternative Paradigm." In *New Perspectives on Racial Identity Development: A Theoretical and Practical Anthology*, edited by Charmaine L. Wijeyesinghe and Bailey W. Jackson III, 129–52. New York: New York University Press.

———. 2012. "The Intersectional Model of Multiracial Identity: Integrating Multiracial Identity Theories and Intersectional Perspectives on Social Identity." In *New Perspectives on Racial Identity Development: Integrating Emerging Frameworks*, 2nd ed., edited by Charmaine L. Wijeyesinghe and Bailey W. Jackson III, 81–107. New York: New York University Press.

Woodford, Michael R., Jessica Joslin, and Kristen A. Renn. 2016. "Lesbian, Gay, Bisexual, Trans, and Queer Students on Campus: Fostering Inclusion through Research, Policy and Practice." In *Transforming Understandings of Diversity in Higher Education: Demography, Democracy and Discourse*, edited by Penny A. Pasque, Noe Ortega, John C. Burkhardt, and Marie P. Ting, 57–80. Sterling, VA: Stylus.

5

Race and Power in Transracial and Transnational Adoption

Historical Legacies, Current Issues, and Future Challenges

JAERAN KIM

Child adoption is typically seen as a win-win-win for adoptive parents, the adoptee, and the adoptee's parents of origin (usually referenced as a birth/first mother or sometimes as birth/first parents) in our society. In this narrative, adoptive parents, often presumed to be unable to have a child by birth, get to parent a child. Although birth/first parents are presumed to be unable or unwilling to parent—not a "win" per se—they are still seen as doing the right thing by virtue of allowing their child to be adopted for what is assumed to be a better life. In reality, adoption is far more complex than what we see in most media representations, and when these adoptions involve the transfer of children into adoptive families across races and nations, the power, privilege, and oppression related to socioeconomic class, gender, age, and disability inherent in adoption to begin with are complicated by the additional factors of race, culture, nationality, and immigration. Adoption is a series of transactions—legal, social, and financial. And as with any other type of transaction, those with the most power get to define the terms and create the policies and practices that most benefit them.

Racist policies and ideas permeate transracial adoption practices in the United States, particularly regarding the interpretation of the "best interests of the child." All adoptive families—even white same-race families—are directly impacted by the racialized attitudes and policies that inform every aspect of adoption practice in the United States; however, modern adoption practices specifically negatively impact Black, Indigenous, and other communities of color. In this chapter I trace the ways race and power are embedded in the intimate sphere of family making in transracial/transnational adoption and how their dynamics affect the adoptee, their families, and communities of origin.

While there are exceptions, most transracial and transnational adoptions involve a child of color and white adoptive parents. Black and Indigenous children are extremely overrepresented in foster care compared to their representation in the general population and people of color are underrepresented as adoptive parents overall (Boyd 2014; Crofoot and Harris 2012). Black children made up 23 percent of the children in foster care compared to 14 percent in the overall child population, and Native American children were 2 percent of the youth in foster care, despite being 1 percent of the general child population (US Department of Health and Human Services 2019).

The majority of transracial adoptions (78 percent) involve white parents with children of color, and for private intercountry adoptions, 73.8 percent of the adopted children under eighteen years of age came from Asia, South and Central America, and Africa (Kreider and Lofquist 2014). These facts should prompt us to interrogate what underlying social and institutional ideologies and policies support this disparity. Transracial adoption is not merely another option for creating a family. Otherwise, we would see a world in which it is just as likely to see white children adopted by Black, Indigenous, Latinx, or Asian parents as it is the other way around. And, contrary to the narrative that people of color "don't adopt their own," research has found that people of color have historically been discriminated against in the adoption process whether because of individual agency worker bias or institutional/agency practices that rule out prospective parents of color. Transracial adoption emerged from historical child welfare practices that privileged monoracial white adoptive families, discriminated against communities of color, and used adoption as a means to assimilate and acculturate children seen as not white (or not white enough).

Context of Adoption in the United States

Public adoption, what most people know as foster care adoption, was founded on the principles of paternalism and *parens patriae* in which the government has the right to serve as the pseudoguardian for children whose parents are determined to be unable or unwilling to parent (Jimenez 2006). With public adoptions, the state serves as the child's guardian until a suitable adoptive home is found or until the child becomes a legal adult. Private adoption, on the other hand, operates in the private free market. In private adoption programs an adoption agency, attorney, or facilitator serves as a mediator between expectant parent(s) who are planning to relinquish a child and prospective adoptive parents. Intercountry (also known as international or transnational) adoption involves a child who was born in a country different from that of the adoptive parents' citizenship. Finally, the adoption of a spouse or partner's child is stepparent or second parent adoption; in the case of same-sex couples, second parent adoption is required in order to have legal rights to a partner's child whether by birth or adoption. Transracial adoption occurs in all of these types of adoption, but the policies influencing how these transracial adoptive families are formed varies.

Prior to the late 1930s, adoption as we know it today was not generally practiced. Children were typically placed in orphanages and asylums if their parents died or if their families were too poor to care for them. Children were more likely to be absorbed into extended family than by nonrelated adults and more likely to be fostered, not legally adopted. Adoption itself was stigmatized, both for the child and for the adoptive parents. The roots of more modern child adoptions reflect a cultural shift occurring during the Progressive Era, when children were recognized and valued for their emotional contributions rather than merely for their economic potential (Zelizer 1994). An emphasis on marriage and domestication following the return of the GIs after World War II contributed to a greater acceptance of legal adoption as a way to build a family. Adoption became a way to integrate a child "so seamlessly that adoptive families did not appear to be designed at all" (Herman 2008, 212). Per law, in most states biological parents' names are replaced with the adoptive parents' names on birth certificates; the original birth certificate and all other documentation related to family of origin are sealed (Carp 1998; Herman 2008).

Historical Eras of Race-Based Adoption Policies

Race-based adoption policies have always existed in the United States. Like most other federal and state programs serving citizens, child welfare services for Indigenous and Black children were largely provided internally through their communities. Many scholars have noted that when Black and Indigenous families were finally included in child welfare and adoption services in the 1950s and 1960s, white social workers assessed child safety and well-being based on best practice paradigms modeled on white, middle-class parents (Billingsly and Giovannoni 1972; Hollingsworth 1998; Slaughter 2000). Some of these scholars argued that this standard continues because current child welfare practices continue to be grounded in a system of white supremacy (Hill 2004; Roberts 2009).

Racialized policies and ideologies regarding how race and culture figure into the interpretation of the "best interests of the child" are greatly influenced by the historical patterns of race relations in the United States. Throughout these historical eras, larger philosophies of race-based policies and practices overlap and demonstrate that sometimes cultural shifts occur because of policies, and sometimes policies shift because of cultural changes.

Mass Child Placement and Assimilation: 1800s–1930s

Two large-scale mass child placement movements began in the nineteenth century: the orphan trains and the Native American boarding schools. At the heart of both of these movements was the explicit goal of assimilating children whose cultural origins were deemed problematic. Beginning in the early nineteenth century, Native American children were sent to government-run and church-run boarding schools. The children were often removed from their families by force, given Anglicized names, prohibited from participating in their cultural and religious practices or speaking their home language, and forced to wear Western clothing and hairstyles. As historian Margaret Jacobs describes, boarding school proponents claimed that assimilating Native American children through a systematic and institutionalized process of removal and education was meant to improve their economic futures, but in reality these policies were "part of a continuum of colonizing approaches, all aimed ultimately at extinguishing Indigenous people's claims to their remaining land" (Jacobs 2009, 25).

During the same time period Native American boarding schools were in operation, immigrant children were also being placed away from their families. In *The Dangerous Classes of New York* (Brace [1872] 1973, 28), Charles Loring Brace, a Presbyterian minister and head of the New York Children's Aid Society, wrote,

> Thousands are the children of poor foreigners, who have permitted them to grow up without school, education, or religion. All the neglect and bad education and evil example of a poor class tend to form others, who, as they mature, swell the ranks of ruffians and criminals. So, at length, a great multitude of ignorant, untrained, passionate, irreligious boys and young men are formed, who become the "dangerous class" of our city.

Brace believed that placing urban immigrant children with farming families was the cure for these children because "the cultivators of the soil are in America our most solid and intelligent class" (Brace [1872] 1973, 225). From 1854 until 1929 an estimated 200,000 children were placed out. The majority of the children sent out on the orphan trains were children of Eastern and Southern Europeans; a large number were estimated to be Catholic and Jewish, and many were placed without parental consent (Holt 1992; O'Connor 2001). Some of these children were formally adopted, but most ended up as farm or domestic labor (Holt 1992; Herman 2008). Both of these child placement programs assumed that assimilation was in the best interests of the children involved, because of the belief that assimilating to "American" values was more important that remaining in their ethnic and Indigenous communities.

Same-Race Matching and Assimilation: 1930s–1950s

Racial policies and cultural ideologies also impacted adoption practices for white children and continued the theme of assimilation. During the Progressive Era, social work became professionalized and the largely white, educated, privileged female workforce began focusing on adoption (Herman 2008; Kunzel 1995). Best practice meant placing children in adoptive homes that mirrored them racially and culturally to protect the family from the stigma of adoption (Herman 2008). Matching was valued in every aspect of the adoption process; social workers carefully considered the child's race, birth parents' religion, socioeconomic class, and, for many years by presumed intelligence, determined by employing

IQ tests on infants and children (Herman 2008). The Child Welfare League of America's first *Standards for Adoption Service*, published in 1958, advocated matching children with parents based on race and religion (Carter-Black 2002).

Early transnational adoptions immediately after the Second World War followed the race-matching ideologies of the times. In addition to the numbers of children orphaned in Europe and Asia as a result of war, another consequence was the children fathered by US servicemen. The first transnational adoptions of children of color were mixed-race white and Japanese children and mixed-race Black and white German children following World War II. In most cases, these children were placed in US adoptive homes where the parents matched the race of the child's father; the Black German children thus went to African American homes and the mixed-race Japanese children went mostly to white homes (Herman 2008; Choy 2013). Technically, these children were multiracial and often were visibly different in appearance from their adoptive families, but the predominant matching criteria was the presumed father's race. Child Welfare League of America documents from 1958 describe the challenge in finding adoptive homes for mixed-race children, partly because prior to the *Loving v. Virginia* court decision in 1967, over thirty states had antimiscegenation laws and finding a match for a multiracial child with an interracial couple was almost impossible (*Loving v. Virginia* 1967). Adoption agencies would match by the child's skin tone; if the child's skin color was light enough, they would be placed with a white family.

Following the end of the Korean armistice in 1953, a campaign to promote the adoption of Korean war orphans began (Choy 2013). What makes these examples of transnational, transracial adoptions unusual is that the United States was still deeply invested in both anti-immigration and Jim Crow policies. In fact, because of several immigration exclusion laws specifically targeting Asians, prospective adoptive parents had to appeal for special legislation under the Refugee Relief Act of 1953 in order to receive permission to adopt from Korea (Lee 2015; Kim and Park Nelson 2020). Similar to the adoptions of mixed-race German and Japanese children, the adoption of Korean children began with efforts to place mixed-race children, but the program proved popular and soon full-Korean children were being sent for adoption. Adoptive parents were advised to downplay their child's racial and cultural heritage in an effort to help them adjust to their new lives (Oh 2015; Patton 2000). The Korean adoption program became a template for other intercountry adoption programs to follow (Winslow 2017).

The Indian Adoption Project (IAP), created by the US Children's Bureau and the Bureau of Indian Affairs, began in 1958 and over its nine-year run placed nearly four hundred Native American children into white adoptive homes. The IAP was explicitly an assimilation program much like the boarding schools, which were still in operation (Jacobs 2013). Once again, most of the children were placed in homes far from their tribal communities (Thibeault and Spencer 2019).

The first transracial adoption of a Black child to white parents is reported to have occurred in 1948 in Minnesota, facilitated by one of the few Black social workers in the state (Ladner 1978). Transracial adoptions of Black children were not common; several states did not allow transracial adoption of Black children into white families, and most of the programs that sought adoptive homes for Black children were focused on recruiting Black families. Transracial adoptive placements were considered a last option (Ladner 1978).

Fighting Back: 1970s–1980s

Following the civil rights movement, Black and Native American activists began to push back on the systematic discrimination against their communities. The increasing number of Black children in foster care was the result of biased child welfare practices that negatively impacted Black families as well as larger cultural shifts that created a new "market" for Black transracial adoption for prospective white adoptive parents (Roberts 2009). Intercountry adoptions began to increase, and the rising numbers of transracial adoptions of Black children prompted the National Association of Black Social Workers (NABSW 1972) to publish the now-famous position statement opposing transracial adoption at the association's 1972 annual meeting. The organization argued that transracial adoption was more about fulfilling the desires of white adoptive parents than meeting the concerns of Black children, questioned whether white parents could meet a Black child's cultural and racial identity development needs, and called out the discriminatory practices against Black families in the home study and licensing process.

Following the NABSW position statement, more agencies focused on recruiting families for Black and Puerto Rican children, and the Child Welfare League of America revised its Standards for Adoption Practice guide in 1973, reversing its earlier position (McRoy 1989). The combination of the boarding school era and the Indian Adoption Project resulted in an astonishingly high number of Native American children (an estimated 25–35 percent) separated from their families and communities (Jacobs 2013). Years of continuous child removal and discriminatory child welfare policies led to the creation and ultimate passage of the Indian Child Welfare Act (ICWA) in 1978 (Crofoot and Harris 2012). Under the ICWA, child welfare agencies are required to notify federally recognized tribes when children who are enrolled or eligible for enrollment in their tribe have come to the attention of the agency. Foster and adoptive placements must follow specific guidelines that allow the child's placement in non-Native American homes only after other options have been exhausted (National Indian Child Welfare Association 2020).

Transracial Adoption as a Civil Right for White Parents: 1990s to the Present

The women's rights movement affected the numbers of white infants available for adoption. Greater access to birth control options and abortion, as well as changing cultural attitudes toward divorced and working women, meant that women who might have relinquished a child for adoption had other options (Solinger 1992). As white infants available for adoption became scarce, more prospective adoptive parents began to consider transracial adoption.

Racialized drug enforcement policies that penalized possession of crack, used more in communities of color, with longer sentences compared to possession of powder cocaine, used more by whites, led to increased child welfare and criminal justice involvement in Black communities and more Black children in foster care by the 1990s (Ortiz and Briggs 2003; Roberts 2009). By 1994, 54 percent of the children in foster care waiting for an adoptive home were Black, and they spent nearly twice the number of months in care (Hollingsworth 1998). Federal and state policies incentivized foster parents to adopt, but white adoptive parents who petitioned to adopt Black foster children because agencies were looking for a Black family claimed they were victims of "reverse racism." In one article from 1995, a legislator from Texas advocating for a white family stated, "There is no question in my mind that this is a vestige of the Jim Crow era as far as using race as a criterion for social policy" (Holmes 1995).

The Multiethnic Placement Act (MEPA) was passed in 1994, intended to encourage transracial adoptions over letting children remain in foster care if a same-race placement was not available. In a 1995 guide to MEPA from the Administration on Children and Families, Senator Howard Metzenbaum, the sponsor of MEPA, recognized that a child's cultural needs were important:

> Although an appropriate transracial placement is often a positive experience, it is also true that a same race, language or ethnic group placement can go a long way in helping children make the psychological, social, and cultural adjustment to their new family. Given the obvious benefits of same race placement, the Multiethnic Placement Act also makes it clear that race, color or national origin can be a factor in making foster care and adoptive placements, if and only if: First, the consideration of these factors are in the child's best interest, and second, race, color, or national origin is considered along with other factors. (US Department of Health and Human Services 1995, 35)

In 1996 the Interethnic Provisions Act (IEPA) was passed, removing the "permissible consideration" aspect of MEPA (US Department of Health and Human Services 1997). The Child Welfare League reviewed the impact of MEPA and found that Black children still experienced significantly longer periods of time in foster care than white children (Child Welfare League of America 2007).

How Racism Shapes the Best Interest of the Child

It is not a surprise that transracial adoption has become a practice that largely benefits white adoptive parents and harms Black, Indigenous, and other communities of color because the laws and policies that support these practices were created by and for white people. US adoption laws were designed in the context of free market capitalism and based on children as property during times when only free white men had property rights. The social work profession assumed responsibility for the facilitation of matching children with prospective adoptive parents and developed the ideologies and assessment protocols used to determine the "best interests of the child." From the beginning, the majority of the social work practitioners were college-educated white women, and the best interests of the child were practiced through this lens. And even though adoption is couched in the sentiment of "finding families for children, not finding children for families," the "client" who pays the service fees are also majority white, middle-/upper-class adoptive parents. Social workers who acknowledge the racial disparities involved in transracial adoption and want to intervene are often hampered by the existing laws and policies that support inequities—including MEPA/IEPA and the knowledge that adoption agencies compete with other agencies and parents can choose agencies that will cater to their desires—including the desire to eliminate any conversation or prerequisite activities related to race and racism (Raleigh 2018).

When communities of color have pushed back against the removal of their children, white prospective parents, supported by white-dominated child welfare and adoption agencies and legislators, created laws (e.g., MEPA/IEPA) or challenged laws (e.g., ICWA) in order to advance their rights to adopt across racial lines. The underlying assumption that propelled the creation of MEPA/IEPA was that the practice of racial matching was delaying adoptive placements for Black children, leaving them to remain in foster care until they reached adulthood. However, MEPA/IEPA was less about Black children remaining in foster care than about white families being denied the opportunity to adopt their Black foster children. Others argued that placement delays were misrepresented; for example, particularly in the Black community, relatives did not want to formally adopt but would foster; these children were considered to be languishing in foster care (Hollingsworth 1998). The Black community also highlighted discrimination against Black prospective adoptive parents. A National Urban League/African American Pulse survey revealed that only two of eight hundred Black families that had applied for adoption between 1981 and 1993 were approved (McRoy, Olgesby, and Grape 1997).

Under MEPA, an agency was able to consider a child's cultural, ethnic, or racial background and assess the capacity of the prospective foster or adoptive parents to meet those needs as long as it was not the *sole* consideration for placement. With IEPA, race, culture, and ethnicity were no longer acceptable as the basis for any placement delay or denial (US Department of Health and Human Services 1997). Agencies that violate MEPA/IEPA by denying or delaying the placement of a child based on race, affecting mostly white prospective adoptive parents, can be heavily fined; there are no repercussions for agencies that violate the recruitment part of the law, affecting prospective families from communities of color (Hollingsworth 1998).

Since the Indian Child Welfare Act was enacted in 1978, several legal attempts have been made to eliminate the law. Most of these challenges have come from white adoptive parents whose adoption petitions were denied or reversed because the child welfare or adoption agency did not notify the child's tribe or follow the placement protocols. One of the more recent cases that went to the Supreme Court was the case of *Adoptive Couple v. Baby Girl*, in which the child, whose father was enrolled in the Cherokee Nation, was placed with a couple in South Carolina despite the fact that authorities had not notified the tribe (Berger 2015). This case, originally about the child's custody and the adoption agency's violation of ICWA, attempted to challenge the constitutionality of ICWA. In the end, the child was placed with the white adoptive couple over her biological father, who wanted to parent, and the support of the Cherokee Nation.

Race shows up in another sphere connected to power and its uneven distribution: adoption fees. How much an adoption costs depends on a multitude of factors; private agency adoptions are the most expensive and foster adoptions are the least. In addition, children who are designated as "special needs"—children with disabilities or health care conditions, those who are not newborn infants, Black and Indigenous children, and children in foster care—cost less to adopt. Domestic adoption agency fees are highest for white babies and least expensive for Black children, with multiracial Black and white children in the middle. In other words, the healthy white infant comes with the highest fees and this is largely based on demand, revealing the adoption industry's focus on middle-class white prospective adoptive parents as the primary client.

Impact on Transracial Adoptees

Since David Fanshel first studied the children placed through the Indian Adoption Project, most of the social work and psychology research has found that transracial adoptees overall are well adjusted in their families, have a sense of attachment to their parents, and have a healthy sense of racial identity (Butler-Sweet 2011; Fanshel 1972; Hamilton et al. 2015; Simon and Altstein 1996). However, the majority of this research is focused on adopted children, adolescents, and young adults—times in a young person's life when they are more protected by their proximity to whiteness via their parents, family, and friends. Less is known about the experiences of transracial adoptees once they leave the protective family sphere and have to navigate the world as a person of color, and the additional tasks of renegotiating their racial identities throughout their lifetime.

A large percentage of transracial adoptees grow up in predominantly white communities. One analysis found that the average Asian adoptee is more likely to be raised in communities that have less diversity than the average white child (Kreider and Raleigh 2016). This leads some transracial adoptees to reject their racial and cultural heritage. In Jane Jeong Trenka's memoir, *The Language of Blood*, she recounts how she checked the box for "white" on her college application (Trenka 2003). She is not alone; read through narratives of transracial adoptees and many describe themselves or share that others describe them as "Oreos," "bananas," "coconuts," and "apples." Transracial/transnational adoptees often feel that they need to be the exception to the stereotypes about their racial communities. Once transracial adoptees are outside the protective spheres of white families, they are seen as any other person of color. College and young adulthood are times when many transracial/transnational adoptees first really confront their racial identities because the bulk of their daily lives no longer includes the familiar white family and friends who provided that proximal white privilege (Hoffman and Peña 2013; Samuels 2009).

Another reality is that transracial/transnational adoptees are seen as suspect in their communities of origin or seen as not authentic. For people of color, code switching is an adaptive strategy used to manage having to work and live in white-dominant spaces without sacrificing their culture (Cross 2012). Transracial adoptees have difficulty code switching because they do not have racial references for expected behaviors and attitudes in their communities of origin. In 2019 Facebook's *Red Table Talk*, a show hosted by Jada Pinkett Smith and her mother, Adrienne Banfield-Jones, and daughter, Willow Smith, presented two shows on transracial adoption. Their first show featured celebrity Kristin Davis, who is white and adopted two Black children. The second included Angela Tucker, a Black adoption professional who grew up in rural Washington state. In the episode with Davis, the hosts rushed to console her when she teared up over the racism her children face. In contrast, the hosts were outraged when in one scene Tucker described her fear of Black people. Tucker clarified by stating that her fear is about feeling inauthentic. Banfield-Jones immediately criticized Tucker, advised her to "counsel herself," and chastised her for not learning about her culture instead of attempting to understand the larger environmental and systemic forces that would cause a Black transracial adoptee raised in a rural white town to fear being rejected by the Black community (Patton 2000). Transracial adoptees have had to take on the task of creating their own strategies for reintegration into their communities of origin. One example of this is Sandy White Hawk's Gathering for Adoptees ceremonies. Since 2003 White Hawk, a transracial adoptee, has worked with tribal communities to facilitate special ceremonies that "welcome back" transracial fostered and/or adopted Native Americans (Whipple 2018).

Transracial Adoption Justice

For a half century, discussions related to race and culture for transracial adoptees on the part of adoption professionals, researchers, and parents have focused largely on encouraging adoptive parents to support their child's ethnic and racial identity, usually through activities such as attending culture camps; going on "homeland visits"; incorporating ethnic food in the home; and purchasing clothing, art, and books representing the transracial adoptees' ethnic or cultural heritage. Many of these activities focus on folk items that can be purchased; adoption professionals are less likely to encourage white adoptive parents to engage in relationships with their child's community of origin. As a result, white adoptive families are supported in what Heather Jacobson (2008) calls "culture keeping"—a celebratory approach to transracial adoptee identity—and not on transracial adoption justice.

A transracial adoption justice framework requires us to shift from believing that the add-on approach of celebrating diversity through culture keeping is enough to support a transracial adoptee's racial identity; instead, we must recognize that isolation from one's community of origin is harmful. A transracial adoption justice framework thus requires society to minimize the potential harms to transracial adoptees and their communities of origin and to incorporate practices that work to repair harm.

Transracial Adoptees' Lives Are Impacted by Both Race and Adoption

When Trayvon Martin was killed in 2012 while walking in his neighborhood because his killer, George Zimmerman, saw the Black teenager as an intruder, transracial adoptees were fearful. They inherently understand the suspicion from others in their own communities—the realities of not being recognized as the next-door neighbor's adopted child but some other person of color who does not belong.

Transracial adoptees are often asked to choose sides by people who do not understand that lives are not lived as either/or but as both/and. Transracial adoptees are largely raised to be white by omission—raised without (or with few) people of color in their neighborhoods, schools, churches, and communities. Transracial adoptees need relationships with others from their communities. Too often a transracial adoptee's middle-class white upbringing reinforces negative stereotypes about other racial groups because of the emphasis on "good schools" and "good neighborhoods"—codes for white. A transracial adoptee who identifies as white and rejects their racial or ethnic group probably had to, for their emotional, psychological, or physical survival. In addition, the pressure placed on the lone few transracial adoptees in these white communities to be the exceptional "model minority" and sole representative of their race can be debilitating. Transracial adoptees need people in their lives who understand that racial, ethnic, and cultural needs are as important as a stable home, loving parents, education, physical and mental resources, and spiritual development.

Understand How Race, Power, Privilege, and Oppression Are Connected to Transracial Adoption

A transracial adoption justice framework asks white adoptive parents and adoption professionals to question why transracial adoption almost always defaults to white parents adopting children of color rather than a phenomenon in which you might just as easily find an Asian adoptive parent of a Latinx child, a Black adoptive parent of an Asian child, or a Latinx adoptive parent of a white child. A transracial adoption justice framework means that white adoptive parents understand how adoption policies benefit white parents over prospective adoptive parents of color.

Transracial adoption justice asks white adoptive parents and adoption professionals to learn about the discrimination and oppression of communities of color in creating "adoptable" children. For example, Black families have a long history in the United States of being separated as a way to weaken community bonds and suppress their power. It also means understanding how Indigenous and Native American families have been separated intentionally as a form of cultural genocide, using white families as a way of erasing Indigenous religions, languages, and cultural practices. Transracial adoption justice means understanding the ways Latinx families, particularly those with mixed status (in terms of citizenship), have been separated. Transracial adoption justice means that white adoptive parents and adoption professionals recognize that they participated in bringing Asian children to the United States during periods when US immigration laws specifically prevented Asians from being able to emigrate. It means recognizing that children are being adopted from South and Central American countries in a time when their classmates and neighbors are chanting "build the wall" and "send them back." It means recognizing that Black children from Ethiopia and Liberia and Haiti are being adopted in a country where media personalities are questioning the Black president's birth certificate and citizenship. Transracial adoption justice means understanding that the majority of the children the United States sends out via intercountry adoption to white parents in Europe and Canada are Black (Naughton 2012).

Believe That Transracial Adoptees Experience Discrimination and Oppression

Transracial adoptees sometimes describe the frustration of feeling as if their experiences with discrimination and oppression are not believed in their white adoptive families or among their white peers (Park Nelson 2016; Smith, Jacobson, and Juárez 2011). White adoptive parents often believe that their own whiteness will protect their children from racism. A transracial adoption justice lens calls for adoptive parents to be proactive in recognizing that racialized incidents will occur and begin the work of preparing their child for discrimination and bias, a process called racial socialization.

Far too often the racial, ethnic, and cultural needs of transracial adoptees get thought of as "add-ons" that would be "nice to have" but not as important as the other stuff. Often, these add-ons are also provided through cultural consumption, what I term "drive-by culture," such as stereotypes of ethnic food, or art and artifacts from the adoptees' folk community. White adoptive parents are less likely to consider the importance of preparing their child to manage future racism and bias (Lee et al. 2006). As a result, transracial adoptees may not share their experiences with racism and discrimination because, as was found in one study by Sara Docan-Morgan (2010), previous attempts to discuss these topics had been ignored or invalidated. Remaining silent about experiences with racism may also be a way to protect adoptive parents from these painful incidents.

A transracial adoption justice framework requires adoption professionals and white adoptive parents to seek out support in strengthening racial literacy skills (Twine 2004); understand that a child's racial and cultural needs are intimately connected to their physical, safety, and social needs; and work toward antiracist policies and practices rather than merely claim to be "nonracist" (Kendi 2019).

Care about Transracial Adoptees' Communities of Origin

A rhetorical tool used by white family members and friends of transracial adoptees is that they can't be racist because of their relationship to the adoptee. The transracial adoptee becomes "my Black friend" or "my Asian daughter" when white people defend themselves in race conversations. The underlying assumption is that the white person's relational proximity to an Indigenous person or person of color is proof of their nonracism. Yet a closer look often reveals that the transracial adoptee is actually more likely to be seen through the lens of an acceptable person of color because of their distance from their communities of origin, not because of their connectedness or ties to those very same communities. This is why adoptive parents can think of their Korean-born or Guatemalan-born child as "all-American" and not as an immigrant whose community of origin should be subject to immigration quotas to the United States or "sent back" because the United States should not be taking in refugees.

Transracial adoption justice means that societies care about adoptees' communities of origin, wherever they are, and care about the issues that matter in those communities, particularly issues of inequity and oppression. A transracial adoption justice lens recognizes how inequity and oppression contribute to the adoption of children from those communities into white adoptive homes and complicates the prevailing narrative that removing children of color and placing them into white families overall harms communities of color in multiple ways; harm as a result of the loss of the community's children adds to community-level trauma. The loss of a community's children is also harmful because many of these children grow up to be afraid of, and disconnected from, their communities of origin as adults.

Transracial Adoption Affects Adoptees throughout Their Whole Lives

Adoption may be an event that ideally happens only once, but the impact of adoption can last a lifetime. Adoption brings added dimensions to a person's psychosocial development. Race, ethnicity, and country of origin are more than demographic descriptors for transracial and transnational adoptees; these characteristics also influence the ways transracial adoptees experience the so-called traditional developmental phases throughout their life (Brodzinsky, Schechter, and Henig 1993). No matter how much a transracial adoptee is raised in a white bubble, some day that adoptee will leave the confines of the world created by the adoptive parent, and the adoptee will have to face what it means to be Indigenous or a person of color in the world without the protective and proximal buffer of white parents. The transracial adoptee may see the world in the same way, but the rest of the world will not reciprocate. As transracial adoptee writer Jaiya John once said at a training for child welfare workers, "I was a cute brown teddy bear when I was a child, but I grew up to be a big Black grizzly."

A transracial adoption justice lens prioritizes research that takes a longitudinal perspective on the impact of transracial adoption on those with that lived experience. A transracial adoption justice perspective considers how the impact of race and adoption affects one's adult relationships, parenting, health, career decisions, and mental health in adulthood. It asks how transracial adoptees come to reconcile or struggle with their racial identity and relationships with their communities of origin throughout their lifetime.

Conclusion

Transracial adoptions are perceived to be more common than in reality, in part because of the cultural and media attention transracial families receive. The 2010 census found that 28 percent of all adopted children under eighteen years old were transracial adoptions and, of these, 10 percent were multiracial Black and white, 15 percent were Black, and 28 percent were Asian or Pacific Islander. The high rate of Asian/Pacific Island children was a result of transnational transracial adoptions, as Asian children made up nearly half of the transnational adoptions (Kreider and Lofquist 2014).

Transracial and transnational adoptions have been largely conceptualized through the lens of individual choice and profamilial ideologies in which the "best interests of the child" exclude a child's racial and cultural needs. These ideologies, in large part, benefit white adoptive parents and harm Black, Indigenous, and other communities of color. These ideologies and practices have also contributed to generations of transracial/transnational adoptees who often find themselves trying to navigate their identities between a white world that only sees them as the "other" and their racial and cultural communities that see them as inauthentic.

These attitudes and beliefs have largely been supported by research that is often conducted by scholars who base their findings about the transracial adoptees' adjustment and racial identity on adoptive parents' perceptions rather than the experiences of the adoptees. Many of the earlier scholars on transracial adoption are also white adoptive parents. Only more recently has research explored transracial adoption identity in adulthood, in part because more transracial adoptees themselves began entering the academy and influencing the research questions.

Transracial and transnational adoption does not exist merely because of individuals making choices about growing their families; if it was simply a matter of freedom to choose how each family decides to come together, transracial adoption would not be largely white parents with children of color. Racialized policies and ideologies have systematically positioned communities of color as deficient and white adoptive parents as child rescuers. While there have been increased attempts to provide racial and cultural socialization opportunities for transracial and transnational adoptees, most of these strategies come in the form of "celebrating diversity" rather than a deeper look into the discriminatory practices and policies that continue to support white parents at the expense of transracial adoptees of color and their communities of origin. We need transracial adoption reform and we can begin by shifting toward a framework of transracial adoption justice.

REFERENCES

Berger, Bethany R. 2015. "In the Name of the Child: Race, Gender, and Economics in Adoptive Couple v. Baby Girl." *Florida Law Review* 67, no. 1: 295–362.

Billingsley, Andrew, and Jeanne M. Giovannoni. 1972. *Children of the Storm: Black Children and American Child Welfare*. New York: Harcourt Brace Jovanovich.

Boyd, Reiko. 2014. "African American Disproportionality and Disparity in Child Welfare: Toward a Comprehensive Conceptual Framework." *Children and Youth Services Review* 37 (January): 15–27.

Brace, Charles Loring. (1872) 1973. *The Dangerous Classes of New York and Twenty Years' Work among Them*. New York: Wynkoop & Hallenbeck. Reprint, Silver Spring: NASW Press.

Brodzinsky, David M., Marshall D. Schechter, and Robin Marantz Henig. 1993. *Being Adopted: The Lifelong Search for Self*. New York: Anchor.

Butler-Sweet, Colleen. 2011. "'A Healthy Black Identity': Transracial Adoption, Middle-Class Families, and Racial Socialization." *Journal of Comparative Family Studies* 42, no. 2 (March): 193–212.

Carp, E. Wayne. 1998. *Family Matters: Secrecy and Disclosure in the History of Adoption.* Cambridge: Harvard University Press.

Carter-Black, Jan. 2002. "Transracial Adoption and Foster Care Placement: Worker Perception and Attitude." *Child Welfare* 81, no. 2 (March): 337–70.

Child Welfare League of America. 1958. "Introduction—Aim, Purpose and Use of Child Welfare League Standards." Child Welfare League of America Papers, Box 12, Folder 10, Social Welfare History Archives, University of Minnesota, Minneapolis.

———. 2007. "United States Commission on Civil Rights." September 21. www.cwla.org.

Choy, Catherine Ceniza. 2013. *Global Families: A History of Asian International Adoption in America.* New York: New York University Press.

Crofoot, Thomas L., and Marian S. Harris. 2012. "An Indian Child Welfare Perspective on Disproportionality in Child Welfare." *Children and Youth Services Review* 34, no. 9 (September): 1667–74.

Cross, William E., Jr. 2012. "The Enactment of Race and Other Social Identities during Everyday Transactions." In *New Perspectives on Racial Identity Development: Integrating Emerging Frameworks*, 2nd ed., edited by Charmaine L. Wijeyesinghe and Bailey W. Jackson III, 192–215. New York: New York University Press.

Docan-Morgan, Sara. 2010. "'They Don't Know What It's Like to Be in My Shoes': Topic Avoidance about Race in Transracially Adoptive Families." *Journal of Social and Personal Relationships* 28, no. 3 (May): 336–55.

Fanshel, David. 1972. *Far from the Reservation: The Transracial Adoption of American Indian Children.* Lanham: Scarecrow.

Hamilton, Emma, Diana R. Samek, Margaret Keyes, Matthew K. McGue, and William G. Iacono. 2015. "Identity Development in a Transracial Environment: Racial/Ethnic Minority Adoptees in Minnesota." *Adoption Quarterly* 18, no. 3 (March): 217–33.

Herman, Ellen. 2008. *Kinship by Design: A History of Adoption in the Modern United States.* Chicago: University of Chicago Press.

Hill, Robert B. 2004. "Institutional Racism in Child Welfare." *Race and Society* 7, no. 1 (December): 17–33.

Hoffman, Joy, and Edlyn Vallejo Peña. 2013. "Too Korean to Be White and Too White to Be Korean: Ethnic Identity Development among Transracial Korean American Adoptees." *Journal of Student Affairs Research and Practice* 50, no. 2 (May): 152–70.

Hollingsworth, Leslie Doty. 1998. "Promoting Same-Race Adoption for Children of Color." *Social Work* 43, no. 2 (Spring–Summer): 104–16.

Holmes, Steven A. 2005. "Bitter Racial Dispute Rages over Adoption." *New York Times*, April 13. www.nytimes.com.

Holt, Marilyn Irvin. 1992. *The Orphan Trains: Placing Out in America.* Lincoln: University of Nebraska Press.

Jacobs, Margaret D. 2009. *White Mother to a Dark Race: Settler Colonialism, Maternalism, and the Removal of Indigenous Children in the American West and Australia, 1880–1940.* Lincoln: University of Nebraska Press.

———. 2013. "Remembering the 'Forgotten Child': The American Indian Child Welfare Crisis of the 1960s and 1970s." *American Indian Quarterly* 37, no. 1 (January): 136–59.

Jacobson, Heather. 2008. *Culture Keeping: White Mothers, International Adoption, and the Negotiation of Family Difference*. Nashville: Vanderbilt University Press.

Jimenez, Jillian. 2006. "The History of Child Protection in the African American Community: Implications for Current Child Welfare Policies." *Children and Youth Services Review* 28, no. 8 (February): 888–905.

Kendi, Ibram X. 2019. *How to Be an Antiracist*. New York: One World.

Kim, Eleana, and Kim Park Nelson. 2020. "'Natural Born Aliens': Transnational Adoptees and US Citizenship." *Adoption & Culture* 7, no. 2: 257–79.

Kreider, Rose M., and Daphne A. Lofquist. 2014. *Adopted Children and Stepchildren: 2010*. Current Population Reports P20-572. Washington, DC: US Census Bureau. www.census.gov.

Kreider, Rose M., and Elizabeth Raleigh. 2016. "Residential Racial Diversity: Are Transracial Adoptive Families More Like Multiracial or White Families?" *Social Science Quarterly* 97, no. 5 (February): 1189–207.

Kunzel, Regina G. 1995. *Fallen Women, Problem Girls: Unmarried Mothers and the Professionalization of Social Work, 1890–1945*. New Haven: Yale University Press.

Ladner, Joyce. 1978. *Mixed Families: Adopting across Racial Boundaries*. New York: Anchor.

Lee, Erika. 2015. *The Making of Asian America: A History*. New York: Simon and Schuster.

Lee, Richard M., Harold D. Grotevant, Wendy L. Hellerstedt, and Megan R. Gunnar. 2006. "Cultural Socialization in Families with Internationally Adopted Children." *Journal of Family Psychology* 20, no. 4 (January): 571–80.

Loving v. Virginia 388 US 1 (1967).

McRoy, Ruth G. 1989. "An Organizational Dilemma: The Case of Transracial Adoptions." *Journal of Applied Behavioral Science* 25, no. 2 (May): 145–60.

McRoy, Ruth G., Zena Oglesby, and Helen Grape. 1997. "Achieving Same-Race Adoptive Placements for African American Children: Culturally Sensitive Practice Approaches." *Child Welfare* 76, no. 1 (January–February): 85–104.

National Association of Black Social Workers. 1972. "Preserving Families of African Ancestry." Position statement. https://cdn.ymaws.com.

National Indian Child Welfare Association. 2020. "About ICWA." www.nicwa.org.

Naughton, Dana. 2012. "Exiting or Going Forth? An Overview of USA Outgoing Adoptions." In *Intercountry Adoption: Policies, Practices, and Outcomes*, edited by Karen Smith Rotabi and Judith L Gibbons, 187–98. Philadelphia: Routledge.

O'Connor, Stephen. 2001. *Orphan Trains: The Story of Charles Loring Brace and the Children He Saved and Failed*. Chicago: University of Chicago Press.

Oh, Arissa H. 2015. *To Save the Children of Korea: The Cold War Origins of International Adoption*. Palo Alto: Stanford University Press.

Ortiz, Ana Teresa, and Laura Briggs. 2003. "The Culture of Poverty, Crack Babies, and Welfare Cheats: The Making of the 'Healthy White Baby Crisis.'" *Social Text* 21, no. 3 (January): 39–57.

Park Nelson, Kim. 2016. *Invisible Asians: Korean American Adoptees, Asian American Experiences, and Racial Exceptionalism*. New Brunswick: Rutgers University Press.

Patton, Sandra Lee. 2000. *Birthmarks: Transracial Adoption in Contemporary America*. New York: New York University Press.

Raleigh, Elizabeth. 2018. *Selling Transracial Adoption*. Philadelphia: Temple University Press.

Red Table Talk. 2015a. Season 2, episode 10 (Davis). https://redtabletalk.com.

———. 2015b. Season 2, episode 15 (Tucker). https://redtabletalk.com.

Roberts, Dorothy. 2009. *Shattered Bonds: The Color of Child Welfare*. New York: Basic Civitas.

Samuels, Gina Miranda. 2009. "'Being Raised by White People': Navigating Racial Difference among Adopted Multiracial Adults." *Journal of Marriage and Family* 71, no. 1 (February): 80–94.

Simon, Rita J., and Howard Altstein. 1996. "The Case for Transracial Adoption." *Children and Youth Services Review* 18, nos. 1–2 (December): 5–22.

Slaughter, Marty M. 2000. "Contested Identities: The Adoption of American Indian Children and the Liberal State." *Social & Legal Studies* 9, no. 2 (June): 227–48.

Smith, Darron T., Cardell K. Jacobson, and Brenda G. Juárez. 2011. *White Parents, Black Children: Experiencing Transracial Adoption*. Lanham: Rowman and Littlefield.

Solinger, Rickie. 1992. *Wake Up Little Susie: Single Pregnancy and Race before Roe v. Wade*. New York: Routledge.

Thibeault, Deborah, and Michael S. Spencer. 2019. "The Indian Adoption Project and the Profession of Social Work." *Social Service Review* 93, no. 4 (December): 804–32.

Trenka, Jane Jeong. 2003. *The Language of Blood: A Memoir*. St. Paul: Borealis.

Twine, France Winddance. 2004. "A White Side of Black Britain: The Concept of Racial Literacy." *Ethnic and Racial Studies* 27, no. 6 (November): 878–907.

US Department of Health and Human Services. 2019. "Preliminary Estimates for FY 2018 as of August 22, 2019." AFCARS Report no. 26. www.acf.hhs.gov.

US Department of Health and Human Services, Administration for Children and Families. 1995. "Guide to MEPA." www.acf.hhs.gov.

———. 1997. "Guide to IEPA." www.acf.hhs.gov.

Whipple, Cat. 2018. "Powwow Welcomes Returning Natives." *Circle News*, November 1. http://thecirclenews.org.

Winslow, Rachel Rains. 2017. *The Best Possible Immigrants: International Adoption and the American Family*. Philadelphia: University of Pennsylvania Press.

Zelizer, Viviana A. 1994. *Pricing the Priceless Child: The Changing Social Value of Children*. Princeton: Princeton University Press.

6

How Did Black Folks Become Indians?

What Lived Experiences Say about Belonging, Culture, and Racial Mixture in Native America

ROBERT KEITH COLLINS

Like most chicken and egg problems, it's hard to know which came first. Did Jews and other Euroethnics become white because they became middle class? That is, did money whiten? Or did being incorporated in an expanded version of whiteness open up the doors to a middle-class status? Clearly, both tendencies were at work.
—Karen Brodkin Sacks (1994, 86)

When activist-scholar Karen Brodkin Sacks (1994) wrote the book chapter "How Did Jews Become White Folks?" in Steven Gregory and Roger Sanjek's edited volume *Race*, one of her goals was to illuminate how changing notions of white racial group affiliation were a component of America's system of institutionalized racism. In this institution, being recognized and belonging as ethnically "white" were the results of processes of cultural change that led to Jewish men benefiting from federal programs, particularly GI Bills and Federal Housing Association (FHA) and Veterans Administration (VA) mortgages. These resources enabled Jewish men to acquire social roles in a growing post–World War II US economy as white-collar professionals and facilitated their belonging to the white middle class.

In the introductory quote, Sacks reminds us that it is hard to know whether people become members of ethnic groups because they adopted cultural practices of those groups or because they were accepted into a new US culture that was expanding its definitions of belonging by opening doors to white suburban affiliation status. This chapter takes a person-centered ethnographic approach to the expansion of this discourse, by examining how African cultural change within Native American communities and families led to new definitions of being and belonging, and the relationship these definitions shared with larger race-making practices in the United States. Focusing on why enslaved Africans, Native Americans, and their African-Native American children (i.e., individuals of blended cultural and/or racial ancestry) said what they said and did what they did, I draw upon Works Progress Administration (WPA) slave narratives researched during the creation of the Smithsonian's traveling banner exhibit *IndiVisible: African-Native American Lives in the Americas* to support the argument that African cultural change within Native America must be understood according to the nature of changing Native American attitudes toward race within their communities and families. Furthermore, Native American cultural impacts on Africans in these communities and families are by-products of these attitudes (*IndiVisible*, n.d.).

Like Sacks, who was "surprised to read that America does not always regard its immigrant European workers as white, that they thought people from different nations were biologically different" (Sacks 1994, 2), I am constantly surprised that many Americans do not know that Africans and Native Americans were once enslaved alongside one another and that Africans were enslaved by Native Americans. If we listen to some African Americans and descendants of Indian Freedmen whose ancestors were slaves among the Five Civilized Tribes (Cherokee, Chickasaw, Choctaw, Creek, and Seminole nations), and read the narratives former slaves told to WPA fieldworkers, we learn of the shared bondage, kinship (both voluntary and involuntary), and forced servitude that shaped senses of belonging, cultural practices, and racial mixtures that their ancestors embodied. Key questions for this chapter thus become, Did Africans become "American Indians" because they lived among Native Americans? In other words, did Native American cultures "Indianize" Africans? Or did incorporation into Native American communities and families and expanding views on belonging lead to Africans "being Indian" through social role and status acquisition?

Although these points and questions may seem revisionist, they are consistent with nineteenth- and twentieth-century anthropological and historical analyses that illuminated the impact of changing and varied racial attitudes among Native Americans toward African populations living among them as citizens and slaves. Such analyses often utilized terminology and concepts that are recognized as problematic today. For example, descriptors like "full-blood" and the reliance on principles of blood quantum when describing individuals and communities have been critiqued more recently for not attending to the complexities of race and legitimizing false notions of distinct racial categories. In order to avoid revising the words of early writers, this chapter reflects the original terms these authors used when referencing or quoting their works.

Understanding African Cultural Change in Native America

The notion of African cultural change in Native America has been central in the work of many anthropologists and historians between 1890 and 1960 (Abel 2014; Chamberlain 1891; Cobb 1939; Foster [1935] 1978; Herskovits 1964; Woodson 1920). Subjectively, through the lens of assimilation, acculturation studies in the United States examined the impact that European cultures had on African and Native American cultures. In the United Kingdom, studies centered on the nature of culture contacts that occurred and the adaptation of both populations to imported European lifeways in the United States and throughout the Western Hemisphere, including the ways slavery facilitated the incorporation of Africans and Native Americans into European cultures. Both analytical frameworks focused on cultural change as a direct precipitate of European expansionism; however, the impact of African and Native American cultures on European cultures and their impacts on one another remained elusive (Hallowell 1963).

Although Alexander Francis Chamberlain alluded to this phenomenon in his works, "The Contribution of the American Indian to Civilization" in 1903 and "The Contribution of the Negro to Human Civilization" in 1911, it was not until Cuban scholar Fernando Ortiz (1947) published *Cuban Counterpoint: Tobacco and Sugar* that the dynamic nature of cultural change was illuminated. Ortiz's contribution was paying particular attention to the *agency exerted by colonized populations* in the face of acculturation, which led to the coining of the term "transculturation." For Ortiz, there was a direct linkage between changes in social roles and cultural change that could be seen in the collective contribution and history of sugar and tobacco production in Cuba.

For A. Irving Hallowell (1963), however, cultural change included more than processes of assimilation into the lifeways of colonial populations. Following in the footsteps of Chamberlain, Hallowell determined that cultural change also comprised processes of lifeway acceptance, changing self-understandings, identity formation, rejection, and social role acquisition on the part of the individuals encountering and being incorporated into a new culture. To account for the identification practices of individuals who broke or modified their own cultural group affiliations while experiencing acculturation, Hallowell coined the term "transculturalization" to illuminate "the process whereby individuals under a variety of circumstances are temporarily or permanently detached from one group, enter the web of social relations that constitute another society, and come under the influence of its customs, ideas, and values to a greater or lesser degree" (Hallowell 1963, 523). Transculturalization further deconstructed the experiences of individuals in contact with new cultures, as they navigated and negotiated being, belonging, and social role acquisition.

Examining the experiences of Africans enslaved alongside Native Americans and by Native American slaveholders, Hallowell (1963) noted that this concept could be applied to examples of "Indianization" found in the fieldwork conducted by his mentor Frank Speck (1908) and later Laurence Foster (1935). To "Indianize" or "adopt the ways of Indians" were American expressions that dated back to the 1600s (Hallowell 1963, 520). Hallowell described Africans as representing a third dimension of contact, which had been conventionally analyzed through focal points of European and Native American contact and Native American contact with Europeans. As slaves, Africans and Native Americans shared the same social roles and status under European and Native American slaveholders. Speck's fieldwork revealed that slavery was a major catalyst for African integration into Native American households, communities, and societies. According to Speck, among the Creeks, "It is said among the descendants of these slaves today that the Indians were easy masters, and that the servitude to the Negro was more like a form of hired services, where they were supported and protected by the Indians to whom in return they tendered their aid in agriculture and household labor" (Speck 1908, 107).

Academic understandings of how African cultural change occurred as a result of contact with Native Americans as well as Europeans came as a result of field studies prior to Hallowell and Speck that sought to understand the state of Native Americans prior to 1820. Anthropological and historical investigations into the nature and sources of contact between Africans and Native Americans would follow as early as 1890. Prior to these empirical explorations, African cultural changes had occurred within Native American communities and societies according to tribal-specific aims, rules of trust, and values for welcoming in outsiders, to a degree that many scholars have not recognized or recorded (Herskovits 1964). Of the 500,000 Africans brought since 1619 into the territories that would eventually comprise the boundaries of the United States, the vast majority would concentrate in the major slavery-practicing regions of the northeastern and southeastern seaboard where cotton, fur, rum, sugar, tobacco, textiles, and whale oil were produced (Hallowell 1963; Morse [1822] 1970; Woodson 1920).

It must be remembered that prior to the 1830s, Native Americans still comprised the majority population in many rural areas of northern states such as New York and Massachusetts; northern midwestern states such as Illinois and Minnesota; and southern states such as Alabama, Louisiana, and Mississippi, and thus played vital integral roles as both forced servants and slaveholding entrepreneurs. Consequently, rural and urban areas contained a significant presence of enslaved and free Africans, Native Americans, and their African-Native American children of blended cultural and racial heritage once referred to as Mustees (Morse [1822] 1970; Forbes 1983).

As early as 1889, scholars studying "the African in Canada" noted that Mohawks such as Joseph Brandt possessed slaves (Hamilton [1889] 2011). Although some claimed that Brandt was giving shelter to runaway slaves, there was no dispute about the admixture of African blood among Mohawks. It is important to mention that academic understandings of African cultural change as a result of contact with Native Americans in New England had been noted since 1633. These notations also included evidence of African agency and social roles in New England. George Washington Williams ([1883] 2014) in *History of the Negro Race in America* also documented the prevalence of intermarriage between Native American women and enslaved African men in Massachusetts. The frequency of this intermarriage may have impacted Chief Justice Parker's decision that the children born to such marriages were free (Williams [1883] 2014).

Nathaniel Southgate Shaler's (1890) article "Science and the African Problem" in the *Atlantic Monthly* explored the extensive mixture between Africans and Native Americans and the impact of this intermingling on the appearance of both groups. Population records from the Massachusetts Historical Society Collections reveal population data on intermarriage between Africans and Native Americans (Woodson 1920). For example, in 1763 approximately 440 individuals lived in Chappaquiddick, all of whom were full-blood Native Americans or mixed African and Native American. The US census of 1790, which included residents of Massachusetts with residents of Maine, noted 4,000 Africans, of which 2,000 were of blended African and Native American ancestry (US Census Bureau, n.d.). As early as 1833, Historical Collections of the Essex Institute noted the mixture between Native Americans of Cape Cod and Africans who were both free and slaves (Woodson 1920; Chamberlain 1891).

In 1833 the Groton Pequot in Connecticut, numbering forty individuals, were recognized as being of white, Negro, and Pequot ancestry. The Shinnecock of Long Island had been recognized as being mixed with African ancestry since the time of slavery in the northern states. Intermarriage occurred with such frequency that Dr. Daniel Brinton's (1887) study of Nanticoke language revealed the presence of non-Algonquin words, found to be Mandingo, resulting from African immigration into their nation. It should not come as a surprise that these intermarriages occurred at a time when Native Americans were the majority population in the colonies and later the United States. Even Thomas Jefferson (1800), in his *Notes on the State of Virginia*, recorded that the Mattapony had intermixed with Africans to a degree that suggested to European Americans that they may have had more African than Native American ancestry. Documentation of historical interactions were not limited to population numbers. Their shared kinship ties were also examined. John De Forest and Felix Octavius Carr Darley's (1853) *History of the Indians of Connecticut* documented families, for example, such as the Hatchetts of the Paugussett or Wepawaug nation, who were all mixed with African ancestry by 1850.

In the southern states, Seminoles not only received runaway slaves, but also engaged in slaveholding. Mick-e-no-páh, for example, owned no fewer than a hundred slaves. Enslaved Africans lived by themselves, away from Seminole slaveholders. Their social roles included cattle herding, cotton agriculture, and so forth, from which they shared a portion of their gains with Seminole slave owners. In Texas, enslaved Africans performed the same daily hunting and agricultural practices as their Native American slave owners (Hallowell 1963). Among descendants of Seminole slaves, Foster (1935) learned that "some of these Indians were rich and were holders of Negro slaves whom they did not treat as the colonists treated theirs. The slaves were permitted to live together and to have their own homes, grains and herds, but they had to pay a certain amount of money at a given time to their masters" (Foster 1935, 21). He further found that like their ancestors, "Seminole Negroes continued to live an 'Indian life,' and that many of the older ones were 'Indian' in their religion as well as in their social and economic practices" (Foster 1935, 66). How African cultural change has been understood is inextricably linked to the nature of academic interest. Despite significant interest prior to 1960, several analytical gaps still exist in the literature.

Explanatory Gaps in the Analysis of African Cultural Change in Native America

The literature describing cultural change among enslaved Africans in Native American communities, families, and societies is grounded in some of the earliest empirical ethnological, ethnographic, and vital statistics data on African and Native contact evident in the anthropological and historical records, and narrated life experiences that comprise the WPA slave narratives (Collins 2009; Lauber 1913; Nash 2014; Katz 2012; Shaler 1884). Nevertheless, three explanatory gaps remain.

First, the perspectives of all Africans serving as fellow slaves alongside enslaved Native Americans cannot be found in the literature. Such absence of experiential data was noted as early as 1890 by Chamberlain (1891). While he was concerned that data could never be gathered on the phenomenon prior to 1890 due to limits in academic interest, analysis of the WPA slave narratives may provide insight into the breadth of interactions that occurred between the populations in shared bondage.

Second, anthropological and historical records contain significant evidence on the existence of Africans and African-Native Americans within Native American families, communities, and societies; however, the changing attitudes these individuals held toward Native Americans in shared bondage or as bond-servants to Native Americans need further academic investigation. Many scholars have given attention to Africans and Native Americans as "fellow slaves" (Porter 1932). The attention given, however, focuses on the phenomenon, leaving how the two populations experienced one another in shared servitude or master-servant relationship an open question.

Third, there are evident variations in African and African-Native American experiences with Native American slaveholders described in the WPA slave narratives and the Native American attitudes toward African presence explored by scholars. Yet, specifics of how Africans entered these communities, families, and societies, adapted to Native American lifeways, and accepted or rejected their own tribal-specific African lifeways in exchange for Native American lifeways remain in need of further academic investigation (Collins 2009).

These explanatory gaps in the literature also reveal the difficulties encountered by scholars exploring African cultural change as a result of contact with Native Americans. The importance of analyzing this phenomenon continues, as the many dimensions of African experiences with Native American contact remain elusive. To understand the nature of these interactions requires an approach that reveals how enslaved Africans made sense of their experiences (Collins 2009).

African Cultural Change and Native American Racism

The relationship between African cultural change and Native American racism has seldom been a central focus of analysis in either anthropological or historical literature; however, significant evidence of changing Native American attitudes toward African presence exists. Anti-Black racism, whether in emulation or learned from European Americans, made possible the rules of inclusion and exclusion that Africans experienced from Native Americans as fellow slaves and while enslaved by Native American (Collins 2009; Littlefield 1978, 1979; Porter 1932).

On the one hand, in shared servitude, Africans and Native Americans experienced slavery; however, on the other hand both groups also experienced the segregation practices on plantations that preceded those characteristics of Jim Crow segregation in the southern United States. For example, Della Bibles, an enslaved Native American, described her experiences with plantation segregation to WPA fieldworker Ada Davis in October 1937 in Waco, Texas:

> Mammy was a white woman. When she was about fourteen, Marse Snell, he married her to a full-blood Indian that he had on the place named Ephram Snell. He was Marse Snell's slave same as the Negroes, but I never knew how or why. . . . Yes, ma'am, I 'members 'bout the house we lived in, and the beds, and chairs. . . . The slaves had what they called "one-legged" bedsteads. . . . Everybody cooks on a fireplace in the winter, and out-of-doors in the summer. . . . Of course, with us, like with all families 'round us, all the children, white and black, grew up on the yard together. But they didn't eat or sleep together. I never have, in my life, lived with the Negroes. (Minges 2004, 26–31)

As slaves of Native Americans, some Africans also experienced the same racial biases that characterized the relationship between European American slaveholders and Africans.

For example, during his fieldwork among the Seminole, Foster (1935) learned that intermarriage between Seminole Negros and Seminole continued as it had for generations, despite changing attitudes toward individuals of African descent when, in 1908, the state of Oklahoma legislature passed a law that gave American Indians the status of whites and prohibited intermarriage with any person having one drop of Negro blood. For Foster's respondents, this change in status resulted in individuals being classed as "colored" who had siblings classified as "white," and was accompanied by a change in attitude that differed from the positive and friendly behaviors experienced prior to the change. Foster concluded,

> The amount of opposition which the Negro meets from the Indian in any given locality varies directly with the strength and persistency of the race complex in that locality. . . . In most instances, the attitude is definitely traceable to the fact that the Indian has learned that this association with the Negro gives him the status of a Negro, which status is generally a damning one both in the estimation of the man who gives the status and of the man to whom it applies. (Foster 1935, 75)

There is a considerable body of literature that addresses the various racial attitudes Native Americans held over time toward Africans and predates and can be used to build on Foster's conclusion and variations in Native American racial attitudes. In anthropology, for example, Cyrus Thomas's (1903) work examined African racial absorption among the Narragansett and how many of their communities had become accused of being, and mistaken for, Negro communities. Frank Speck's (1908) work revealed how the Narragansett made no distinction between full-blood or mixed-blood children and all were loved equally. In his work among the Nanticoke, however, he learned of the post-Reconstruction tribal split between Nanticoke who freely intermarried with Africans and those who intermarried among Nanticoke and with whites (Speck 1915).

John Reed Swanton's (1926) work revealed how Jim Crow segregation of African Americans lent to African-Native Americans being among the last speakers of American Indian languages—particularly the Houma in Louisiana. Later, Circe Sturm's (2002) ethnography *Blood Politics: Race, Culture, and Identity in the Cherokee Nation of Oklahoma* revealed how racial attitudes created an anti-Black sentiment that lent to Cherokee descendants being rejected for citizenship, despite the Treaties of 1866 that guaranteed their adoption into the nation, while those of blended European ancestry and/or white phenotype were accepted. What these studies have in common are their discussions of African and African-Native American experiences with the racial attitudes of tribal-specific Native American clans, communities, families, individuals, tribes, or nations. For Foster, it is these attitudes that also shaped the extent to which African-Native Americans felt accepted as members of tribal communities or rejected and affiliated to greater or lesser degree with African Americans.

Native American Racism and African-Native American Being and Belonging

Contextualizing African-Native American being and belonging within Native American racism enables us to understand how aspects of the race complex have caused once friendly connections to fade or be ignored (Foster 1935, 74). Such contextualization also enables scholars to understand how such actions may constitute what Naomi Quinn later referred to as "more or less explicit messages from socializing agents, and these lessons extracted from the behavior modeled by these socializers about what is moral and what is natural" (Quinn 1992, 121). Examination of WPA slave narratives reveals that socialization that Africans and Native Americans received in their forced servitude occurred between enslaved Africans and Native Americans, as they taught one another which jobs and roles were to be performed. Socialization also occurred between slaveholders and enslaved Africans and Native Americans, as interpersonal communication conveyed messages of social roles to be performed and who was free, who was slave, and who decided (*IndiVisible*, n.d.).

Africans enslaved by Native American slaveholders were socialized by the slaveholders in accordance with traditional Indigenous slavery practices. This occasionally resulted in full-blood slaveholders adopting Africans into the family and clan or, more commonly among white and Native American mixed-blood slaveholders, perpetual servitude according to the slaveholder's aims and values. These aims and values often mirrored those of their European American counterparts.

Foster (1935) offered the most comprehensive summary of this phenomenon by asserting that it was the race complex that further taught both the African and Native American, for example in Oklahoma, that, "from the point of view of the law of Oklahoma, an Indian who associated with a Negro on terms of equality is a criminal" (Foster 1935, 74). Foster's points were supported by fifty years of anthropological investigations into the dynamics of Native American cultural impact on African populations in the United States. Like Chamberlain, Hallowell, Speck, and Woodson before him, Foster sought to challenge racial expectations of enslaved Africans that created the illusion that enslaved individuals were impacted only by contact with Europeans.

The lives of formerly enslaved individuals among the Cherokee, Choctaw, and Creek that inform and support this analysis were shaped by their knowledge of culture: everyday lifeways that enslaved and enslaving families practiced and agreed to be their understandings of appropriate collective behavior, with which families from similar facets of culture agree, and those from dissimilar facets contest and disagree. Like Foster, I hypothesize that these lifeways enable us to make sense of the world around us and shape self-understandings, and did the same for Africans enslaved alongside and by Native Americans. However, the respondents interviewed by WPA fieldworkers have caused me to further hypothesize that self-understandings among enslaved Africans and African-Native Americans were both private and public. Private formulations were indelibly linked to family and kinship ties, despite the fact that slave families and kindship ties were officially considered illegitimate. Understandings of self were public as well, since social experiences as a slave produced answers to the question "Who am I?" that were both consistent and inconsistent with kinship. This duality was important because of individual needs to navigate race-making practices within US society. However, it also raises other questions pertaining to identity and culture raised by this chapter. More specifically, do these two conceptualizations of self suggest inconsistencies between family-based identification and racial recognition that generate conflict for those who hold racial perceptions of us and expect the two to be synonymous? And what is it about private self-understanding that is so coercive that it encourages us to challenge the perceptions of others? For Africans and African-Native Americans the answers lie in whether or not private and public interpersonal interactions with Native Americans caused race to become salient in self-understanding. Where self-understanding is inconsistent with racial categorization, the potential for resistance or an alternative identity arises. Where self-understanding is consistent with race and part of existential concerns, the need for resistance is reduced. Many of us, like Erik Erikson (1994), who introduced the concept of identity to the social sciences, understand that our mothers and fathers were the first to socialize us into understandings of who we are and where we come from, only to watch these notions challenged by nonfamilial members of community and society attempting to derail these teachings.

The transculturalization approach taken in this chapter enables the exploration of individual self-understandings within the cultures, the family, and society, and the nature and source of these inconsistencies. The remembered lived experiences of the African-Cherokee, African-Choctaw, and African-Creek individuals presented next will exemplify these African-Native Americans' self-understandings and the salience of Native American lifeways in them. Their lives reveal the nature and source of the racism that shaped their senses of being and belonging.

These narratives, collected between 1936 and 1938, are selected excerpts from more than two thousand interviews with former slaves conduct by WPA interviewers. Although the interviewers did not center their question on experiences of what it was like to be enslaved alongside Native Americans or by Native Americans, the respondents' answers to the open-ended questions illuminate what it was like for individuals or their children to live and witness these experiences (Library of Congress, n.d.).

Three salient themes emerge from the WPA slave narratives from individuals enslaved alongside both Africans and Native Americans: being African and Native American, belonging to a Native American parent or slaveholder, and race mixture as an understanding of self. All of these themes are addressed in the previously discussed literature. Excerpts presented here were used in the creation of the traveling banner exhibit *IndiVisible: African-Native American Lives in the Americas*. Nearly three years in the making, and running between 2009 and 2015, this collaboration between the National Museum of the Native American, the National Museum of African American History and Culture, and SITES (Smithsonian Institution Traveling Exhibition Services) illustrated the dynamics of African and Native American contact in North, Central, and South America, as well as the understandings of being, belonging, and self-understanding that African-Native Americans (i.e., individuals of blended African and Native American cultural and racial ancestry) embodied. The narratives presented here illustrate African-Native American understandings of being, belonging, race mixture, and servitude (Collins 2009).

Jefferson Cole described his lived experiences as a slave to a Choctaw slaveholder to WPA fieldworker James Gray in Hawthorne, Oklahoma, in March 1938:

> I am eighty-eight years old, and I was born under slavery. I lived in Eagle County of the Choctaw Nation until I was freed after the Civil War. . . . Our old original mistress was a full-blood Choctaw woman. I think she came from Alabama or Mississippi during the exodus in 1833, or thereabout. . . . She married a white man named Peachler, and of course, that made her children half-breeds. And they were more progressive and ambitious than the full-blood Indians. . . . When I was growing up, I was what was called a houseboy. I worked around the house—getting in wood, taking care of the babies, carrying water, milking cows, and doing other chores around the place. . . . We lived in a community of Choctaws. Within three miles of my master's house were about a dozen families. My master farmed on a large scale, for the times, but the average Choctaw family didn't do much farming. They had small patches of corn, and a small vegetable garden, and that was all. Usually women did what little farming that was done. I have seen an Indian woman make her complete crop with nothing but a grubbing hoe; break the ground, lay off rows, and till the plants. (Minges 2004, 164–65)

Louisa Davis recalled her lived experiences being enslaved and Africans and Native Americans being enslaved alongside one another, as well as belonging to the same family, to WPA fieldworker W. W. Dixon in Winnsboro, South Carolina:

> I was born in de Catawba River section. My grandpappy was a full-blood Indian; my pappy a half-Indian; my mother, coal-black woman. Just who b'long to whem a baby? I'll leave dat for de white folks to tell, but old Marster Jim Lemon buy us all. . . . In de course of time us fell to Marse Jim's son, John, and his wife, Miss Mary. I was a grown woman then, and nursed their fust baby. . . . My pappy rise to be foreman on de place and was much trusted, but he plowed and worked just de same. . . . Once a week I see de farm hands git rations at de smokehouse, but dat didn't concern me. I was a housemaid, and my mammy run de kitchen, and us got de same meals as my marster's folks did. (Minges 2004, 15–17)

Mary Grayson described the lived experiences of her and her mother being enslaved to Creek slaveholders to WPA fieldworker Robert Vinson Lackey in Tulsa, Oklahoma:

> I am what we colored people call a "native." That means that I didn't come into the Indian country from somewhere in the Old South, after the Civil War, like so many Negroes did, but I was born here in the old Creek Nation, and my master was a Creek Indian. That was eighty-three years ago, so I am told. . . . My mammy belonged to white people back in Alabama. . . . When Mammy was about 10 or 12 years old, some of the Creeks begun to come out to the Territory in little bunches. . . . A Creek come to my mammy's master and bought her to bring out here, but she learned she was being sold, and run off into the woods. . . . The Creek man that bought her was a kind sort of man, Mammy said. . . . He took her away and was kind to her, but he decided she was too young to breed, and he sold her to another Creek. (Minges 2004, 100–101)

Felix Lindsey described his family and the race mixture they embodied at the time of their enslavement to WPA fieldworker Lottie Major in Wichita Falls, Texas, in October 1937:

> I's mo' Injun mix dan I is nigger, but make no difference. I's a nigger. You all knows how dat is. I's proud of it. . . . I was borned in Rockey Branch, Kentucky, on October 10, 1847. My mother was half-breed Creek Injun—half-Negro, half Injun. Her name was Charity. She dies 'long 'bout 1853. My father's name was Faithful. He was a full-blood Creek. He was killed in the war 'tween Mexico an' 'Nited States. (Minges 2004, 145–49)

Chaney McNair's responses to WPA fieldworker Annie Faulton, in Vinita, Oklahoma, illuminates what it was like to be enslaved by Cherokee slave owners:

> My parents came from Georgia with the Cherokee. They came by boat I 'spect. I didn't know much about 'em, can't even remember my mother, she died when I's so young. So belonged to Vina Ratliff. . . . We lived in the Joe Martin community. I've heard tell how mean he was. Lots the Cherokee had slaves. . . . Most of the Cherokees was good to their slaves, but old Joe Martin wasn't. . . . My last marster, William Penn Adair, was tall, slender man. He was pretty good looking, smart lawyer. Most of the time he was good to his slaves, but crossed up with us sometimes. . . . We had plenty to eat on Marster William's plantation—lots of wild stuff,

turkeys, deers.... You asked me if I feel bad when my father was sold? I don't know if I did or not. I had to make the most of it, slaves did. They come and take you anytime, maybe husband, maybe children. (Minges 2004, 41–42)

Julia Grimes Jones Ocklbary explained her ancestry and that of her enslaved Choctaw father to WPA fieldworker Alfred Menn in November 1937 in Manor, Texas:

My name is Julia Ocklbary, and I was born on March 2, 1855, at Bastrop, down in Bastrop County.... Ma's name was Melissa Grimes.... I called my own fathaw Pa, and his name was Arthur Grimes.... Pa was a full-blooded Choctaw Injun. Mistress Abbie's grandfather captured him f'om de Injun nation, when he was jes' a little boy. He couldn't talk plain, and de white folks had to learn him how to talk dere way. Pa always knowed dat he was a Injun. (Minges 2004, 191–97)

Implications

What implications do the literature and narratives discussed hold for researching the dynamics of African belonging, cultural affiliations, and racial mixture in Native America? The works of Chamberlain, Foster, Hallowell, Woodson, and others reveal that African belonging to Native American families and communities was facilitated through the interpersonal interactions that occurred between enslaved Africans and enslaved Choctaws, Creeks, Pequots, and so on. This belonging was initiated largely through intermarriages and the shared kinship to both parents that enslaved Africans and Native Americans embodied. Although slave status frequently overshadowed tribal-specific affiliations, the WPA slave narratives presented remind us that tribal-specific ancestry and/or parentage was not forgotten, and cultural knowledge was imparted to the children. The mixed-race African-Native American children who recalled their own experiences and those of their parents should serve as a reminder that enslaved Africans and Native Americans were keen observers of the environment in which they were forced to serve. Their servitude did not overpower their ability to love and remember their kinship ties within a system that legally enabled other humans to ascribe to them the status of chattel. Mixed race in this context represented mixture not merely in appearance but also in culture, family, subsistence strategies, and language.

The questions raised by Sacks (1994) shed light on the line of ethnographic questioning necessary to explore the intersections of African belonging, cultural affiliations, and racial mixture in Native America. Did Africans become "American Indians" because they lived among Native Americans? Or did incorporation into Native American families and communities and expanding views on belonging lead to Africans being "Indianized" through social role and status acquisition? Like Sacks's findings related to Jewish cultural and status changes in the United States, African cultural change in Native America occurred through both processes. Enslaved Africans shared slave status with enslaved Native Americans. Therefore, the exchange of culture between slaves occurred largely outside the cultural parameters of European American expectations for racial interactions or the sovereignty that their Native American slave owners embodied. Given that the African and Native American kinship ties slaves embodied were deemed illegitimate by law and social custom, their mixed-race status, as W. Montague Cobb (1939) reminds us, was synonymous with being a slave and seldom documented, except in the memories of the children who called them mother and father. This is evident in the narrative of Felix Lindsey, who by today's blood quantum measurements would be three-quarters Creek ancestry. This is also evident in the narrative of Julia Grimes Jones Ocklbary, who was half Choctaw. Her father was a full-blood Choctaw who was kidnapped and sold into slavery. For scholars interested in the validity of African American claims to Native American ancestry, it seems that further studies of these phenomena and the life histories that the WPA slave narratives represent can reveal answers overlooked by previous scholars.

Hallowell's transculturalization method for describing African cultural change in contact with Native Americans allows for the illustration of how slave status was acquired, the understandings of self that enslaved Africans possessed within servitude, the slave families they created with enslaved Native Americans, the love and trust that motivated their intermarriages, and the understandings of belonging to a family that their African-Native American children remembered. In this context, for enslaved Africans who married enslaved Native Americans and African-

Native children born to enslaved Native Americans, "Indianization" was part of coexistence as a couple and upbringing, despite the illegitimacy of slave status. For Africans enslaved to Native American slaveholders, slave status required adaptation and conformity to tribal-specific Native American cultures through custom and language acquisition, preparation of foods, subsistence strategies, and so forth. For example, in the narrative of Jefferson Cole, his servitude as a "houseboy" brought him in close contact with the Choctaw woman who enslaved him. His duties of taking care of the children, carrying water, cleaning the house, and other tasks helped to maintain her household and caused him to adapt to slave life in Eagle County of the Choctaw Nation. For Chaney McNair, enslavement by Cherokee was inherited through her parents, who came over on the "Trail of Tears" with the Cherokee. Acquisition of slave status and Cherokee language and lifeways were also part of her upbringing and lifeways of her parents before her. Therefore, in both examples, "Indianization" can be said to have occurred by affiliation and social role acquisition.

Another major implication of the literature and narratives discussed in this chapter is that the analysis of African belonging in Native America is not an attempt to revise the history of Africans and African-Native Americans in the United States, it is a continuation of over a hundred years of anthropological and historical investigation of one aspect of the race mixture that some African Americans embody. The person-centered approach taken in this chapter to the study of African transculturalization in Native America is an attempt to illuminate the relevance of enslaved African senses of belonging, cultural affiliation, and race mixture that shaped the lived experiences that inform this analysis. Given the cultural diversity of the Native Americans that enslaved African and African-descended individuals interacted with, academic questions need to be formulated to address the dynamic nature and breadth of these interactions, so as not to reinforce the illusion that there was one cultural practice that shaped African cultural change in Native America.

The discourse contained in this chapter consists of information conducive to future research on the relevance of these interactions to the 269,421 individuals who self-identified as American Indian or Alaska Native and Black and the 230,848 individuals who self-identified as

American Indian or Alaska Native, white, and Black in the 2010 census (Norris, Vines, and Hoeffel 2012).

Conclusion

What implications do the literature and narratives hold for understanding how "Black folk became Indians" and for answering the related questions, Did Africans become Indianized because they lived among Native Americans or did their incorporation into Native American communities and expanding views on belonging lead to them acquiring social roles and status related to being tribal-specific "Indians"? Laurence Foster (1935) reminded us that these interactions ensured that

> there are Indians who are greatly mixed with Negroes who are Indian in their culture and are legally regarded as Indians. In other instances, large numbers of persons who are mixed with Negro and Indian blood accept the status of Negroes because of the fact that their dominant culture is Negro. Yet, in these instances, these peoples often take delight telling about their Indian strain. (Foster 1935, 74)

Foster also reminded us that it is important to note that contemporary Native American attitudes toward Africans are rather different from those historical attitudes that shaped early interactions in the United States and the race complex caused some Native Americans to separate themselves from African-Native Americans. Despite this separation, past interactions—like those that have produced the 182,494 individuals identifying as African American and Native American today—"Indianized" Africans through shared servitude, kinship, language, religion, subsistence strategies, and so on (Norris, Vines, and Hoeffel 2012).

If the processes by which Africans became Native American is to be illuminated, then analyses of African cultural change among tribal-specific Native Americans in the United States must include analyses of the dynamics of these processes and the individual lived experiences that comprise the phenomenon. A major implication of this analysis is that merely being among Native Americans did not facilitate cultural change. Instead, it was through the *social role* acquired as a slave in shared servitude and in servitude to Native American slaveholders that cultural practices were accepted, as illustrated in Davis's narrative; or rejected, as asserted in the narrative of Grayson. However, it was this imposed social role that led to the acquisition of tribal-specific lifeways and understanding of slave duties among African-descended individuals.

The central argument in this chapter is that to understand how "Black folk became Indians" requires an examination of the lived experiences and interpersonal relationships Africans and Native Americans shared as fellow slaves and Africans experienced as bondsmen and women to Native American slaveholders. The larger goal of this argument is to further investigate the origins of Native American ancestry among African Americans and the African presence in Native America. Such investigations can reveal the limitations of analyses of the phenomenon that have little to no salience in the lived experiences of the people who informed the research. Assuming acceptance of being and belonging from physical appearance has always been a pitfall for studies that take the existence of African-Native Americans as the central focus of analysis. Through the investigation of shared experiences of voluntary and involuntary kinship and servitude, we can understand the human agency exercised by Africans and Native Americans within the institutions of slavery practiced by Europeans and Native Americans.

The transculturalization lens through which this analysis has been constructed illuminates additional limitations and the need for exploration of the life histories that describe changing Native American racial attitudes toward Africans. Without such discourse in the academic record, understandings of African experiences among Native Americans will continue to be shrouded in misconceptions. First, understandings of historical relationships between Africans and Native Americans will be premised on casual links between African individuals and Native American societies without a clear explanation of how individuals were incorporated. Second, the fact that not all Africans internalized Native American cultures completely will remain elusive. Third, how different enslaved Africans adapted to and internalized different Native Americans cultures, such as Cherokee, Choctaw, Creek, and so on, which furthered the cultural variation that existed among enslaved Africans will remain underexamined. To understand how Africans became Indians requires analyses of the agency and avenues through which Africans navigated and negotiated Native American attitudes toward their presence. Examining these phenomena through the lens of African transculturalization in Native America can enable such understanding.

REFERENCES

Abel, Annie Heloise. 2014. *The American Indian as Slaveholder and Secessionist*. Scotts Valley: CreateSpace.

Brinton, Daniel G. 1887. "On Certain Supposed Nanticoke Words, Shown to Be of African Origin." *American Antiquarian and Oriental Journal* 9, no. 6 (January): 350–54.

Chamberlain, Alexander Francis. 1891. "African and American: The Contact of Negro and Indian." *Science* 17, no. 419 (February 13): 85–90.

———. 1903. "The Contribution of the American Indian to Civilization." *Proceedings of the American Antiquarian Society* 16 (October): 91–126.

———. 1911. "The Contribution of the Negro to Human Civilization." *Journal of Race Development* 1, no. 4: 482–502.

Cobb, W. Montague. 1939. "The Negro as a Biological Element in the American Population." *Journal of Negro Education* 8, no. 3 (July): 336–48.

Collins, Robert Keith. 2009. "What Is a Black Indian? Misplaced Expectations and Lived Realities." In *IndiVisible: African-Native American Lives in the Americas*, edited by Gabriella Tayac, 183–96. Washington, DC: Smithsonian Books.

De Forest, John, and Felix Octavius Carr Darley. 1853. *History of the Indians of Connecticut from the Earliest Known Period to 1850*. Hartford: Hamersley.

Erikson, Erik H. 1994. *Identity and the Life Cycle: Selected Papers*. New York: Norton.

Forbes, Jack D. 1983. "Mustees, Half-Breeds and Zambos in Anglo North America: Aspects of Black-Indian Relations." *American Indian Quarterly* 7, no. 1: 57–83.

Foster, Laurence. (1935) 1978. *Negro-Indian Relations in the Southeast*. Reprint, New York: AMS.

Hallowell, A. Irving. 1963. "Papers in Honor of Melville J. Herskovits: American Indians, White and Black: The Phenomenon of Transculturalization." *Current Anthropology* 4, no. 5 (December): 519–31.

Hamilton, James Cleland. (1889) 2011. *The African in Canada: The Maroons of Jamaica and Nova Scotia*. Reprint, Charleston: Nabu Press.

Herskovits, Melville. 1964. *The American Negro: A Study in Racial Crossing*. Bloomington: Indiana University Press.

IndiVisible: African-Native American Lives in the Americas. n.d. www.nmai.si.edu. Accessed June 1, 2016.

Jefferson, Thomas, and Samuel Knox. 1800. *Jefferson's Notes, on the State of Virginia; with the Appendixes*. Baltimore: Pechin.

Katz, William. 2012. *Black Indians: A Hidden Heritage*. New York: Atheneum.

Lauber, Almon Wheeler. 1913. *Indian Slavery in Colonial Times within the Present Limits of the United States*. New York: Columbia University Press.

Library of Congress. n.d. "Born in Slavery: Slave Narratives from the Federal Writers' Project, 1936–1938." www.loc.gov. Accessed June 1, 2016.

Littlefield, Daniel. 1978. *The Cherokee Freedmen: From Emancipation to American Citizenship*. Santa Barbara: Greenwood.

———. 1979. *Africans and Creeks: From the Colonial Period to the Civil War*. Santa Barbara: Greenwood.

Minges, Patrick. 2004. *Black Indian Slave Narratives*. Winston-Salem: Blair.

Morse, Jedidiah. (1822) 1970. *A Report to the Secretary of War of the United States on Indian Affairs*. Reprint, New York: Kelley.

Nash, Gary. 2014. *Red, White, and Black: The Peoples of Early America*. New York: Pearson.

Norris, Tina, Paula L. Vines, and Elizabeth M. Hoeffel. 2012. *The American Indian and Alaska Native Population: 2010*. 2010 Census Briefs. Washington, DC: US Census Bureau.

Ortiz, Fernando, and Harriet De Onís. 1947. *Cuban Counterpoint: Tobacco and Sugar*. New York: Knopf.

Porter, Kenneth W. 1932. "Association as Fellow Slaves." *Journal of Negro History* 17, no. 3 (July): 294–97.

Quinn, Naomi. 1992. "The Motivational Force of Self-Understanding: Evidence from Wives' Inner Conflicts." In *Human Motives and Cultural Models*, edited by Roy D'Andrade and Claudia Strauss, 90–117. Cambridge: Cambridge University Press.

Sacks, Karen Brodkin. 1994. "How Did Jews Become White Folks." In *Race*, edited by Steven Gregory and Roger Sanjek, 78–102. New Brunswick: Rutgers University Press.

Shaler, Nathaniel Southgate. 1884. "The Negro Race in America." *Atlantic Monthly*, September.

———. 1890. "Science and the African Problem." *Atlantic Monthly*, July.

Speck, Frank. 1908. "The Negroes and the Creek Nation." *Southern Workman* 37, no. 1: 106–10.

———. 1915. *The Nanticote Community of Delaware*. New York: Museum of the American Indian, Heye Foundation.

Sturm, Circe. 2002. *Blood Politics: Race, Culture, and Identity in the Cherokee Nation of Oklahoma*. Berkeley: University of California Press.

Swanton, John Reed. 1911. *Indian Tribes of the Lower Mississippi Valley and Adjacent Coast of the Gulf of Mexico*. Washington, DC: US Government Printing Office.

———. 1926. "Notes on the Mental Assimilation of Races." *Journal of the Washington Academy of Sciences* 16, no. 18: 493–502.

Thomas, Cyrus. 1903. *Indians of North America in Historic Times*. Philadelphia: Nabu.

US Census Bureau. n.d. "1790 Overview." www.census.gov. Accessed June 15, 2020.

Williams, George Washington. (1883) 2014. *History of the Negro Race in America from 1619 to 1880*. Vol. 2, *Negroes as Slaves, as Soldiers, and as Citizens*. Reprint, New York: Firework.

Woodson, Carter G. 1920. "The Relations of Negroes and Indians in Massachusetts." *Journal of Negro History* 5, no. 1 (January): 45–57.

7

Racializing Faith

The Intersections of Racism and (White) Christian Hegemony

KAMEELAH MU'MIN RASHAD AND D-L STEWART

I've always had to—both as a Black man and as a Muslim (especially in post-9/11)—be very cautious about the way that I move in the world and the way that I interact with people. I've never been able to go into a space and not be aware of my blackness or [not be] aware of my Islam.
—Umar, twenty-five-year-old African American Muslim man

This is an important time in the world and in the United States. We are experiencing the greatest movement of people in human history. With war, terror, and climate change driving international and intercontinental migration at increasingly higher rates, the religious diversity of nations and local communities is also increasing. With that greater demographic diversity is also an increased awareness and visibility of religions and faith traditions, as Diana Eck (2002) observed, an awareness that evolves into the kind of double jeopardy of race and religious faith that people like Umar, quoted above, must face.

In this chapter we discuss the intersection of multiple structures of oppression and domination on the self-perceptions and experiences of Religiously Minoritized People of Color (RMPOC). RMPOC experience religious extremism and hegemony in a Christian society, as well as racism in a white supremacist society. The need to navigate these intersecting and reinforcing systems distinguishes the experiences of RMPOC from other People of Color who are not religiously minoritized as well as from other religiously minoritized people who are white. Through this chapter, we seek to explain the context of intersectional oppression, elevate awareness of the experiences of RMPOC, and offer strategies for change and justice within faith communities and the larger society.

Why Us

I (Kameelah) am a daughter of parents who converted to Sunni Islam in the late 1970s. I am one of seven children raised in a predominantly African American Muslim community in Brooklyn, New York. I recall with fondness my mother's deep engagement in this community as well as her emphasis on self-determination, education, and social justice. Her carefully curated home library included Islamic texts focused on theology, prayer, and purification, alongside books by authors such as J. A. Rogers, Marcus Garvey, Na'im Akbar, and Yosef Ben-Jochannan. One of my earliest memories is attending a protest and rally at the well-known Slave Theatre in Bed-Stuy, Brooklyn. "No Justice! No Peace!" was a familiar chant to my precocious eight-year-old ears. These formative experiences left an indelible impression and fueled my interest in race, religion, and psychology. My doctoral research was a qualitative examination of the lived reality of Black Muslim emerging adults with respect to identity and psychological well-being. This study considered how these young adults cope with intersectional invisibility (Purdie-Vaughns and Eibach 2008), double marginalization, well-being, and belonging. The pioneering scholarship of my esteemed coauthor, D-L, served as a rich foundation upon which I was able to theorize about Black Muslim emerging adults specifically and the intersections of spirituality, faith, race, and identity broadly. This present collaboration with D-L offers an incredible opportunity for me to deepen my knowledge of RMPOC, identity formation, and the impact of multiple forms of oppression, including Christian hegemony, on this process of exploration and integration.

I (D-L) approach this topic from a family background steeped in Christianity, yet having awareness, knowledge, and skills in engaging with others across religious differences, especially members of the Nation of Islam. My personal religious background is marked by Christian ecumenism, having been raised in various Protestant denominational churches while attending Catholic schools. This background came to inform my scholarship as well when I began my doctoral program in higher education and the early years of my career as an academic scholar. I have considered how race and religion intersect (Stewart and Lozano 2009), enunciating the ways that racially minoritized people may experience their faith tradition differently than those who are white. I also have written about the spirituality of Black college students (Stewart 2002, 2010, 2013). However, all of those publications were written through a Christian lens. Christian hegemony was deep in my scholarship. I would later expand my viewpoint and my competence in religious pluralism by sharing leadership of a professional association entity group focused on religion, faith, secularism, and meaning. I also began to write about the need for student affairs professionals to become competent in discussing matters of religion, faith, and secularism with college students (for example, Stewart 2015). Collaborating with Kameelah on this chapter and colearning with her are part of my ongoing personal and scholarly spiritual evolution.

Centering the Experiences of Religiously Minoritized People of Color

Increased immigration to the United States from the Global South (e.g., Africa, South Asia, Oceania) has made more Christians in the United States aware of Islam, Hinduism, Sikhism, and Buddhism. This, along with successes in primary and secondary multicultural education initiatives, means that awareness of religious diversity has become infused in many sectors of public life.

On the other hand, this awareness is often accompanied by news of political and sectarian conflicts around the world. In other words, knowledge of Islam may be reduced to associations with terror attacks or Judaism with the Holocaust. Certain parts of the world may also be understood through the lens of sectarian violence. For example, the island comprised of the two nations of Northern Ireland (a member of the United Kingdom) and Ireland may be understood simplistically as a matter of intrasectarian discord between Catholics and Protestants. Consequently, although Eck (2002) proclaimed the United States the most religiously diverse nation across the globe, it is not necessarily the most religiously well-informed or competent in religious pluralism.

Framing the Conversation in Terms of Oppressive Systems

Discussing the intersectional oppression of RMPOC is necessary due to the realities of US settler colonialism, racism, and religious hegemony. We take a moment here to briefly explain each of these terms and recommend resources for further information. The term "US settler colonialism" refers to the ongoing occupation, settlement, and domination of Indigenous lands by white European settlers. The United States exists due to the colonization of North America by England, France, and Spain and the subsequent revolution(s) fought to take control of these lands away from Indigenous nations by white people. All the institutions that support the national sovereignty of the United States came at a direct cost to Native people, in terms of land, livelihood, and life. Roxanne Dunbar-Ortiz (2014) presented an informative and well-documented history of US colonialism. Eve Tuck and K. Wayne Yang (2012) also offered a useful lesson in what settler colonialism is and what calls for decolonization often lack but, nevertheless, must entail.

"Racism" refers to the institutionalized laws, policies, practices, and norms that created the fiction of race while structurally positioning white people at the top of the fictive racial hierarchy. Racism is best understood as a system or structure of white supremacy that benefits certain people over others and with which people of any racial classification may collude. Racism is pervasive in US society and was part and parcel of the country's founding in the eighteenth century. Further discussion of racism and its persistent effects can be found in the work of Derrick Bell (1993) and Richard Delgado and Jean Stefancic (2017).

"Religious hegemony" refers to the institutionalized dominance of one religion or faith tradition. Religious hegemony is apparent when government, public schools, places of financial transactions, and other nonreligious organizations and institutions all observe the significant religious holy days of a singular religion. Religious hegemony is also evident in daily practices and cultural norms and figures of speech that are informed by a singular religious tradition. In the United States, religious hegemony is held by Christianity. For more on Christian religious hegemony, Paul Kivel (2013) offered a detailed analysis.

Intersectional Oppression

Although we have discussed the terms "settler colonialism," "racism," and "religious hegemony," we need to go further to really demonstrate the unique burden faced by RMPOC. As Crenshaw (1991) discussed regarding intersectionality, people with multiple minoritized identities encounter multiple systems of domination and they do not encounter those systems singly. In other words, when a Black Muslim is automatically suspected of having committed a violent act, of being nasty even, that person is not just experiencing racism, they are also experiencing Christian hegemony in the form of Islamophobia. US white supremacy and Christian hegemony have compounding effects on the experiences of RMPOC. In this section we explore how settler colonialism, white supremacist racism, and Christian religious hegemony came to be intertwined. We then explore the effects of this on attitudes of white Christians toward, and their interactions with, RMPOC. Finally, we give attention to the ways that this intersectional oppression affects RMPOC's self-perceptions and engagement with each other in religious spaces. But first we want to illustrate what these concepts or terms mean in folks' lived experiences.

> I live in the South. There are streets . . . that are still named after Confederate heroes. In middle school and early high school was the time in my life where I heard terrorist jokes. That was the first time in my life I got called a nigger. I've had to stop at a gas station with a big Confederate flag in the window. Walking into this place and thinking, "They don't like me because I'm Black, . . . they don't like me because I'm Muslim." I've always had to—both as a Black man and as a Muslim (especially in post-9/11)—be very cautious about the way that I move in the world and the way that I interact with people. I've never been able to go into a space and not be aware of my blackness or [not be] aware of my Islam. The racist history . . . is alive. I have to make sure I'm watching how people are looking at me, the threat of danger is a real thing. It happens to anyone who's not a straight, white man, . . . you're at risk of being harmed. I find myself in my travels always looking around making sure, seeing all possible threats. Even if they don't come to pass, I know where all the exits are in a building. I know if I need to run out this way, I can go this way. It's sad to say, but you get used to it. It comes to a point where it's just

automatic. I think because it was so indoctrinated to me at an early age, at a certain point I didn't notice it. It was just the way that I was. It wasn't necessarily something that I had to cope with. It was a building block of my personality just because from the point that I was born to now, I've been in certain ways trained to assess threat. We had no way of predicting in 2001 the public opinion of Muslims would change drastically, but when it did happen, we (Black Muslims) didn't have to get ready because we were already ready.
—Umar, twenty-five-year-old African American Muslim man

Being a Black Muslim—or a Black, Muslim woman, rather—is like having three layers of constant struggle and discrimination that all intersect into this one identity. . . . I guess being Black Muslim means, to me, not being part of one or the other completely. Being Black, at least in my community, is strongly attributed to being part of this community of Baptists and Catholics . . . heavily involved in the Christian community and expressions of Christianity such as, Black Christmas, Black Easter and having all those experiences and as a Muslim I can't really experience that. Then on the other side being Muslim, a lot of my identity as a Black person, can't necessarily fit into what people think is Muslim. It's only in communities of both Black and Muslim people that you actually feel like you are with people you belong with, in that you're a complete person.
—Salima, twenty-two-year-old African American Muslim woman

Christianity, Racism, and Colonialism

As illustrated by the narratives offered above, Christian hegemony, racism, and colonialism are intertwined. As Ibram Kendi (2016) traced in his powerful text, racist ideas were developed to justify already existing practices that had economic and sociopolitical benefits for white people. Likewise, religious hegemony was used to camouflage nativist and racist ideologies. The argument for Indigenous land grabbing by white settlers was shrouded in the language of "civilizing savages." Beasts. Brutes. Savages. These were the epithets flung at Indigenous and African peoples for having religious, spiritual, cultural, governance, and familial structures and practices that were unfamiliar to European settlers.

Even Harvard and Dartmouth Colleges raised donations to found these schools by claiming that Native students would be granted admission to civilize them through Western classical education (Thelin 2019; Wilder 2013). Harvard and Dartmouth were decidedly sectarian institutions, like most colleges in the colonies at the time (Thelin 2019). Western classical education of the seventeenth and eighteenth centuries was inherently Christian in its curricular posture and daily regimen, requiring chapel attendance and Puritan student discipline conduct codes (Thelin 2019). Consequently, aims to civilize Native peoples inherently involved attempts at religious conversion as well as identifying as supposedly savage any peoples who did not profess Christianity, simply on the basis of their lack of profession. However, those proclamations were reserved for Indigenous and African peoples. Upon failing to convert Indigenous students and their fatal susceptibility to European-borne diseases, Harvard and Dartmouth both aborted attempts to educate Native students. Once again, Native peoples were made to be savages. On the other hand, Africans were never thought fit to be educated. Rather, Africans were thought to be fit only for manual and reproductive labor in a system of chattel slavery justified by the religious hegemonic belief that African peoples had no souls capable of Christian salvation (Kendi 2016). Christianity was used as a tool of imperialism and settler colonialism, but it would not have been nearly as effective had racism and white supremacy not been entangled with it.

White Christians' Attitudes and Interactions

Kivel (2013, 4) asserted that one clear outcome of Christian hegemony is that "Christians internalize feelings of superiority, entitlement and judgement." However, Ferber (2012, 72) noted that calling out "Christonormativity" and privilege is vociferously rejected and perceived as an offensive attack on Christianity. Due to the privilege afforded by white supremacy and Christian hegemony, individuals who possess these dominant identities are socialized to believe that their thoughts, behaviors, and worldview are objectively normal, wholesome, moral, and superior. RMPOC are cast as dangerous and malevolent, grossly transgressing the boundaries or possibilities of salvation or redemption due to their racial and religious minority status.

This socialization also influences RMPOC to believe that the normalcy of whiteness and inherent danger of POC are indisputable facts or objective truth. Further, the racialization of religion (Joshi 2006; Singh 2013; Selod 2015) in the United States post-9/11 has introduced additional layers of discrimination for RMPOC. For example, Muslims face additional scrutiny at airport security and border crossings (Considine 2017) and Sikhs have been attacked by those mistakenly assuming them to be Muslims (Ahluwalia 2011; Ahluwalia and Pellettiere 2010). What these incidents have in common is the nonwhiteness of their victims interlaced with other physical evidence of non-belongingness. Indeed, as Jaideep Singh (2013, 123) noted, "Race and religion have comingled to form indispensable aspects of an othered identity which is not only clearly outside of the nation's mainstream, but one that has been criminalized by the state."

Effect on Interactions with White Christians and Their Attitudes toward RMPOC

It is this fraught context of denial, fragility, and superiority that leads to RMPOC being subjected to environments that are often inherently and overtly demeaning and hostile. RMPOC find themselves navigating pressures to conform and assimilate to white hegemonic norms while simultaneously resisting the internalization of negative racial stereotypes and religious biases. For example, they are forced to choose between work and religious commitments because time off is not allowed, or they are mocked and harassed for bringing their religious practices into work spaces (Mujtaba, Cavico, and Senathip 2016). The psychological strain this produces is tremendous and leads to susceptibility to stereotype threat (Spencer, Logel, and Davies 2016), race-related stress (Franklin, Boyd-Franklin, and Kelly 2006), and impression management (Shams 2015).

Tahseen Shams's (2015) qualitative study of Bangladeshi American Muslims living in Mississippi, a Bible Belt state, offered a searing example of the effect of white Christian norms and assumptions on the everyday lives of RMPOC. Due to the relative isolation and marginalization faced by this community, individuals engaged in "impression management," or the construction of public identities that might be more palatable to the white and Christian majority. Individuals in this study described three distinct strategies to navigate interactions with majority individuals: distancing themselves from Islam or minimizing any display of religious affiliation; highlighting their ethnic and cultural affiliation; and challenging stereotypes in an indirect or tentative manner so as to avoid confrontation or escalation of tension.

In yet another example of impression management, the National Sikh Campaign (NSC) launched a $1.3 million "We Are Sikhs" campaign in 2017 to raise awareness of the Sikh religion and Sikh American communities throughout the United States. In fact, the campaign logo was a "star-spangled" turban. Gurwin Ahuja (2017, para. 5), the cofounder and executive director of the campaign, stated that "Sikh values are American values and Sikh Americans have been making positive and significant contributions to American life for more than a century. We run local businesses, sing our national anthem with pride, serve on local Parent Teacher Associations and lead Boy Scout Troops.... The American dream is fundamental to our identity here in America." Impression management is evident in this campaign's framing of Sikhism as related to and aligned with quintessential "American" iconography such as the national anthem and Boy Scouts of America. Despite the fact that Sikhism is the fifth-largest religion in the world, in the US context, many Sikhs may feel that they have no choice but to suppress public displays of their faith and espouse these white Christian normative views in order to be accepted.

Relatedly, interpersonal interactions with white Christians and those benefiting from Christian privilege include subtle demands for RMPOC to prove their humanity and innocence (i.e., "This RMPOC is a threat until proven otherwise"). Kameelah has named these *performative spectacles of goodness* (K. Mu'Min Rashad, personal communication, January 2020). These spectacles are displays of extraordinary acts of patriotism, grace, or moral sacrifice in order to prove one's worth, citizenship, and uncritical adoption of (white Christian) American values. The demand to prove humanity and innocence manifests itself in the subconscious and behavior of RMPOC. The tendency for RMPOC to capitulate to this demand is another type of impression management. The ultimate goal is the alleviation of white Christian discomfort rooted in the belief that if one can effectively demonstrate or embody the markers of the white

Christian majority, this will reduce one's likelihood of being read as foreign, inferior, dangerous, and un-American.

Khizr and Ghazala Khan are Pakistani Muslim immigrants to the United States and the parents of Army Captain Humayn Khan, who was killed in 2004 while on active duty in Iraq. In the *New York Times* review of Khizr Khan's book, *An American Family: A Memoir of Hope and Sacrifice*, journalist Linda Chavez (2017, para. 14) wrote,

> Their faith imbues every facet of their lives; but it is a tolerant, modern Islam. . . . "I am an American patriot," Khan writes near the end of his book, "not because I was born here but because I was not. I embraced American freedoms, raised my children to cherish and revere them, lost a son who swore an oath to defend them, because I come from a place where they do not exist."

The implication here is that one must be "tolerant, modern," and willing to die for the United States in order to gain acceptance by the white Christian majority.

It must be noted that highlighting the above examples is in no way an indictment against these RMPOC, but demonstrates instances in which religiously and racially minoritized people feel compelled to construct counternarratives and public identities in order to defy deeply entrenched stereotypes that demonize them as the Other.

In addition to these performative spectacles, RMPOC have everyday interactions with white Christians and People of Color with Christian privilege that are rife with microaggressions. Microaggressions are "subtle assaults on one's identity" (Sue et al. 2007). The detrimental impact on minority communities has been well documented (Wang, Leu, and Shoda 2011; Ong et al. 2013; Nadal et al. 2014). However, the microaggressions experienced by RMPOC must be understood using an intersectional framework because the marginalization experienced by this community occurs as a result of systems of power related to multiple stigmatized identities.

Misrecognition is a microaggressive act on the part of white Christians that has had lethal consequences. Sikh Americans routinely experience misrecognition as Muslims due to their skin color, beards, turbans, and other religious and racial markers. Tragically, misrecognition has resulted in Sikh Americans being subjected to lethal violence at the hands of white Americans. On September 15, 2001, just four days after the Twin Towers fell in New York City, Balbi Singh Sodhi was murdered at his gas station in Arizona by Frank Roque in an apparent hate crime. Roque allegedly bragged that he had killed a "towel head" as "revenge for 9/11" (Elizondo 2011, para. 15). Roque's intention was to attack someone he believed to be Muslim (a "towel head") in retaliation for the 9/11 terror attacks. The senseless killing of Sodhi is just one egregious example of the consequences of microaggressive misrecognition. However, the consequences of microaggressions also include subtle slights and invalidations whose cumulative impact over time can be extremely emotionally damaging.

Shareefah Al'Uqdah, Sahran Hamit, and Sabrina Scott (2019, 143) offered examples of "intersectional microaggressions" against African American Muslims, including the "patholog[izing] of Muslim religion and [the] African American race." Several years ago, I (Kameelah) received a request for an interview from a white Christian journalist. I was asked the following questions: "Where are you from originally? When did you become Muslim? What drew you to Islam? How did your parents feel about your adopting another religion? What was your birth name? What is it about American culture that you might find offensive as a Muslim?" Inherent in these questions are numerous microinsults and microinvalidations, including that I (Kameelah) as an African American must have converted to Islam, my faith represented a denunciation of my parents' identity (presumably Christian), and my racial-religious identities are undoubtedly incompatible with American (Christian) values. These slights become painful reminders that as a RMPOC, I—and many in my community—are viewed as outcasts from mainstream (i.e., white Christian) American society. My history as a descendant of enslaved Africans (with southern and midwestern roots dating as far back as the early nineteenth century) does little to change that perception, and my identity as a Muslim reinforces the stigma of outsider.

Whiteness is held up as an aspirational goal in the United States through the reinforcement of norms, ways of being, and ways of believing that create and reinforce white Christian supremacy. RMPOC doubly defy whiteness when they are identifiably both nonwhite and non-Christian. This reality has material consequences, including psychological, emotional, and physical violence.

Self-Perception and Engagement among Religiously Minoritized People of Color

As we noted earlier, intersectional oppression has multiple effects on RMPOC, including traumatic injury, internalized devaluation, depression, anxiety, and self-blame, as well as collective guilt and shame. RMPOC are simultaneously hypervisible and invisible in white Christian-dominated spaces. These communities are reduced to exoticized caricatures—deviations from the white Christian hegemonic norm—with little to no value assigned to their deeply rich and complex lives and experiences.

> There is an assault on Christianity. . . . There is an assault on everything we stand for, and we're going to stop the assault.
>
> Now, in these hard times for our country, let us turn again to our Christian heritage to lift up the soul of our nation.
>
> Some bad things are happening and a lot of them are happening in the mosque. . . . I'm not the only one saying this, other countries are saying this, frankly, but some really bad things are happening.
> —Donald Trump, as quoted by Whitehead, Perry, and Baker (2018, 151)

These remarks by a president of the United States demonstrate the enforcement of white Christian hegemony. These words and their underlying beliefs contribute to the oppressive effects experienced by RMPOC. The Muslim ban, the war on terror, incarceration, detention, and physical attacks on RMPOC contribute to a profound sense of vulnerability at the personal, familial, and communal levels. Due to intersectional oppression and hidden wounds of devaluation, voicelessness, and an assaulted sense of self (Hardy 2013) experienced by RMPOC, their perceptions of safety, rootedness, and belonging are constantly being questioned, negotiated, and renegotiated.

Effect on RMPOC's Self-Perceptions and Engagement with Each Other

It is important to also consider how RMPOC treat each other as a result of white supremacy and Christian hegemony. We assert that there are two ways RMPOC's self-perceptions can manifest in relationships with other RMPOC and groups that reflect different symptoms of internalized oppression (David and Derthick 2013). First is *consciousness*, an awareness of and solidarity due to shared experiences and relative status to white supremacy and Christian hegemony. An example was reported by the Carnegie-Knight News21 Initiative (News21 Staff 2018, para. 21). In their report about solidarity among Jewish and Muslim communities in Victoria, Texas, the authors extrapolated to national trends, "As religious hate crimes rise in America, faith groups across the country have come together to protect themselves and help others who have been attacked for their religion." This reflects *stigmatized solidarity* (David and Derthick 2013) a positive form of internalized oppression.

Second, internalized oppression can manifest negatively through *collusion* (David and Derthick 2013). This desire for proximity to whiteness leads to derogation, distancing, and enactments of colorism. Engaging with other RMPOC in these ways supports white supremacy and Christian hegemony, maintaining oppressive systems and structures. The vast diversity within Islam has often been the site of tensions, particularly between Black Muslims and immigrant Muslims in the United States (Elliott 2007). As Andrea Elliott (2007, para. 34) reported, "Divisions between African-American and immigrant Muslims remained pronounced long after the first large waves of South Asians and Arabs arrived in the United States in the 1960s." US Black Muslims and immigrant Muslims are attempting to narrow the divide to achieve a unity anchored in their faith. However, both faith leaders and congregants find that their efforts are challenged by deep differences (Elliott 2007): in racial politics steeped in the history of surveillance and state-sanctioned violence experienced by Black Americans; and in social class schisms fostered by generations of US white supremacy against Black Americans and recent US immigration policies that have favored those who are well educated and financially stable.

It must be emphasized that internalized oppression and the collusion of minoritized people with their own or others' oppression occur because white Christian hegemony exists. The underlying belief that People of Color who are not Christians are uncontrolled, violent, lascivious, and dirty still exists and is sometimes enunciated by political leaders. The racist and religiously hegemonic ideology of the seventeenth and eighteenth centuries has not gone away. It has merely evolved into more subtly coded language and practices, and the effect on RMPOC is deep and sustained. White Christian hegemony fundamentally corrupts the ways RMPOC engage both their faith and each other.

Malidoma Patrice Somé (1999) wrote about the ways that People of Color internalize oppression and its spiritual impact. Having accepted the message that they are dirty and lacking in self-control, some People of Color in Westernized religious traditions take on that self-image and focus on making themselves clean, pure—white—in order to be seen as virtuous. That connection is always felt to be tenuous. One misstep and they are no longer righteous in the eyes of others. All of this is rooted in a white supremacist, Christian hegemonic idea born to justify imperialist domination of certain people varying in skin pigmentation, facial features, and hair texture.

Individual and Collective Struggles of Identity Integration and Disconnection

As psychologists and developmental theorists have noted, the adolescent and young adult years are liminal periods of development and maturation, especially concerning one's social identities (Arnett 2015; Tatum 2017). During this season of life, one engages in meaning-making about the self, others, and one's place in community and society. For individuals with multiple minoritized identities, coming to an integrated understanding of the self supports positive and affirming social identity development (Stewart 2002).

Meaning-making that reflects an integrated approach resists external pressures to isolate one's identities, using just one to represent the whole self. As Audre Lorde, the Black lesbian feminist warrior woman mother poet, observed, the pressure to "pluck out some one aspect" of her identity and to "present [it] as the meaningful whole" was constant, but doing so would "eclipse or deny" the other aspects of who she was (Lorde 1984, 120). RMPOC who have internalized an understanding of the self as integrated accept that their social identities are not, as Lisa Bowleg (2012, 1268) noted, "independent and unidimensional but rather multiple, interdependent, and mutually constitutive." Their racial and religious identities do not stand in isolation, but rather help to shape and inform the other.

Intersectional Oppression of Identity Integration

This work of resisting internalized self-hatred and oppression is done amidst pressure for RMPOC to identify solely with their racially minoritized group or solely with their religiously minoritized group, but not with both. They are expected to let their difference from the larger group fade into the background for the sake of a false sense of community. As racially minoritized people within a Christian hegemonic society, they are subjected to invocations at community events that acknowledge a Christian God and call for the surrender to a Christian understanding of Jesus, which presume a commonality of experience with liturgical traditions. The ways that Christian imperialism and orthodoxy have literally destroyed or sought to annihilate Indigenous cultural spiritual practices are washed over in favor of religious oppression.

On the other side, within their faith communities, RMPOC's racial and phenotypic differences are erased in favor of organizational practices and norms that enact and collude with whiteness, white supremacy, and colorism. The call to unite in defense of the faith against Christian hegemony can elide the various ways that People of Color in these worship and community spaces are treated as less than white people. As in the larger society, racially minoritized people in predominantly white faith communities are talked over and dismissed, are not afforded leadership roles, and experience microaggressions that attack their knowledgeability and morality.

The phenomena of misrecognition, microaggressions, and impression management evident in the interactions and examples highlighted in this chapter are corrosive—eroding self-esteem and self-efficacy. Yet the psychological toll of white supremacy and Christian hegemony on RMPOC is often neglected. According to Kivel (2013, 7), "The impact on people who are not Christian but who live inside Christian-dominated cultures is, perhaps, more complex as we are forced to resist the constant aggressive pressure to accept the dominant worldview." The "constant aggressive pressure" manifests in overt and subtle ways, in multiple contexts (school, work, public spaces) and on a nearly daily basis. Internalized oppression, the cognitive depletion caused by attributional ambiguity (Hoyt et al. 2007), and symptoms of race-based traumatic injury and stress (Carter et al. 2017) are just a few of the detrimental consequences experienced by RMPOC as a result of white supremacy and Christian hegemony.

Strategies for RMPOC Communities to Engage with One Another

Radical healing can restore belonging, kinship, and community among and between RMPOC communities. The Cycle of Liberation (Harro 2018) is the spiritual base for this radical, collective healing. There are seven points in Harro's (2018) Cycle of Liberation: waking up, getting ready, reaching out, building community, coalescing, creating change, and maintaining. These are particularly relevant for healing in RMPOC communities. Waking up to white supremacy and Christian hegemony, and reaching out to and building community with other RMPOC in acts of solidarity are necessary first steps to realizing healing and new community engagement patterns.

Part of waking up requires that we acknowledge the fear and despair that may be felt in recognizing the impact of white supremacy and Christian hegemony. RMPOC must create affinity spaces in which they express pain and grief about oppression as well as to celebrate resilience and joy in the face of devaluing contexts.

Reaching out, building community, and coalescing can be enacted when RMPOC engage in dialogue with other RMPOC communities that decenters whiteness and desire to conform to hegemonic Christian norms. For example, a multiracial interfaith dialogue between Black and Latinx Muslims, Black Jews, Sikh, and Hindu communities would help foster connections and build awareness of shared experiences. However, we must consider what the barriers are to solidarity. We must question how we foster understanding when we feel overwhelmed by our own experiences of marginalization. Finally, a central aspect of even getting ready to engage with each other includes addressing the gaps in our own knowledge about each other and identifying how white supremacy and Christian hegemony benefit from our isolation from one another.

Strategies for Change and Justice

As Tuck and Yang (2015) and Leigh Patel (2015) have discussed, *theories of change* are necessary for liberation. Although critique and identification of problems, challenges, and oppressive systems and structures are necessary, they are not enough to sustain hope and galvanize resistance. These movements toward liberation need to acknowledge the ways RMPOC are affected by the multiplying effects of both white supremacy and Christian hegemony. This intersectional approach leads to better enactments of social justice by more thoroughly understanding the problem and constructing solutions that serve those on the margins of the margins. It is important that we envision the world as we want and desire it to be. We must not allow oppression to handcuff our imagination or vision of what could be beyond what is.

In that spirit, we offer our thoughts on strategies for change and justice in the lives of RMPOC. As we do so, we first discuss how definitions of belonging, kinship, and community have been affected by intersectional oppression and strategies for healing. Next, we discuss the implications of intersectional oppression for RMPOC identity integration and disconnection, as well as offer strategies. Our strategies focus first on religiously minoritized faith communities and then on US society as a whole.

Strategies for Faith Communities

Religiously minoritized faith communities have an opportunity to be allies and accomplices for the People of Color in their midst. This can be done in three ways. First, faith communities must acknowledge the different racial histories among the members and what role their faith tradition might have played in colluding with white supremacy, historically and currently. This open acknowledgment of race and racism in the experiences of members is the first step toward racial healing.

Second, leaders of faith communities need to examine the ways that whiteness and white supremacy inform patterns of who is in leadership, who receives attention and support, and who can access the services offered to members. Rarely do leaders make decisions that are openly identifiable as racist, colorist, or white supremacist. Rather, these decisions reveal what Kimberlé Crenshaw (2019) calls *baseline assumptions*. These tacit assumptions privilege ways of knowing, being, and living that reflect and support white supremacy and light-skinned colorism.

Third, leaders in faith communities should educate themselves and their members on the issues that affect the life chances and possibilities for those among them who are racially minoritized. Those political and social issues must become issues relevant for the whole faith community. What affects one, affects all. For example, police brutality against Black and Brown people might be further heightened for those who are visibly members of religiously minoritized groups. As such, white and white-passing people in religiously minoritized communities ought to stand alongside their faith siblings against police brutality, recognizing the additional burdens RMPOC people face, including gender, sexuality, and social class. These effects are multiplied for these members. Through these three strategies, faith communities can engage in racial healing, begin to practice antiracism (Kendi 2016), and become accomplices to People of Color in their own congregations and throughout the society. Change and justice begin within.

Strategies for the Larger Society

As a whole, US society has a lot of work to do to repair and reform the damage done by settler colonialism, racism, and religious hegemony. However, there are steps that can be taken—indeed, must be taken—to advance change and justice for RMPOC. These strategies are manifold, but we will highlight two here. First, government entities (local, state, and national levels) need to examine and disrupt the myriad ways that Christian hegemony actively informs business operations and cultural operations. One common example is the closure of offices to coincide with Christian holidays and cultural observances. However, another illustration involves refusing to structure the workday in ways that support religious practices of other faiths. Because race and religion are tied together, Christian hegemony often reflects and advances white supremacy, as we have illustrated in our discussion here. For example, standards of professionalism often demean cultural and faith-based hairstyles, certain lengths of facial hair, skin markings, coverings, and attire as unprofessional. To be a so-called professional means showing up to work in a manner consistent with norms based in white Christianity. If officials take a hard look at the ways that white Christian hegemony informs the norms and practices of government and then work to disrupt and dismantle them, they will be able to more justly conduct government that is supposed to be "for the people, by the people."

Second, the mechanisms of socialization include educational, religious, legal, and political institutions as well as popular culture (Harro 2018). All of these institutions are comprised of people whose *baseline assumptions* (as coined by Crenshaw 2019) help to run the engine of intersectional oppression in the society. Change and justice will be realized only when power that flows from the people is directed toward change and justice. This is massive work. Yet it begins small—within local-level groups, community centers, neighborhoods. Beverly Daniel Tatum (2017), Eboo Patel (2012), and others call for deeper conversations person to person that begin from the broad base of our commonalities rather than the narrow precipice of our differences. These dialogic approaches are important and necessary, but they do not address the ongoing oppression built in to our structural edifices. Alongside dialogue there must also be political activism, a groundswell movement that makes a demand upon systems and structures of power. Sustainable change and justice require both personal and institutional transformation.

Future Possibilities

The sociocultural, racial, religious, and political landscape in the United States is shifting. According to the Pew Research Center (2015), in the next thirty years, both the number of Christians and the number of white people will dramatically decline and Islam will grow faster than any other religion, with more Americans identifying as Muslims than those who identify as Jewish. In fact, globally, there will be nearly equal numbers of Christians and Muslims. As Eck (2002) has noted, immigration in the 1960s and 1970s heightened religious diversity in the United States with the arrivals also of B'hai, Buddhist, Hindu, and Sikh practitioners. Yet despite these substantial changes, white supremacy and Christian hegemony as systems of oppression will endure in the absence of a commitment to deep and sustained positive transformation. Indeed, Andrew Whitehead, Samuel Perry, and Joseph Baker (2018, 167) asserted that "while white Christians might be declining demographically, one of their primary cultural creations (Christian nationalism) will remain a powerful political force for years." However, we can work toward this deep and sustained transformation by embracing radical healing and hope as frameworks from which to ground solidarity, understanding, and community connectedness.

Conclusion

The current sociopolitical moment in the United States and globally presents us with an urgency and an opportunity. The ongoing effects of Christian hegemony and the intersectional oppression it has fostered are being increasingly acknowledged and resisted. At the same time, religion and faith are playing an ever-larger role in multicultural, diverse, and democratic societies like the United States. From the election of Muslim political representatives to cultural shifts in our language about the winter holidays, religious multiculturalism is gaining ground. Yet intertwining oppressions have resulted in the corruption of sacred relationships with self and others. We have a religiously multicultural society but not one that is deeply connected soul to soul.

We encourage you to read and reflect on the ideas discussed in this chapter and, upon deep reflection, to do the following. One, note what resistances you felt as you read this chapter and consider where they came from. What further work do these resistances teach you that you need to engage? Two, look around at your personal and social networks and examine what minoritized perspectives are missing or absent from those with whom you are connected. Instead of seeking out token RMPOCs to add to your social circles, take the onus on yourself to read, listen to public talks, follow public figures who are Religiously Minoritized People of Color, and go to open community events. In expanding your world, by extension, you will expand your worldview. Third, take the bold step to engage others like yourself to join you in your journey. This means being willing to have hard conversations with those most like yourself, privilege to privilege. Christians must talk to Christians about Christian hegemony, including among People of Color. White people must engage other white people about racism and white supremacy, as well as their manifestations in colorism, including among religiously minoritized groups. Challenging oppression on these fronts must not be left only to Religiously Minoritized People of Color.

REFERENCES

Ahluwalia, Muninder K. 2011. "Holding My Breath: The Experience of Being Sikh after 9/11." *Traumatology* 17, no. 3 (September): 41–46. https://doi.org/10.1177/1534765611421962.

Ahluwalia, Muninder K., and Laura Pellettiere. 2010. "Sikh Men Post-9/11: Misidentification, Discrimination, and Coping." *Asian American Journal of Psychology* 1, no. 4 (December): 303–14.

Ahuja, Gurwin. 2017. "National Sikh Campaign Launches 'We Are Sikhs.'" National Sikh Campaign press release, April 14. www.wearesikhs.org.

Al'Uqdah, Shareefah N., Sahran Hamit, and Sabrina Scott. 2019. "African American Muslims: Intersectionality and Cultural Competence." *Counseling and Values* 64, no. 2 (October): 130–47. https://doi.org/10.1002/cvj.12111.

Arnett, Jeffrey. 2015. *Emerging Adulthood: The Winding Road from the Late Teens through the Twenties*. Oxford: Oxford University Press.

Bell, Derrick. 1993. *Faces at the Bottom of the Well: The Permanence of Racism*. New York: Basic Books.

Bowleg, Lisa. 2012. "The Problem with the Phrase *Women and Minorities*: Intersectionality—An Important Theoretical Framework for Public Health." *American Journal of Public Health* 102, no. 7 (May): 1267–73. https://doi.org/10.2105/AJPH.2012.300750.

Carter, Robert, Veronica E. Johnson, Katheryn Roberson, Silvia L. Mazzula, Katherine Kirkinis, and Sinead Sant-Barket. 2017. "Race-Based Traumatic Stress, Racial Identity Statuses, and Psychological Functioning: An Exploratory Investigation." *Professional Psychology: Research and Practice* 48, no. 1 (January): 30–37. http://dx.doi.org/10.1037/pro0000116.

Chavez, Linda. 2017. "What Trump Can Learn from a Gold Star Family." *New York Times*, October 20. www.nytimes.com.

Considine, Craig. 2017. "The Racialization of Islam in the United States: Islamophobia, Hate Crimes, and 'Flying While Brown.'" *Religions* 8, no. 9 (August): 165–84. https://doi.org/10.3390/rel8090165.

Crenshaw, Kimberlé. 1991. "Mapping the Margins: Intersectionality, Identity Politics, and Violence against Women of Color." *Stanford Law Review* 43, no. 6 (July): 1241–99.

———. 2019. "The Marginalization of Harriet's Daughters: Perpetual Crisis, Misdirected Blame, and the Enduring Urgency of Intersectionality." *Kalfou* 6, no. 1: 7–23. https://doi.org/10.15367/kf.v6i1.226.
David, E. J. R., and Annie O. Derthick. 2013. "What Is Internalized Oppression, and So What?" In *Internalized Oppression: The Psychology of Marginalized Groups*, edited by E. J. R. David, 1–30. New York: Springer.
Delgado, Richard, and Jean Stefancic, eds. 2017. *Critical Race Theory: An Introduction*. 3rd ed. New York: New York University Press.
Dunbar-Ortiz, Roxanne. 2014. *An Indigenous People's History of the United States*. Boston: Beacon.
Eck, Diana. 2002. *A New Religious America: How a "Christian Country" Has Become the World's Most Religiously Diverse Nation*. San Francisco: Harper Collins.
Elizondo, Gabriel. 2011. "No Bitterness 10 Years after Sikh Killing over 9/11." *Al Jazeera* blog, September 6. www.aljazeera.com.
Elliott, Andrea. 2007. "Between Black and Immigrant Muslims, an Uneasy Alliance." *New York Times*, March 11. www.nytimes.com.
Ferber, Abby L. 2012. "The Culture of Privilege: Color-Blindness, Postfeminism, and Christonormativity." In "Systems of Privilege: Intersections, Awareness, and Applications," edited by Kim A. Case and Jonathan Iuzzini. Special issue, *Journal of Social Issues* 68, no. 1 (March): 63–77.
Franklin, Anderson J., Nancy Boyd-Franklin, and Shalonda Kelly. 2006. "Racism and Invisibility: Race-Related Stress, Emotional Abuse and Psychological Trauma for People of Color." *Journal of Emotional Abuse* 6, nos. 2–3 (October): 9–30.
Hardy, Kenneth V. 2013. "Healing the Hidden Wounds of Racial Trauma." *Reclaiming Children and Youth* 22, no. 1 (Spring): 24–28.
Harro, Bobbie. 2018. "The Cycle of Liberation." In *Readings for Diversity and Social Justice*, 3rd ed., edited by Maurianne Adams et al., 627–35. New York: Routledge.
Hoyt, Crystal L., Lauren Aguilar, Cheryl R. Kaiser, Jim Blascovich, and Kevin Lee. 2007. "The Self-Protective and Undermining Effects of Attributional Ambiguity." *Journal of Experimental Social Psychology* 43, no. 6 (November): 884–93. https://doi.org/10.1016/j.jesp.2006.10.013.
Joshi, Khyati Y. 2006. "The Racialization of Hinduism, Islam, and Sikhism in the United States." *Equity & Excellence in Education* 39, no. 3 (August): 211–26. https://doi.org/10.1080/10665680600790327.
Kendi, Ibram X. 2016. *Stamped from the Beginning: The Definitive History of Racist Ideas in America*. New York: Bold Type.
———. 2019. *How to Be an Antiracist*. New York: One World.
Kivel, Paul. 2013. *Living in the Shadow of the Cross: Understanding and Resisting the Power and Privilege of Christian Hegemony*. Gabriola Island: New Society.
Lorde, Audre. 1984. *Sister Outsider*. Berkeley: Crossing.
Mujtaba, Bahaudin G., Frank J. Cavico, and T. Senathip. 2016. "Managing Stereotypes toward American Muslims in the Modern Workplace through Legal Training,

Diversity Assessments and Audits." *Journal of Human Resources Management and Labor Studies* 4, no. 1 (June): 1–45. https://doi.org/10.15640/jhrmls.v4n1a1.

Nadal, Kevin L., Katie E. Griffin, Yinglee Wong, Sahran Hamit, and Morgan Rasmus. 2014. "The Impact of Racial Microaggressions on Mental Health: Counseling Implications for Clients of Color." *Journal of Counseling & Development* 92, 1 (January): 57–66. https://doi.org/10.1002/j.1556-6676.2014.00130.x.

News21 Staff. 2018. "As Intolerance Grows, Targeted Religious Groups Join Forces." Center for Public Integrity, August 27. https://publicintegrity.org.

Ong, Anthony D., Anthony L. Burrow, Thomas E. Fuller-Rowell, Nicole M. Ja, and Derald Wing Sue. 2013. "Racial Microaggressions and Daily Well-Being among Asian Americans." *Journal of Counseling Psychology* 60, no. 2 (April): 188–99. https://doi.org/10.1037/a0031736.

Patel, Eboo. 2012. *Sacred Ground: Pluralism, Prejudice, and the Promise of America.* New York: Beacon.

Patel, Leigh. 2015. *Decolonizing Educational Research: From Ownership to Answerability.* New York: Routledge.

Pew Research Center. 2015. *The Future of World Religions: Population Growth Projections, 2010–2050.* Washington, DC: Pew Research Center. www.pewforum.org.

Purdie-Vaughns, Valerie, and Richard P. Eibach. 2008. "Intersectional Invisibility: The Distinctive Advantages and Disadvantages of Multiple Subordinate-Group Identities." *Sex Roles* 59, nos. 5–6 (April): 377–91. https://doi.org/10.1007/s11199-008-9424-4.

Selod, Saher. 2015. "Citizenship Denied: The Racialization of Muslim American Men and Women post-9/11." *Critical Sociology* 41, no. 1 (December): 77–95. https://doi.org/10.1177/0896920513516022.

Shams, Tahseen. 2015. "Bangladeshi Muslims in Mississippi: Impression Management Based on the Intersectionality of Religion, Ethnicity, and Gender." *Cultural Dynamics* 27, no. 3 (November): 379–97. https://doi.org/10.1177/0921374014548281.

Singh, Jaideep. 2013. "A New American Apartheid: Racialized, Religious Minorities post-9/11 Era." *Sikh Formations* 9, no. 2 (October): 115–44. https://doi.org/10.1080/17448727.2013.822138.

Somé, Malidoma Patrice. 1999. *The Healing Wisdom of Africa: Finding Life Purpose through Nature, Ritual, and Community.* New York: Tarcher/Putnam.

Spencer, Steven J., Christine Logel, and Paul G. Davies. 2016. "Stereotype Threat." *Annual Review of Psychology* 67, no. 1 (September): 415–37. https://doi.org/10.1146/annurev-psych-073115-103235.

Stewart, Dafina Lazarus. 2002. "The Role of Faith in the Development of an Integrated Identity: A Qualitative Study of Black Students at a White College." *Journal of College Student Development* 43, no. 4 (July): 579–96.

———. 2010. "Knowing God, Knowing Self: African American College Students and Spirituality." In *The Evolving Challenges of Black College Students*, edited by Terrell L. Strayhorn and Melvin C. Terrell, 9–25. Sterling, VA: Stylus.

———. 2013. "Complicating Belief: Intersectionality and Black College Students' Spirituality." In *Living at the Intersections: Social Identities and Black Collegians*, edited by Terrell L. Strayhorn, 93–108. Charlotte: Information Age.

———. 2015. "The Role of Professional Associations in Advancing Spirituality, Faith, Religion, and Life Purpose in Student Affairs." In *Making Meaning: How Student Affairs Came to Embrace Spirituality, Faith, Religion, and Life Purpose*, edited by Jenny L. Small, 82–96. Sterling, VA: Stylus.

Stewart, Dafina Lazarus, and Adele Lozano. 2009. "Difficult Dialogues at the Intersections of Race, Culture, and Religion." *New Directions for Student Services*, no. 125 (December): 23–31. https://doi.org/10.1002/ss.304.

Sue, Derald Wing, Christina M. Capodilupo, Gina C. Torino, Jennifer M. Bucceri, Aisha Holder, Kevin L. Nadal, and Marta Esquilin. 2007. "Racial Microaggressions in Everyday Life: Implications for Clinical Practice." *American Psychologist* 62, no. 4 (May): 271–84.

Tatum, Beverly Daniel. 2017. *Why Are All the Black Kids Sitting Together in the Cafeteria? And Other Conversations about Race*. New York: Basic Books.

Thelin, John H. 2019. *A History of American Higher Education*. 3rd ed. Baltimore: Johns Hopkins University Press.

Tuck, Eve, and K. Wayne Yang. 2012. "Decolonization Is Not a Metaphor." *Decolonization: Indigeneity, Education, and Society* 1, no. 1: 1–40.

———. 2015. "Thinking with Youth about Theories of Change." In *Youth Resistance Research and Theories of Change*, edited by Eve Tuck and K. Wayne Yang, 125–38. New York: Routledge.

Wang, Jennifer, Janxin Leu, and Yuichi Shoda. 2011. "When the Seemingly Innocuous 'Stings': Racial Microaggressions and Their Emotional Consequences." *Personality and Social Psychology Bulletin* 37, no. 12 (September): 1666–78. https://doi.org/10.1177/0146167211416130.

Whitehead, Andrew L., Samuel L. Perry, and Joseph O. Baker. 2018. "Make America Christian Again: Christian Nationalism and Voting for Donald Trump in the 2016 Presidential Election." *Sociology of Religion* 79, no. 2: 147–71. https://doi.org/10.1093/socrel/srx070.

Wilder, Craig Steven. 2013. *Ebony and Ivy: Race, Slavery, and the Troubled History of America's Universities*. New York: Bloomsbury.

8

The Dangers of Being Too Certain

How White Desires for Racial Innocence Hinder Meaningful Racial Justice Work

ZAK FOSTE

As white, you must be open to a kind of death—a death of your stubbornness, a death of your denials, a death of your "innocence," a death of your arrogance, a death of your racial comfort, a death of your narcissism, a death of your "goodness," a death of your fears, a death of your color evasion, a death of your self-righteousness . . . a death of all those tricks you play to convince yourself that you are fine, that you are the good ones, the sophisticated ones, the nonracist ones, the ones who truly care about justice and a world without oppression, hatred, and racist violence.
—George Yancy (2018, 58)

Despite the omnipresence of racism in contemporary American life, and the increasing number of white people willing to acknowledge that race shapes a host of life outcomes (Mayorga-Gallo 2019), you would be hard-pressed to find yourself in a conversation in which a white person actually names their racism. While we, as white people, are rhetorically capable of naming the myriad ways race functions elsewhere, it seems to be just that: always elsewhere and never close to home. But in doing so we keep our own racial selves at a safe distance from any implication in the larger discourse about racism, white supremacy, and the ugly and violent history of racial domination in this country. We speak with a certainty about our knowledge of the racial world while keeping the messy details of complicity at arm's length (Applebaum 2010).

But as George Yancy reminds us, if we white people are going to commit ourselves to the struggle for racial justice and equity, we must first release ourselves from attachments to certainty, innocence, and goodness. Over the last three years I have conducted multiple studies that critically examine white people's relationship to, and understanding of, race and whiteness. While the individuals I interviewed come from a variety of class backgrounds, geographic regions, and political affiliations, there often appears to be a consistent thread throughout their accounts: deep investments in white racial innocence. The investments in racial innocence that surface in these interviews mirror many of the attitudes and behaviors of white students with whom I have worked in community service learning, as well as my own ongoing journey in unlearning the oppressive conditioning of whiteness. It is from this place, at the intersection of my research, my work with students, and my own personal journey that I consider the deep and enduring investments in racial innocence among many white people. My use of the pronoun "we" is intentional, as my own journey has been, and continues to be, marked by the lure of racial innocence and moral goodness. In the writing of this chapter I have been reminded of my own need and desire to be seen as the white person who gets it.

The white people who are centered in this chapter are not the ones attending a racist theme party or being reported for overtly racist language in the workplace. Rather, these are the seemingly well-meaning, supposedly liberal and progressive white people who traverse college campuses, workplace environments, and the communities in which we live. This chapter considers four key questions. First, what is racial innocence and how does it manifest among individual white people? Second, what are the conditions and contexts that produce such investments in racial innocence? Third, what are the consequences of these investments in broader struggles for racial justice? And finally, what kinds of interventions and practices might challenge our deeply held desires for racial innocence?

Naming Our Investments in Racial Innocence

Just what is racial innocence? Deep investments in racial innocence refer to a fundamental belief in white moral goodness (Applebaum

2010; Sullivan 2014). To talk about white racial innocence is to center the intentions and desires of white people at the expense of any meaningful critique of white supremacy and one's own relationship to such a system of racial domination. This type of innocence is central to the production of white racial identities, for it provides a psychological buffer between white people's perceptions of themselves and larger discussions of racist violence, deeply ingrained racial inequities, and racial privilege. In short, our desires for racial innocence encourage individualistic analyses of race and racism, where some whites are perpetrators while others stand outside culpability, ensuring that our own character and sense of goodness are not threatened by both the ugly history and contemporary manifestations of white supremacy in the United States. To illustrate this phenomenon, I share two vignettes.

While working on my doctorate in the fall of 2015 I taught two sections of a community service-learning course each semester. As a part of the course, students completed thirty hours of service at designated community organizations such as food pantries, after-school programs, and community houses. A central goal of the course was for students to make connections between the experiences at their service sites and weekly readings on topics such as racial privilege, poverty, and underlying patterns of inequality in the United States. During our weekly check-in at the start of class, where I asked students to offer updates on their service experiences, two white women looked visibly frustrated and angry. These women had been two of the most active white students in the class, frequently naming the ways racism and white privilege produced inequitable educational outcomes. They were volunteering at an after-school homework help center and had come to see the overwhelming representation of Black and Brown children who used the service. On this day, however, they expressed their frustration that the third-grader they had been tutoring for the prior six weeks shared that he would be working with other volunteers from now on. When they asked him why, he shared that his father had recently told him never to trust white people. The two women were incredulous. They decried the father's perspective as racist and wondered how he could ever impart such a message to his young son, whom they believed they'd come to know over the six-week period.

Over the course of the semester, both women spoke fluently about the prevalence of racism in shaping life outcomes, both for people of color and for white people. They lamented all semester about educating their peers to think more critically about the nature of racial privilege and the daily impacts of microaggressions on communities of color. Yet, when they were directly implicated as a part of the problem, when they were gazed upon as racial subjects, their intellectual understandings of racism gave way to an all-out effort to defend their own moral goodness. They paternalistically questioned how the child's father could impart such a racist message about white people, especially about *them*, given the work they had put in with his son over the course of the term. All of this came just one week after we had read a portion of Ta-Nehisi Coates's *Between the World and Me* (2015), in which the author writes to his young Black son about what it means to grow up in a Black body in a white supremacist world. In the moment I was surprised. How could these white students not square their own encounter with the young child at the homework help center with the accounts offered by Coates and the pleas from communities of color to stop killing young Black men? In that moment, however, I was trapped by my own investments in racial innocence—my hope that if only these white women would read Coates, their minds would be significantly altered and they might understand, as bell hooks (1997) explained, how people of color come to recognize and name the terror of whiteness, not out of superficial stereotypes, but from generations of the Black experience in America.

During the fall semester of the next academic year, I again found myself teaching service-learning classrooms of predominantly white students. It was early in the term and a young white man, just beginning his sophomore year on campus, raised his hand during our weekly check-ins. He explained that during his first few visits to his service site, a food pantry on the west side of the city, he felt unwanted and out of place. He noted that the food pantry serviced primarily Black and Latinx communities and that he was one of the only white people on site. I was unsure where the conversation was about to go. Before I was able to interject, he shifted his body to the rest of the class and asked, "What if they don't want us there?" I was struck by this question and the humility that grounded his thinking. He was not angry. He was not defensive. Instead, he engaged with the uncertainty inherent in the very question. After a few weeks at the food pantry, he had come to recognize the skepticism among community members of white student volunteers amidst a sea of Black and Brown bodies. His question offered an opportunity for the class to engage in critical discussions about white narcissism and savior complexes, the ways white students typically use such community centers for the hours they need and then leave, and the broader patterns of mistrust toward white people who claim they wish to help people of color.

I could not help but consider his questions in the context of the two students from the semester before. For weeks I tried to find language to express what it was that differentiated their accounts. Eventually it dawned on me: it was the extent to which they exhibited a deep investment in racial innocence and, subsequently, their ability to see themselves as seen through the eyes of people of color. The two white women from the semester before simply refused to entertain why the young child's father would impart what they experienced as a racist message to his son. Their accounts were grounded in a sense of certainty in their knowing (Leonardo 2009) and subsequently produced a form of arrogance in their paternalistic appraisal of the Black father. They could not—or simply refused to—grapple with the historic and contemporary abuse, violence, and terror imposed by whiteness, and white people, in the lives of communities of color. As Audrey Thompson (2003, 8) explained, "For the white student who is new to colored epistemologies . . . it can be devastating to realize that people of color—people who, not by coincidence, do not really even know you—can make judgements about you and just assume that you are racist without giving you the chance to prove otherwise." In this regard, their ignorance protected them from any sustained critique of their own situatedness in larger systems of racism and white supremacy (Leonardo 2009). The white man who questioned his place at the food pantry, however, exhibited a willingness to enter into a space of self-critique, to consider the historical and contemporary realities that produced the skeptical and wary looks he received while completing his service hours. In one instance the class was marked by white certainty and arrogance that result from deep investments in innocence; in the other, humility and self-critique opened up new possibilities and ways of thinking.

Where Do These Desires Come From?

It is important to make something clear. The two white women in the service-learning course that spring semester were not anomalies. In fact, their accounts mirrored much of what I have heard in interviews with white college students and administrators over the last three years (Foste 2020). During the fall of 2016 I interviewed a number of student leaders as part of a study exploring the ways white undergraduates assign meaning to whiteness. A major takeaway from my time with these students was the ways that a majority of them used their involvement on campus as surefire evidence of their own racial innocence. They routinely offered their time in resident assistant trainings, diversity workshops, and service-learning programs as a sign that they were different from other white students on campus.

At the conclusion of the second of our two interviews, I typically asked students what it had been like to engage in interviews on race and whiteness. One student remarked that the interview hadn't been too challenging because, due to her leadership experiences that exposed her to content about race and other markers of difference, she surrounded herself with "a group of people that cares more and tries more" (Foste 2020, 38). She explained that while the conversation might be harder for other white students who were not involved in various leadership positions on campus, these dialogues were a routine part of her experience on campus. Another student commented that his time as a student leader in residence life exposed him to ideas and perspectives he believed were not available to other, less involved students. He explained, "When you get into that community everyone wants to learn as well. Like, you don't have the people in there who don't think it's worth anything to know about diversity." He wondered aloud about "other students on this campus, how they're getting to know all of these things" (Foste 2020, 39). At the heart of both of these reactions is the same level of certainty in one's own goodness, often understood to be the result of increased content knowledge and discussions about racial diversity, that permeated the service-learning classroom. But as Yancy (2018, 80) reminds us, "As a white person, you never clearly come to a place of 'arrival'—where such a place suggests a static noun—as a *'nonracist* white.'"

What, then, are the contexts and conditions that encourage white people to desire to be seen as innocent and good? How do we understand this level of certainty in one's ability to make sense of something as messy, violent, and exploitative as white supremacy? In my own time as a white researcher, teacher, and human, I have come to recognize certain conditions that seem especially capable of fueling this desire for innocence and certainty in one's knowing. The underlying foundation for which these conditions rest is a belief that racism is a matter of interpersonal bigotry and prejudice, rather than structural arrangements of power grounded in history that produce unequal life opportunities and frames through which we interpret the world. That is, because so many white Americans see racism as a matter of overt bigotry and hatred, and refuse to consider the larger sociohistorical elements of white supremacy (Bonilla-Silva 2006; Cabrera 2014), it is no surprise that we become so wrapped up in a need to be seen as good, morally virtuous white people. In light of this reality, I briefly review three particular conditions that seem to accelerate this drive for innocence.

One of the central conditions that fuels a desire for racial innocence and goodness is the racially insulated lives we white people live. The very ways whiteness structures and patterns our daily routines, wherein interactions with people of color are almost entirely optional and by choice, make it easy to avoid understanding how communities of color see whiteness. In his book *Tears We Cannot Stop: A Sermon to White America* (2017, 59) Michael Eric Dyson pointedly noted that whiteness "keeps white folk ignorant of Black life. It makes so many of you, if we're honest, largely indifferent to Black life." It is not uncommon for supposedly progressive, enlightened white liberals to leave a diversity training or workshop and artfully recite a list of white racial privileges or the ways implicit bias manifests in daily interactions. While these represent important, incremental steps, and easily quantifiable outcomes to assess (a point to which I return shortly), rarely do I get a sense that these same white individuals are able to seriously entertain how people of color come to see and experience whiteness, *their* whiteness, *our* whiteness. This was the primary concern outlined in the narrative at the outset of this chapter. Our distance from people of color means that we can remain ignorant of what hooks (1997, 165) described as the special knowledge these communities hold about whiteness and white people.

She explained that "Black folks, from slavery on, shared in conversations with one another 'special knowledge' of whiteness gleaned from close scrutiny of white people." The certainty of our understanding of the racial world, and subsequent investments in innocence, are thus at least partially a result of the fact that we have rarely considered the baggage attached to our white bodies—all of the violent history, the exploitation, and the general disregard for communities of color in all of their humanity.

For white people who rarely, if ever, considered what it is that whiteness represents to communities of color, diversity trainings and workshops—in educational contexts, corporations, and nonprofits—often accelerate rather than undermine their investment in innocence. These spaces represent a second significant condition worthy of exploration. A large and mounting body of scholarship has documented how diversity language and programs often mystify, rather than reveal, how structures of oppression such as white supremacy pattern our daily lives and shape our perceptions of racial others (Berrey 2015; Thomas 2018; Warikoo 2016). Such approaches promote a celebratory understanding of difference, or what Joyce Bell and Douglas Hartmann (2007, 906) described as the "happy talk of diversity." Using interviews with participants across four major American metropolitan areas, Bell and Hartmann found that while individuals hold overwhelmingly positive beliefs about the idea of diversity, rarely did they account for issues of politics, power, and inequality. That is, although diversity was routinely embraced by these participants, understandings of the concept were often vague and ambiguous. Their study echoes the work of sociologist Ellen Berrey (2015), who has documented the evolution of diversity, in both education and the workplace, from a means of remedying structural inequities to a celebratory approach that prizes positive interpersonal interactions across difference. This framing of diversity insists that everyone holds some form of difference worth sharing and that if we can just consume enough of that difference, learn as much as possible in our two hours together, then we will have reached a desired goal. In this regard, the very approaches that have some sliver of potential to invite white people to consider our location in the world, and most importantly our location vis-à-vis people of color, actually cater to our desires for comfort and safety. Put otherwise, a majority of diversity trainings and workshops do not critically invite white people to consider ourselves relationally against the backdrop of people of color (Foste and Jones 2020). As Nolan Cabrera, Jesse Watson, and Jeremy Franklin (2016, 130) note, white people need to experience a sense of agitation and discomfort to avoid the racial arrested development produced by these types of environments.

To experience such agitation, and in turn consider our relational location vis-à-vis people of color, would require that we consider how the privileges granted by whiteness, those we learn about and are eager to recite to our like-minded white friends, come at the expense of racially marginalized communities and are the product of violent and exploitative histories of white supremacy (Dyson 2017; hooks 1997; Yancy 2018). That is, the contemporary reality of white racial privilege is the result of historical violence against Indigenous communities and people of color. Critical race philosopher Zeus Leonardo (2009, 78) reminds us that too often white privilege is communicated as a contemporary state of being without any attention to the underlying histories and structures that produced this relationship of domination and subordination. I am often struck at how easily many white students with whom I have worked recite the bevy of privileges associated with whiteness. They rattle them off, flippantly at times, similar to how they might discuss content in biology or chemistry courses. "A Band-Aid that matches the color of my skin!" one might proclaim. Others note how painfully obvious it is that they, as a white person, need not worry about being followed around in a store due to their race. It is the tone with which they recite these newfound privileges that one can sense the absence of any historical or structural understanding of racism and white supremacy, an understanding that *our* privilege is connected to *their* oppression. There seems little in the way of understanding that Band-Aids match our skin because whiteness has long been framed as the standard of beauty and humankind (Feagin 2013). Likewise, this newfound awareness lacks any relational understanding that people of color are followed around in stores because they are not white. Their bodies are marked by historical constructions of Blackness and Brownness as dangerous against the innocent whiteness of our bodies. As Toni Morrison (1992, 52) once noted, "Africanism is the vehicle by which the American self knows itself as not enslaved, but free; not repulsive, but desirable; not helpless, but licensed and powerful; not history-less, but historical; not damned, but innocent; not a blind accident of evolution, but a progressive fulfillment of destiny."

I am struck, but not surprised, because this particular trajectory toward racial enlightenment absent any deep, critical structural reflection mirrors my own journey. I could attend a training or workshop on whiteness and return home to lecture my friends and families on the myriad of ways white people are privileged by race. However, if I am honest with myself, I never seriously entertained the violent and oppressive histories that produced these privileges. To do so would have required serious reflection on how whiteness became associated with beauty, rationality, and intelligence, while Blackness and other nonwhite bodies were deemed irrational, deviant, criminal, and in need of civilizing. This type of thinking would demand some understanding of how my own white racial privilege was the result of the systematic dehumanization of nonwhite bodies. Further, such an analysis would have required that I understand the history of American Reconstruction, Black codes, and policies like redlining that all but ensured that progress toward racial equity was halted to maintain the privileges and power of whiteness. Each of these tasks would have demanded that I more critically connect my own state of being to a broader sociohistorical analysis of racial domination (Foste and Jones 2020; Yancy 2018).

In short, having rarely considered the ways people of color see whiteness, we white people often enter into diversity trainings and programs that are stripped of history, power, and critical attention to the violence imparted in the name of whiteness. We leave feeling good about the progress made during our short time in said workshops. This is, at least partially, related to the third and final condition that I want to touch on in this chapter: an assessment-driven culture that prizes certainty and assuredness over humility and complexity. An assessment-driven culture, coupled with the uncritical embrace of diversity language, prizes quantifiable and attainable outcomes such as cultural competency and other so-called best practices (Berrey 2015; Warikoo 2016). Unlearning the conditioning of whiteness and white supremacy is a messy, lifelong endeavor. This is not to imply that we should take our time meandering through the wilderness of self-exploration and critical reflection. Indeed, the daily experiences of people of color demand attention to the ways systems of white supremacy can be challenged and undone. Rather, so much of the (un)learning and development necessary is not quantifiable or easily measurable. Despite this reality, our assessment-driven culture often requires deliverable and quickly achievable goals. Indeed, the rise of implicit bias tests is in part the result of a desired cure-all for racial justice and diversity work (Chun and Feagin 2019). What is required of white people, however, is much more than naming how we are privileged by whiteness, superficial awareness of our racial identities, consumption of ethnic differences, or recognition of implicit bias.

As Joe Feagin (2013) argues, white Americans require a sociohistorical framework that allows us to recognize how historical forms of racial domination and terror have patterned both structural inequities and cognitive patterns of interpreting people and communities of color. Feagin calls on white people to consider how centuries of racial oppression have created and maintained what he describes as the white racial frame, or a perspective of the world that includes beliefs, cognitive elements, images, and emotions. The white racial frame moves beyond stereotypes and instead captures "an overarching and generally destructive worldview, one extending across white divisions of class, gender, and age. Since its early development in the seventeenth century, this powerful frame has provided the vantage point from which white Americans have constantly viewed North American society" (Feagin 2013, 10). In a similar vein, Barbara Applebaum (2010) has challenged white people to consider the ways we are complicit in systemic white racial domination, regardless of our intentions. She posits that by virtue of benefiting from racial privilege, we reproduce racial domination, regardless of how racially enlightened or aware we may be. Neither of these approaches—Feagin's call for a broader sociohistorical framework or Applebaum's invitation to consider complicity—is easily captured via assessment and quantifiable outcomes. They require not only content knowledge but a capacity of mind and a sense of humility. Instead, however, we are left with approaches to diversity education that allow for white people to maintain a distance between our own being, our own positioning in society, and the creation and maintenance of difference we seek to better understand. Under such conditions, then, we are left with the message that if only one consumes enough content on racial difference, learns how to spot a microaggression, or recognize white racial privilege, we have engaged in the work necessary to move toward more inclusive communities.

What Are the Consequences of Deep Investments in Innocence?

These types of desires for racial innocence, rooted in a sense of certainty about our knowing of the racial world, have major implications for the broader project of racial justice. Perhaps most notable among these is that, in our attempt to locate ourselves as racially enlightened and progressive, we imply that we somehow exist outside the problem of whiteness and white supremacy (Applebaum 2010; Sullivan 2014; Yancy 2018). In my own experiences I have come to understand that our desires for innocence are only matched by, and in large part a result of, the certainty of our own knowledge about the racial world. By proclaiming our own racial innocence, we somehow insist that we are no longer a part of the problem, that we somehow have escaped the tangled web of whiteness. Matt, one of the students in my study on white college students' relationship to race, underscores the connection between a certainty in one's knowledge and a belief in one's racial innocence. During our time together he recalled a particular encounter with a faculty member of color who challenged his white students to think about how they might articulate a genuine commitment to cultural competency in an admissions interview for medical school. Matt perceived that the instructor was directing his question to white students:

> And I'm sitting there, like here I am, obviously I would never say that I am fully culturally competent. There is always more to learn. But to say that a white person has to struggle more with understanding diversity, like just because you're (the instructor) Indian, it felt really bad. Because here I am. This is the second year I've gone through a lot of training. And um. And uh made a real effort to understand different cultures and go to [multicultural] programs and had talks with my residents, and you know, had programs about diversity . . . and here he was, who, I mean, these are types of people who might be interviewing me. And they already have these perceptions about me and white kids that they don't understand diversity. So that just kind of hurt. Just because now I feel like I have to really prove myself. (Foste 2017, 176–77)

Matt's account is especially notable for a few reasons. First, like many of the students with whom I met in the fall of 2016, Matt was quick to establish his record of diversity trainings and programs that were the product of his involvement on campus. In doing so, he set particular conditions for how our conversation might proceed. Elsewhere I have described this phenomenon as the *enlightenment narrative* (Foste 2020), wherein students use their exposure to diversity programs and experiences as evidence of their racial goodness. Second, Matt's account underscores the certainty in his own knowledge about the racial world. He appears completely unwilling to engage the prompts offered by his faculty, instead finding it nonsensical that "white kids... don't understand diversity." Later in our time together, when asked to discuss his role as a resident assistant on campus responsible for engaging other white students on matters of diversity and inclusion, Matt responded,

> You have the opportunity to kind of break some barriers as a white person, kind of purging the gap for maybe other white people who don't think the same. Like for me I think it's neat to be able to kind of like bridge as an RA, as a white RA, for maybe white people who don't think the same as me to be more culturally competent. (Foste 2017, 254)

Here again, Matt locates himself outside the problem. In his words, it is neat to engage "white people who don't think the same as me." In this regard, Matt clearly demarcates boundaries between himself and other supposedly less culturally competent students.

Locating oneself outside the problem of white supremacy via one's proclamations of innocence is far from a new phenomenon. Shannon Sullivan (2014) has documented how middle-class white Americans have historically used poor, southern whites as a reference group against which to paint a sense of white racial goodness. Similarly, James Baldwin described his encounters with white people who refused to grapple with the weight of history and white supremacy in the United States. In his essay "White Man's Guilt," he explained the refusal of whites to enter into the world as understood by Black Americans: "The nature of this stammering can be reduced to a plea: Do not blame *me*. I was not there. I did not do it. My history has nothing to do with Europe or the slave trade" (Baldwin 1965, 47–48). Baldwin's writing mirrors in many ways the approach of the two white women in the service-learning course described at the outset of the chapter. But there is a certain level of arrogance in believing that one can simply stand outside whiteness. If we are to understand whiteness as Peter McLaren (1998) described, as a type of sociohistorical consciousness that is grounded in genocide, the theft of land, and chattel slavery, it becomes all the more difficult to imagine that one could simply remove oneself from this troubling history.

Second, and relatedly, regardless of how woke, how aware, how enlightened we are, we are still read as white and thus granted privileges associated with such a racial location. No matter how many times we recite Peggy McIntosh's knapsack of white privilege (1990), read Patricia Hill Collins's *Black Feminist Thought* (2000), or engage the groundbreaking work of James Baldwin (1965) and his critiques of whiteness, we are still seen, read, and understood as white bodies. This is, I believe, a critically important point that is often lost on us white folks who do aspire to challenge and deconstruct white supremacy. Content knowledge alone will not save us. No matter the amount of self-work we do, we will continue to occupy white bodies in a world that loves whiteness at the expense of Blackness and Brownness (Brown 2018). This is not to disavow the very real self-critique we white people must undertake as we unlearn the oppressive conditioning of whiteness. And indeed, much of this work does come via the written word and engagement in cross-racial dialogues, trainings, and workshops. Much of my own journey has been influenced by scholars of color like George Yancy, James Baldwin, and bell hooks. The ways they have written about whiteness, not as an identity but a force of terror and dehumanization in the lives of people of color, have been critically important to my growth. But to rely on their works as evidence of our own goodness feels shallow at best and exploitative at worst (Thompson 2003).

In short, then, what I hope to convey here is that our desires for racial innocence only further obscure and mystify the ways whiteness has functioned historically and manifests in our contemporary lives. Reducing whiteness to distinctions between good whites and bad whites does little, if anything, to challenge the racial status quo in our communities, in our schools, and in our organizations. As the historian Ibram Kendi (2019) reminds us, you would be hard pressed to find anyone who actually identified with the term "racist" throughout American history. In many ways these deep investments in innocence actually function to obscure this work by mystifying historical and structural analyses required to challenge white supremacy.

How Might We Guard against Desires for Innocence?

So far in this chapter I have detailed troubling patterns related to white racial innocence and a certainty in one's racial knowledge. How, then, might we engage white people in our schools, universities, and organizations in ways that guard against such desires? Before concluding, I would like to offer three recommendations for developing increasing levels of criticality about white racial locations in a world that prizes whiteness. I offer each in hopes of reducing our desire to be seen as morally good, innocent white people.

As I have documented throughout this chapter, ahistorical understandings of race broadly, and whiteness in particular, set a strong and enduring foundation for racial innocence among white people. Without an adequate understanding of how whiteness has functioned over time, socially, culturally, economically, and politically, our analyses will continue to begin and end with the individual. As such, many of us will default into familiar good white/bad white dichotomies that reaffirm a belief in our own inherent goodness. To this point, it is imperative that those of us white individuals who endeavor to fight for racial justice and equity seriously engage the history of white racial domination in the United States. Further, we must do so in a way that allows for us to locate ourselves within this historical equation. Doing so opens up the possibility that we might grapple with the relational nature of racism and white supremacy: that bodies of color are marked as deviant and other only in relation to whiteness as the norm or that the wealth gap between white families and Black and Brown families is the product of economic exploitation, to name but a few. This type of thinking asks that we focus our attention far beyond the immediate context of white racial privilege. Instead, we orient ourselves to historical and structural understandings of racism and white supremacy, and our own complicity in said systems.

During a recent trip to Atlanta, Georgia, I began listening to the newest audiobook of Henry Louis Gates Jr., *Stony the Road: Reconstruction, White Supremacy, and the Rise of Jim Crow* (2019). Gates documents in excruciating detail the ways white Americans worked diligently to craft master narratives about recently freed Black slaves during the Reconstruction. These narratives of Black people as dangerous, irrational, and unintelligent have long persisted in the white American imagination far beyond the years following the Civil War. Indeed, much of the struggle for racial justice in this country has been, in part, challenging this white racist framing of Black and Brown bodies. As I listened to Gates, I was struck by how much of this type of analysis is often absent in trainings and workshops about race and whiteness. How can we white people begin to grapple with the magnitude of whiteness and white supremacy if we are not willing to confront, or even so much as engage, its brutal and violent history?

Beyond such a historical analysis, there is much to be gained by critical engagement with those voices of color who have long named and critiqued whiteness throughout American history. It is important to clarify the detail of "critical engagement." Nancy Leong (2013) coined the phrase "racial capitalism" to describe how white people and institutions draw on people of color as a form of currency to advance our own interests. In short, Leong posits that white people associate ourselves with people and communities of color in order to advance an image as progressive and in support of diversity. Racial capitalism dehumanizes people of color by reducing their being to no more than a form of capital in our own advancement, be it in graduate education, medical school, or corporations. When I say "critical engagement," then, I am arguing for contexts that challenge us white people to stay in the messiness of critique. We should not be totally immobilized by these critiques, but we should sit with them and take their words seriously.

As I noted previously, one of the major foundations of white racial innocence is the racially insulated and segregated nature of our lives. Rarely are we white people asked to enter into the world as experienced by people of color. Further, when we do engage with diversity-related topics and events, such efforts are typically safe, sanitized, and ahistorical in nature. What might it mean for us well-meaning, supposedly progressive white folks to see ourselves through the eyes of people of color? How might our sense of certainty and innocence be called into question through the writings of authors like Baldwin, Du Bois, hooks, Morrison, Coates, and others who have explicitly and unapologetically critiqued how whiteness functions as a form of terror and violence in communities of color? And how might hearing about the many ways people of color have resisted whiteness and flourished in spite of its presence prompt us to pause and consider the enormity of the problem that is white supremacy? Finally, what might it mean to prize feelings of humility and uncertainty in the process of unlearning the oppressive conditioning of whiteness (Aanerud 2015)? Both of the recommendations I have offered here, entering into the oppressive history of whiteness and hearing those voices most impacted by its brutal presence, demand a sense of humility. If we are to truly grapple with the enormity of whiteness, we must be willing to confront all of the ways we have come to misunderstand the racial world (Applebaum 2010). Such an effort requires that we hold out and rethink lessons learned from those closest to us, including parents, peers, and trusted teachers.

During my study on white college students and race, I was struck by the absolute certainty with which a number of them spoke about issues of race and racism. All of these students were in some form of leadership positions on campus, many of which required them to directly engage their peers about issues like diversity, race, and whiteness. When I asked Lucas, a resident advisor, what it was like to learn about racial privilege in his role as a peer educator in the residence halls, he explained a rather straightforward process:

> And um, it's usually very like, let's get this done, let's talk about it, let's understand it and we have that conversation further, it's like we will have a one-on-one with (my supervisor). And we will talk with him and just sort of be like, let's understand this. Give me more examples. Help me understand what is going on. I don't want to say it is business like, but it is a part of our job . . . how do we get students to understand it, just so that we don't understand it, they (students) also understand it, kind of a thing. (Foste 2017, 252–53)

Lucas would go on to explain that "once you understand, you understand." As I engaged with Lucas, I began to sense that his assuredness was not simply the reflection of some inner state, but the product of trainings and initiatives within the department for which he worked. He exhibited a sense of confidence in his understanding of the racial world, so much so that he could consume a few examples from a supervisor and then communicate the issue to residents on his floor. While I understand the instinct to assess growth and development in trainings and programs related to whiteness and racial justice, too often these efforts imply a linear pathway toward a designated end point. Emphasizing humility and uncertainty requires that white people like Lucas step back and avoid a rush to understanding and action. During a recent meeting I sat with colleagues as we discussed the climate for racial diversity and broader efforts for social justice and equity on campus. The conversation started late due to other agenda items, and thus lasted no more than twenty-five minutes before the meeting came to a close. We'd barely scratched the surface, yet multiple individuals in the room asked, "Okay, so what can we do with this information?" Like Lucas, we were so focused on the actionable item that resulted from some perceived new form of knowledge about difference without any real critical interrogation or reflection. I was left to wonder how the meeting may have looked different if we prized uncertainty and humility at the outset of our gathering.

Conclusion

In writing this chapter I had four primary aims. First, I have sought to detail the ways white racial innocence manifests among individual whites who believe themselves to be good, aware, and even woke about racial injustice. Central to this desire for innocence is a certainty in one's own racial knowledge, which produces a sort of arrogance that keeps oneself at arm's length from the morally threatening implication in white supremacy. This was evident in the narrative of the service-learning classroom and the multiple accounts offered by participants in my interview studies. Second, I have highlighted the conditions and contexts that I have seen, be it in my own research, teaching, and personal journey as a white person, that seem to amplify, rather than challenge, these investments in racial innocence. These include the racially insulated and segregated nature of white people's lives, diversity trainings and programs that are often ahistorical and void of critical literacy, and an assessment-driven culture that seeks easily identifiable outcomes that are at odds with the inherently messy and lifelong process of unlearning the conditioning of whiteness. Central to these experiences is the reduction of unlearning whiteness and white supremacy to a form of content mastery that is easily achievable via enough quantifiable experiences. Rarely, however, do these experiences invite white participants to see whiteness through the eyes of people of color.

Third, I wanted to not only document how white racial innocence manifests, but also think more critically about the consequences of these desires. Most notably, desires for innocence locate individual white people outside a larger social and historical context. In doing so we further perpetuate a good white/bad white binary that has evolved throughout the history of race relations in this country. Finally, I have reflected on potential ways we white people might begin to caution against the need to be seen as innocent and good. These efforts include deeper engagement with the history of whiteness and white supremacy in the United States, a willingness to see how whiteness is understood and experienced through the eyes of people of color, and the capacity to prize humility and uncertainty in our journeys.

REFERENCES

Aanerud, Rebecca. 2015. "Humility and Whiteness: How Do I Look without Seeing, Hear without Listening?" In *White Self-Criticality beyond Anti-Racism: How Does It Feel to Be a White Problem?*, edited by George Yancy, 101–14. Lanham: Lexington.

Applebaum, Barbara. 2010. *Being White, Being Good: White Complicity, White Moral Responsibility, and Social Justice Pedagogy*. Lanham: Lexington.

Baldwin, James. 1965. "White Man's Guilt." *Ebony* 20, no. 10 (August): 47–48.

Bell, Joyce, and Douglas Hartmann. 2007. "Diversity in Everyday Discourse: The Cultural Ambiguities and Consequences of 'Happy Talk.'" *American Sociological Review* 72, no. 6 (December): 895–914.

Berrey, Ellen. 2015. *The Enigma of Diversity: The Language of Race and the Limits of Racial Justice*. Chicago: University of Chicago Press.

Bonilla-Silva, Eduardo. 2006. *Racism without Racists: Color-Blind Racism and the Persistence of Racial Inequality in the United States*. 2nd ed. Lanham: Rowman and Littlefield.

Brown, Austin Channing. 2018. *I'm Still Here: Black Dignity in a World Made for Whiteness*. New York: Convergent Books.

Cabrera, Nolan L. 2014. "Exposing Whiteness in Higher Education: White Male College Students Minimizing Racism, Claiming Victimization, and Recreating White Supremacy." *Race Ethnicity and Education* 17, no. 1: 30–55.

Cabrera, Nolan L., Jesse S. Watson, and Jeremy D. Franklin. 2016. "Racial Arrested Development: A Critical Whiteness Analysis of the Campus Ecology." *Journal of College Student Development* 57, no. 2 (March): 119–34.

Chun, Edna B., and Joe R. Feagin. 2019. *Rethinking Diversity Frameworks in Higher Education*. New York: Routledge.

Coates, Ta-Nehisi. 2015. *Between the World and Me.* New York: Random House.
Collins, Patricia Hill. 2000. *Black Feminist Thought: Knowledge, Consciousness, and the Politics of Empowerment.* 2nd ed. New York: Routledge.
Dyson, Michael Eric. 2017. *Tears We Cannot Stop: A Sermon to White America.* New York: St. Martin's.
Feagin, Joe R. 2013. *The White Racial Frame: Centuries of Racial Framing and Counter-Framing.* 2nd ed. New York: Routledge.
Foste, Zak. 2017. "Narrative Constructions of Whiteness among White Undergraduates." PhD dissertation, Ohio State University.
———. 2020. "The Enlightenment Narrative: White Student Leaders' Preoccupation with Racial Innocence." *Journal of Diversity in Higher Education* 13, no. 1 (June): 33–43.
Foste, Zak, and Susan R. Jones. 2020 "Narrating Whiteness: A Qualitative Exploration of How White College Students Construct and Give Meaning to Their Racial Location." *Journal of College Student Development* 61, no. 2 (March–April): 171–88.
Gates, Henry Louis. 2019. *Stony the Road: Reconstruction, White Supremacy, and the Rise of Jim Crow.* New York: Penguin.
hooks, bell. 1997. "Representing Whiteness in the Black Imagination." In *Displacing Whiteness: Essays in Social and Cultural Criticism,* edited by Ruth Frankenberg, 165–79. Durham: Duke University Press.
Kendi, Ibram X. 2019. *How to Be an Antiracist.* New York: One World.
Leonardo, Zeus. 2009. *Race, Whiteness, and Education.* New York: Routledge.
Leong, Nancy. 2013. "Racial Capitalism." *Harvard Law Review* 126 (June): 2151–226.
Mayorga-Gallo, Sarah. 2019. "The White-Centering Logic of Diversity Ideology." *American Behavioral Scientist* 63, no. 13: 1789–1809.
McIntosh, Peggy. 1990. "White Privilege: Unpacking the Invisible Knapsack." *Independent School,* Winter, 31–36.
McLaren, Peter. 1998. "Whiteness Is . . . The Struggle for Postcolonial Hybridity." In *White Reign: Deploying Whiteness in America,* edited by Joe L. Kincheloe, Shirley R. Steinberg, Nelson M. Rodriguez, and Ronald E. Chennault, 63–75. New York: St. Martin's.
Morrison, Toni. 1992. *Playing in the Dark: Whiteness and the Literary Imagination.* New York: Vintage.
Sullivan, Shannon. 2014. *Good White People: The Problem with Middle Class White Anti-Racism.* Albany: State University of New York Press.
Thomas, James M. 2018. "Diversity Regimes and Racial Inequality: A Case Study of Diversity University." *Social Currents* 5, no. 2 (April): 140–56.
Thompson, Audrey. 2003. "Tiffany, Friend of People of Color: White Investments in Antiracism." *International Journal of Qualitative Studies in Education* 16, no. 1: 7–29.
Warikoo, Natasha K. 2016. *The Diversity Bargain and Other Dilemmas of Race, Admissions, and Meritocracy at Elite Universities.* Chicago: University of Chicago Press.
Yancy, George. 2018. *Backlash: What Happens When We Talk Honestly about Race in America.* Lanham: Rowman and Littlefield.

9

Islam and Hip Hop in Black America

Oral Tradition as Critical Liberatory Praxis

AMER F. AHMED

The history of Black America is typified by resistance against consistently imposed systemic racism in the United States. Throughout centuries of racial oppression, various methods of resistance and subversion have been undertaken by Black people, including affiliations with Islam and other non-Christian religious perspectives (Gomez 2005; Turner 1997). Islam offers an alternative socioreligious model and can provide a redefined ritual order that may have been part of a Black American's broken African lineage. For many, Islam holds the key to their resistance in its overt stressing of the equality of all human beings, which is at the heart of its message. Islam presents an opportunity for Black people, who had become accustomed to suppression, to redefine their identity according to a new set of principles independent of Christianity (Gomez 2005; Turner 1997). For some, it is simply a welcome change from Christianity, which is frequently associated with the hegemony of a Western-established order imposed through the process of slavery. As a result, Islam allows some people to adapt their ritual order without having to totally deconstruct their previous religious knowledge while they also reclaim a sense of identity connected to pre–Atlantic slave trade Africa.

In evaluating the significance of religion for Black Americans, we see the centrality of its role when it is formulated within paradigms of resistance to power. Debra Washington Mubashshir (2001, 1) discussed this core role in her definition of "Black religion":

> A distinct social phenomenon with roots traceable to . . . the spiritual yearnings of African peoples, black religion has been used to describe

the path through which ... adherents of various faith systems experience the presence of what they acknowledge as holy, sacred or of the highest value as they journey through life and death in search of justice and in the celebration of inner and external liberation.

In this definition, the interdependence of spiritual belief and notions of justice and liberty is crucial. This connection is significant and central in Black religion because the metaphysical dimension of practice attempts to transcend real-world circumstances imposed by the dominant order. As a result, the circumstances of individuals often cause a redefinition of spiritual and religious concepts (Dirks 1994). These redefinitions, grounded by the search for justice and liberty, are able to offer a mode of subversion for the individual resisting the imposition of dominance.

James C. Scott's *Weapons of the Weak: Everyday Forms of Peasant Resistance* (1985) discussed "everyday resistance" as a way that oppressed people engage in action that is subversive to hegemony in daily life. In *Domination and the Art of Resistance: Hidden Transcripts*, Scott (1990) noted that resistance can be expressed through social transcripts that can be "public" or "hidden." He defined "public" transcripts as open interactions between the dominant and subordinate individuals, while "hidden" transcripts are disguised "offstage" (4, 24) and represent discourses that critique and resist various aspects of social domination. Layered with the themes of redefinition, justice, subversion, and resistance offered by Nicholas Dirks (1994), religion and its associated rituals can be seen as central modes of resistance enacted through outright defiance or through "everyday" resistance that produce either public or hidden transcripts. Tricia Rose (1994) argued that rap music, as an extension of Black oral tradition, is both a public and hidden transcript of resistance containing overt expressions of resistance as well as coded messages that often mask expressions of resistance. Furthermore, Hip Hop culture is an example of "everyday resistance" regarding the manner in which its subversive aesthetics are embedded into the daily lives of its participants.

This chapter draws on Paulo Friere's (1970) notions of *critical pedagogy* and *praxis* to investigate Hip Hop as a source of dialogue and reflection resulting in transformative action to resist oppression and seek liberation. It addresses complexity and intersectionality within race, faith, resistance, and art by specifically exploring Islamic-based ideologies in Hip Hop and their connection to Black American experiences, both historically and in more contemporary settings. Existing scholarship on Islam in Black America (Gomez 2005; McCloud 1995; Turner 1997) has generally not focused on its role and relationship to Hip Hop, although in recent years some scholars have engaged this connection (Abdul Khabeer 2016; Daulatzai 2012). However, such research has not explored the connection between Islam and Hip Hop in Black America as liberatory critical pedagogy. Before turning to the main analysis, I describe my relationship to Islam and Hip Hop as a form of resistance and liberation in a racially oppressive US context.

Personal Narrative

I have been involved in Hip Hop activism for most of my adult life. As I am a South Asian Muslim American, many people are surprised by my engagement in Hip Hop, yet Hip Hop has been a critical component of the social justice work I have participated in within the United States and around the world. As I am a member of the Hip Hop generation, Hip Hop culture has facilitated numerous encounters, particularly with Black American Muslims, that have helped me to develop a deeper understanding of issues, inequities, and injustice.

I was born and raised in Springfield, Ohio, by Indian-Muslim immigrants. My family was part of a small South Asian Muslim community in a blue-collar town. Like many cities in the Midwest, Springfield was relatively segregated across racial and class lines, with the majority of Black and lower economic groups living on the South Side and most white and upper-middle-class people living on the North Side. My high school was about 60 percent white and 38 percent Black; I was part of the tiny percentage of students categorized as "other." Like most adolescent youth, I just wanted to fit in. This proved to be challenging since I was raised in a cultural environment vastly different from that of most of my peers.

I often moved between white and Black people with varying experiences of acceptance. One thing that was abundantly clear to me was that Black folks empathized with me about being different, while white folks seemed to expect me to be like them. Those differences led me to cultivate relationships, learn, and understand the marginalizing experiences that were so deeply part of being Black in the United States. Meanwhile, my Islamic upbringing uniquely connected me to Black American Muslims in my community in a manner that was not the same for non-Muslim South Asians.

I went to high school and college in the 1990s, when Hip Hop became an integral part of mainstream popular culture in the United States. As a Muslim who experienced significant invisibility in the pre-9/11 United States, I was shocked to hear so many Islamic references in Hip Hop by various artists. I wanted to learn more about why rappers knew so much about Islam and expressed it in their music. Over time, I found that there was a disproportionate representation of Muslims and/or other Islamic-based ideologies (e.g., Nation of Islam, Five Percent Nation) among Hip Hop artists. This representation was intriguing to me and led me to want to know more about why this connection existed. As a result, my master's thesis research at Indiana University focused on this topic.

As a young adult, I began performing spoken word poetry and engaging in social and racial justice activist movements. Hip Hop culture provided me a space for expression of my ideas, feelings, and emotions, particularly regarding my anger and frustration about racism and oppression. This became an even more acute feeling following more direct experiences of racism after the attacks of September 11, 2001. This intersection in my life experience led to my involvement in the Hip Hop activist movement in the United States and around the world. *Hip Hop activism* means using the foundational principles, definitions, values, and environments in which the culture originally emerged (the South Bronx) and is re-created as inspiration that motivates and grounds our work to challenge injustice, empower through education and creativity, and utilize the culture as a facilitator of social change. In addition, given that Hip Hop culture is often engaged by marginalized youth all over the world, it provides a vehicle to communicate, create, and organize activism (Chang 2005).

I started organizing Hip Hop festivals as a student and later as an administrator for various colleges and universities to promote diversity and social justice education. I utilized a network of artists, activists, educators, and organizers to bring together diverse constituencies committed to utilize Hip Hop culture as a tool for creating social change. In each city in which I lived, I reached out to people working with youth, particularly the most marginalized populations in the area. In our workshops, I consistently saw how excited young people would be to see role models who used Hip Hop in a positive way. Young people walked away from these summits more confident, more expressive, and more interested in education. Suddenly, the gulf between their lives and higher education did not seem as wide. Many youths realized that they, too, could potentially be college students and participate in programs they would find interesting and relevant. They did not feel ashamed of expressing themselves through Hip Hop, which is a major barrier in the lives of many young people who are frequently told that Hip Hop is not positive.

Parallel to my positions and efforts in higher education, I also worked with an organization called Inner-City Muslim Action Network (IMAN) based on the South Side of Chicago. Through its work I observed the direct relationship between Islam, Hip Hop, and social justice as related to Black American Muslims and others. It is at IMAN that I saw the praxis of Islam and Hip Hop in Black America most explicitly on display.

Hip Hop's Connection to Liberation and Islamic-Based Ideologies

Hip Hop is a reformulated postindustrial cultural experience originally cultivated in the South Bronx and drawn from Black historical traditions rooted in their once African past. It is a cultural form that attempts to negotiate the experiences of marginalization, brutally truncated opportunity, and oppression within the cultural imperatives of African American and Caribbean history, identity, and community. It is the tension between the cultural fractures produced by postindustrial oppression and the binding ties of Black cultural expressivity that sets the critical frame for the development of Hip Hop.

Hip Hop as Oral Tradition

Tricia Rose (1994, 21) noted that "some analysts see Hip Hop as quintessentially postmodern practice, and others view it as a present-day successor to premodern oral traditions." The assessment of Hip Hop as a cultural phenomenon in many ways mirrors much of how Islamic-based ideologies have operated in Black America since the 1960s. Islam has been a spiritual, religious, and sociocultural form that has also allowed Black Americans to negotiate the experience of marginalization in postindustrial America with cultural connections to an African past. In this negotiation, the oral tradition has remained a key cultural component in the contextualization of both Islam and Hip Hop as part of the development of modern Black American culture. This is because written language cannot convey the physical resonance that is experienced by listeners of these rhythmic patterns of speaking, irrespective of the message attached to them.

These modes of delivery bypass logical reasoning by invoking passion and deep emotional responses that leave listeners moved and empowered by indescribable feelings. Such oral traditions are widely recognized as a central mode of communication with regard to the history and evolution of African and Black American music, religion, and culture. Ethnomusicologist Portia Maultsby (1991, 326) discussed how this tradition has translated into Black culture:

> The continuum of an African consciousness in America manifests itself in the evolution of an African-American culture. The music, dance, folklore, religion, language, and other expressive forms associated with the culture of slaves were transmitted orally to subsequent generations of American blacks.

Maultsby's observation is grounded in the work of Lawrence Levine (1977, 5), who articulated that traditions are not static, but rather ongoing transformations within changing contexts regardless of circumstances, such that culture is

> the product of interaction between the past and present. Its toughness and resiliency are determined not by a culture's ability to withstand change, which indeed may be a sign of stagnation not life, but by its ability to react creatively and responsively to the realities of a new situation.

Scholars widely note that Black culture is a dynamic example of such evolution that draws from the past yet evolves according to circumstances. Since culture is a constantly evolving and fluid process rooted in tradition, both Islam and Hip Hop play an inherent role in Black culture grounded in its historical relationship with Africa. Therefore, Hip Hop's incorporation of oral dissemination of knowledge (known as *rapping*) fits into a relationship with Africa that continues to evolve and change according to contemporary circumstances.

Hip Hop and Islamic-Based Ideologies

As we evaluate current contexts that create adaptation in culture and tradition, it is clear that the maintenance of African oral tradition through rapping as well as the evolving presence of Islam in Black America exist within an interwoven, ongoing resistance to oppression. The history of Black Americans is a quest for ways to affirm one's self-worth and value in a society that typically devalues and suppresses the expression of one's cultural reality. Without a determination to express their evolving collective experience, there could never have been opportunities to create any sense of dignity that would provide meaning, purpose, and significance to continue forward.

Richard Brent Turner (1997, 185) offered the idea of the Black American Muslim's "*jihad* (struggle) of words," referring to the use of the oral tradition as a method of delivering messages of resistance to oppression. Juan M. Floyd-Thomas (2003) extended this notion to rap music as related to Islamic-based ideologies. He noted that "there has been a synergy of African American Islam and Hip Hop over the past few decades which has forged a profound and complicated relationship between these two phenomenological forces that must be studied more closely" (51). Floyd-Thomas helped to identify the "*jihad* of words" as an ongoing dynamic in the historical continuum of Islamic-based ideologies in Black America that brought "attention to *both* the historical development of various modalities of Islam in black communities and the articulation of these developments in the lyrical content of rap music" (51).

William Eric Perkins (1996) noted that numerous individuals who are credited with the formulation of rapping into its modern expression were people who identified with Islamic-based ideologies. Whether Black revolutionary poets like The Last Poets or public speakers such as Malcolm X, Muhammad Ali, and Minister Louis Farrakhan, a number of individuals who are credited with influential reformulations of Black oral expression were Muslim. Beyond the forerunners to rap, Perkins also indicated that many of the artists who emerged in the 1980s were also associated with Islamic-based ideologies, and that "the Islamic rap styles of political or message rap are represented by Lakim Shabazz, the Poor Righteous Teachers, Rakim, Pete Rock and C. L. Smooth, Brand Nubian, Two Kings in a Cypher, and women rappers Star & Crescent" (27). In the modern postindustrial context, Hip Hop culture, and more specifically rap music, has been a significant part of this method of sharing Islamic-based knowledge in Black America.

Early Intersections of Hip Hop, Islam, and Black Nationalism

Given the impact of Islamic-based ideologies on Black America, particularly through Black Nationalism, it is not surprising that the foundation and formation of Hip Hop culture intersect with the ongoing power and influence of Islamic-based ideologies in Black America. In fact, numerous individuals who preceded modern rappers were Black Nationalists associated with Islamic-based ideologies, including poets such as Gil Scott-Heron and members of the group The Last Poets. A central figure in the foundation of Hip Hop culture known as Afrika Bambaataa (founder of the Universal Zulu Nation and commonly referred to as the "Godfather" of Hip Hop culture) credited these poets and many others for drawing on traditions from their African ancestry, including the use of the oral tradition and call-and-response techniques:

> Rap in general dates all the way back to the motherland where tribes would use call-and-response chants. In the 1930's and 1940's, you had Cab Calloway pioneering his style of jazz rhyming. The sixties you had the love style of rapping with Isaac Hayes, Barry White, and the poetry style of rapping with the Last Poets, the Watts poets and the militant style rapping with brothers like Malcolm X and Minister Louis Farrakhan. (Afrika Bambaataa quote from 1993 in Perkins 1996, 4)

Bambaataa, recognized as an elite member of Hip Hop's old-school era, was part of the New York City community of individuals who, in the late 1970s, helped cultivate Hip Hop as a cultural form that spoke to the conditions and circumstances of marginalized urban youth. Although this cultural form was a new reformulation of Black expression, founding fathers of Hip Hop culture like Bambaataa had a solid understanding of its roots and groundworks drawn from evolved African tradition. As a result, Bambaataa ensured that influential figures who preceded Hip Hop culture are credited with its creation. Bambaataa also echoed the rhymes of Muhammad Ali, whose poetic couplets during the peak of his career between 1964 and 1972 provided new inspiration to inner-city youth who specialized in "signifying" or "playing the dozens." This particular form of verbal jousting continues to be quite common in African American and urban culture (Perkins 1996).

We begin to see a collage of foundational influences that cross cultural realms within the Black community. References to figures like The Last Poets, Gil Scott-Heron, Malcolm X, Muhammad Ali, and Louis Farrakhan paint an early picture in which the formation of Hip Hop culture was dependent on direct cultural influences by figures who associated with Islamic-based ideologies. Lusane (2004, 355) noted that particularly "minister Louis Farrakhan and his Nation of Islam have had tremendous influence on the political views of black youth, in general, and [on] rappers, more specifically." All of these individuals can be credited as key influencers in the intersection of Islam and Hip Hop. In addition, Malcolm X played a central role in influencing the Hip Hop generation. As Daulatzai (2012, 98–99) noted,

> Just as the hip-hop generation did, Malcolm represented ideas of an "authentic" Blackness that did not sell out or compromise to white America. Both Malcolm and hip-hop also gave voice to the poverty and difficulties of urban existence while also speaking truth to power against the Black bourgeoisie, white power, and state authority. Both . . . faced accusations of reckless violence, while ironically, both were also subject to incarceration and the constant threat of imminent violence. . . . Malcolm had transcended the violence and despair of the ghetto and incarceration, providing a redemptive possibility to Black youth who had already been locked up or were constantly subjected to that possibility in the era of mass incarceration. . . . Finally, and possibly most important, like Malcolm, hip-hop was deeply invested in the power of words as a weapon, and . . . it used its rhetoric rebellion to speak its truth to power.

The power of Black Muslim figures, particularly Malcolm X, influenced youth and urban culture, and helped cultivate the ideals and principles from which Hip Hop culture would then draw. Both cultural movements resonated among those who felt marginalized by the American political and sociocultural landscape and sought to reclaim their identity through self-determined expression, "reeducation," and action. These individuals drew from their African heritage to express a newly reformulated political, social, and/or spiritual framework that was cultivated within the nexus of postindustrial American social marginalization and African tradition. Those who identify with Islamic-based ideologies and/or Hip Hop culture typically seek to subvert the oppression they have inherited and experienced in their lives.

Individuals who identify with Islamic-based ideologies and people drawn to Hip Hop share historical connections and interests, and thus the representation of rap artists who identify with Islamic-based ideologies seems to be disproportionately larger than their general representation in Black America. Although rooted in a common political and social commentary on the circumstances of Black people within the broader American social dynamic, this overlap reveals a significant spiritual component to Hip Hop culture expressed through ritual that also appeals to the Islamic-based individual.

One of the most overt expressions of spirituality is in a common ritual known as a *cipher*, in which individuals crowd around in a circle and disseminate rhythmic phases that are typically improvised in a form of rapping known as *freestyling*. Participants often express feelings of euphoria and spiritual highs when describing the experience of freestyling in a cipher. In a cipher, the group collectively bounces to a common rhythm, often performed by an individual who creates a drum-like beat with his mouth through a technique known as *beatboxing*. Many people describe the cipher as collective human movements that expand and contract like a beating heart in which the energy of the collective group is reinforced by the circle, creating a feeling of unity among participants. According to Perry (2004, 107),

> The best way to describe the term (*cipher*), one popularized by the Five Percent Nation, is that it indicates a mystical and transcendent yet human state, that creates a vibe amid a community, as well as a spirit of

artistic production or intellectual/spiritual discursive moments. A classic example would be the cipher created in a group of freestylers at the moment of their shared rhyming. Access to the cipher is denied to the ignorant or unenlightened. And the negative energy of one person might mess up the cipher.

These practices exemplify evolved historical connections that are tied to African Islamic oral and cultural custom. The circle is an important component of the African spiritual and cultural tradition, as are improvised vocals and the rhythmic syncopated beat to keep the collective in unison. This is a clear example of how "Hip Hop has styles and themes that share striking similarities with many past and contiguous Afrodiasporic musical and cultural expressions" (Rose 1994, 27).

Islam and Hip Hop as Modern Social Commentary in Black America

The notable influence of Islamic-based ideologies within Hip Hop has remained relatively unnoticed by many who engage it. Eric Arnold (2005, 1) articulated this gap in awareness:

> "I think that Islam itself is the unofficial religion of Hip Hop," proclaims Adisa Banjoko, the San Jose-based writer, publicist, radio show host of *One Mic* on KNEW-AM.... "So much hip-hop has come to be that has referenced Islam, that many of the people themselves don't even recognize it."

The lack of knowledge and understanding of the significance of Islam and African influences in Hip Hop can be attributed to two major factors. First, few understand the influence of African traditions on evolving Black cultural traditions. For example, the significance of Islam as an African-diasporic historical influence is not well known or understood. The significance of African oral tradition and how it influences today's Black cultural expressions are not commonly understood either. Second, there are a number of hidden meanings and messages in rap that can go unnoticed. The embedding of messages has been termed *signifying* by ethnographer Claudia Mitchell-Kernan (1990, 311), who described it as a way of encoding messages or meanings which involves, in most cases, an element of indirection. This kind of signifying might best be viewed as an alternative message form, selected for its artistic merit, and may occur embedded in a variety of discourses. . . . The apparent meaning of the sentence "signifies" its actual meaning.

When we apply the meaning of signifying to its common use in rap, it becomes evident that there are numerous expressions that will not be understood by the broader audience. Nowhere is this better exemplified than in raps that use Five Percenter concepts. Also known as the Nation of Gods and Earths and founded by Clarence 13X in 1964, Five Percenters are a group that splintered from the Nation of Islam. Hip Hop phrases like "What up G?" have become common slang language in American pop culture; however, few realize that this phrase comes from the Five Percenter concept of "G" meaning "God," signifying the seventh letter of what they refer to as the Supreme Alphabet. In reality, when Five Percenters were originally saying this phrase, its true intention was to say, "What up God?" in reference to their belief that they, as Black men, are Allah. Supreme Mathematics, a system of numerology among Five Percenters, is also heavily coded into rap language to signify concepts and meanings that are divine by those who understand these concepts (Floyd-Thomas 2003; Rose 1994).

Five Percenter ideologies are extremely pervasive in Hip Hop and are often tied to powerful political statements and social commentary on the state of Black people in America. As Perry (2004, 149) described, "Through lyrics, Five Percenters hope to enlighten their listeners with the truth of their message, and to encourage self-knowledge." Prominent Five Percenter rappers include Rakim, Poor Righteous Teachers, Big Daddy Kane, Busta Rhymes, Guru, Digable Planets, and the entire Wu Tang Clan, among numerous others. Given the ways signifying is used by Five Percenters in their raps, most consumers of their work are not aware of the messages embedded into the music. These expressions by rap artists exemplify how Hip Hop as well as Islamic-based ideologies within Hip Hop function as both public transcripts for a broader audience and hidden transcripts strategically used to invoke various forms of everyday resistance tied to a reformulated ritual order that convey specific messages to specific audiences for the purpose of education, inspiration, and mobilization (Dirks 1994; Rose 1994; Scott 1985, 1990).

Although Five Percenter philosophy and other Islamic-based ideologies have been present throughout much of the history of Hip Hop culture, widespread public acknowledgment of their significance did not really begin until the early 1990s after Black Nationalist and Nation of Islam concepts were used by a prominent political rap group known as Public Enemy. Through their use of Black Nationalist rhetoric, Public Enemy often featured sample recordings of Malcolm X in their songs, wore hats and t-shirts featuring an "X," and in turn caused Malcom X's legacy to return to pop culture status. They also helped create interest in Islam-based influences in Hip Hop. As Perkins (1996, 23) described,

> Islamic rappers bring to Hip Hop a powerful sense of recovering and reinventing history, packaging it as "science" for the visual generation. Invoking much of the eclectic and popular science of the Nation of Islam, its various factions, and the resurgence led by Minister Louis Farrakhan, they represent a submerged voice of the black rap underground.

Perkins's reference to "reinventing history" reinforces the significance of historical imagination in how Islam is perceived in postindustrial Black America. Although it is clear that African Diasporic influences (including Islamic history and tradition) are significant in contemporary Black America, it is also clear that the reformulations occurring over time create significant changes to the tradition. Though these changes draw upon African tradition in subconscious ways, there is also a significant element of intention among many who seek to return to African foundations to bypass their American historical reality. An example of this phenomenon is found in the song "Rock This Funky Joint" by Five Percenters known as the Poor Righteous Teachers (1990). In the song there is a lyric in which the group member Wise Intelligent says, "Assalamalaikum, Walaikumsalaam; a universal greeting from the people of Akon." This rhyme articulates a direct connection between the universal Muslim greetings used globally with specific African Muslim tribes in West Africa from which numerous slaves were brought through the Atlantic slave trade. Their articulation of this connection clearly communicates that their identification with Islam is not abstract or coincidental.

At the same time, it educates listeners about their ancestral connections to specific traditions in West Africa in which one can subvert the oppression of the Black North American experience and reclaim African identity, heritage, and knowledge.

In evaluating heterodox Islamic-based ideologies tied to political and social dissent in Hip Hop, one often sees a marginalized Black male voice expressing frustration through a new identity tied to an idealized historical imagination. Among many Black people, there is a desire to return to an African-based identity that reflects the power and intelligence of the civilized African man (as opposed to a primitive or ignorant man). This Black identity is intended to reverse the self-hatred created through centuries of oppression and reinvent itself as descended from a Utopian African identity. In this identity one may be raised to become a godlike figure elevated higher than one's previous masters (the white devils). Islam directly ties individuals to a "civilized" past but, as discussed earlier, it certainly was not a past free of suppression. However, when one is seeking to subvert oppression, the historical imagination allows an individual to ignore that which may be problematic (Anderson 1991).

It should not be surprising that Hip Hop and Islamic-based expression in Hip Hop are male-dominated phenomena. Rose (1994, 26) noted that "a great deal of the history of black cultural practices has been disproportionately explored via male subjects, the oral and protest roots models for rap's development refer to a male-centered scholarly tradition." Hip Hop descended from the evolving Black traditions that came before it, including blues, jazz, and bebop, which were male-dominated art forms. Furthermore, storytelling and oral traditions in Africa were traditionally male-dominated endeavors. In a postindustrial capitalistic context, this male-centered culture has translated into a culture of competition and bragging. It is also a reflection of the desire of the Black male ego to be acknowledged and raised to a level beyond its demoralized condition in the broader American social context. It creates a realm in which one can prove to others one's worth and value through a voice not often heard or listened to.

Rationalizations within many Islamic-based ideologies are often specifically geared toward the empowerment of Black males as well. In fact, such ideologies are often adhered to and/or learned during terms in prison (much like the experience of Malcolm X), where Black men are disproportionately incarcerated and directly experience the result of postindustrial marginalization (Alexander 2010). Such ideologies provide new perspectives on one's own circumstances, providing inspiration and new options to consider in leading life during and after imprisonment. The intersection of Hip Hop and Islamic-based ideologies offers an opportunity for an individual to have spiritual, religious, political, social, and cultural needs and desires addressed by affirming their own worth through a number of affirmations that transcend social voids as a result of marginalization (Daulatzai 2012).

It should be noted that orthodox Islam has also been significantly expressed through Black rap music. Artists such as Mos Def (now known as Yasiin Bey), Brother Ali, Lupe Fiasco, A Tribe Called Quest, Binary Star, and Jurassic 5, among numerous others, often express mainstream Sunni principles in their raps. Such artists tend to cite more mainstream Islamic principles drawn from Qur'anic and universally Islamic principles. Often Sunni Islamic Hip Hop artists proclaim interests in a universal family that transcends race. Although most promote a less nationalistic approach, many adhere to philosophies similar to Malcolm X's late-life ideals that promoted a universal humanity but continue to prioritize and focus on the uplifting of the Black community in America (Floyd-Thomas 2003).

Sunni Muslim rap articulates a shift in Islamic rap that in many ways reflects the transformation of ideology, philosophy, and spirituality of Malcolm X as he transitioned to become El Hajj Malik Shabazz. Floyd-Thomas (2003, 64) utilized the work of Mos Def as an example in order to articulate this shift:

> In the song "Fear Not of Man," the rapper Mos Def provides a stark contrast to the prevalent trend in hip-hop during the late 1990s. The song begins with Mos Def uttering . . . a solemn Arabic invocation, *Bismillah ir Rahman ir Raheem*, which means "In the Name of God the Most Merciful, the Most Compassionate." . . . By offering the Bismillah as the first words on his album/CD, Mos Def performs *dhikr*, a brief yet poignant prayer intended to assert one's full awareness of the union between God and the faithful believer and to purify the Muslim of all that is bad. Thus,

Mos Def expresses the intention to commit himself and his musical work to divine will by repeating the name and attributes of God in hopes of drawing himself closer to God. This deceptively modest gesture can be seen as a profound shift in the articulation of African American Islam in contemporary rap music.

This example not only illustrates a shift in how Sunni Black Muslim artists tend to infuse Islam into rap music, but also is representative of how many other artists signify Islamic concepts and principles. Similar examples of encoded Islamic Arabic language and ritual can be found in the work of Lupe Fiasco, A Tribe Called Quest, and many others. This approach also demarcates Sunni Muslim rappers in a manner that is identifiable among the various Islamic-based rap artists and delineates their positionality in Islam.

Islam, Hip Hop, and Resistance beyond the United States

As Hip Hop continues to grow as a globalizing force in the world, Muslim rappers are continuing to encounter the global world of Islam. As the global Islamic world increasingly gains interest in Hip Hop culture, the depth of the intersection between Islam and Hip Hop also expands. Not surprisingly, Hip Hop culture and rap music are being articulated by Muslims around the world who face marginalizing and oppressive circumstances in various contexts. Among the more prominent places where this is occurring is among Muslim North Africans in France and other immigrant communities expressing frustration with their conditions throughout Europe, including in the United Kingdom, Germany, and Scandinavia. Many, like Palestinians, have been featured in notable documentaries like *Slingshot Hip Hop* (2008), while Senegalese Hip Hop was featured in *African Underground: Democracy in Dakar* (2007).

In *Black Star, Crescent Moon: The Muslim International and Black Freedom beyond America*, Sohail Daulatzai (2012) draws connections between the shared history of the Muslim Third World and Black freedom struggles in the United States. The global dialogue of resistance to oppression in global Muslim Hip Hop and among Black American Hip

Hop artists highlights an emerging hegemonic dynamic that juxtaposes the "Black Criminal" and "Muslim Terrorist." As Daulatzai described,

> It is deeply ironic that Malcolm X would become the iconic figure for Black radicalism and hip-hop culture late in the twentieth century. For not only had he been incarcerated and labeled criminal at an earlier time, but he also converted to Islam and become a radical Black internationalist who challenged US anti-Black racism and linked these struggles with those in the Muslim Third World. (Daulatzai 2012, 97)

This discourse directly correlates the experiences of Black ghettos in the United States with the experience of imperialism in Muslim lands around the world.

Islamic-based Hip Hop artists have raised the prominence of their "jihad of words" and have now reached a global audience. This has resulted in the Muslim Third World and other Muslims around the world in marginalized circumstances connecting and identifying with the struggles of Black Americans. The connection between Black Nationalism and Western imperialism was facilitated through the music of prominent groups like Public Enemy, whose messages of resistance to oppression, facilitated by embedded iconography of Malcolm X, resonated with the global Muslim Hip Hop generation (Daulatzai 2012).

As Hip Hop culture expands as a global force, the influence of Islam on this counterhegemonic oral tradition is becoming more apparent, not just among Black Americans in the United States, but also among marginalized Muslims throughout the world, including prominent communities in Europe, Africa, and Asia (Swedenburg 2001). These exchanges of information and music, globally and locally, are facilitated by rapid shifts in technology in which messages are disseminated in dynamic and impactful ways. This *"jihad of the tongue, or jihad bil lisaan,* which also includes *jihad bil qalam,* or *jihad* of the pen" (Alim 2006, 35), is facilitating transformational learning experiences and processes of liberatory praxis that draw from African forms of lifelong learning practices that are often unaccounted for in academic literature. This is significant for numerous reasons, including the need to account for non-Eurocentric, counterhegemonic pedagogies that Islamic rap is enacting. Furthermore, it also highlights the need to add discourse to existing Hip Hop pedagogical practices in classrooms that tend to impose Eurocentric modes of structuring formal education, without focusing on informal learning occurring outside the classroom.

Acknowledgment of informal learning facilitated by Islamic rap music allows educators to consider the role of evolved African aesthetics inherent in learning processes that occur through Islamic rap. Furthermore, when educators recognize and embrace these educational experiences as a form of critical pedagogy, they can enact liberatory praxis and create opportunities for learners to construct new self-determined realities in their lives.

Hip Hop and Rap as Critical Pedagogy in Education and Social Movements

In *Pedagogy of the Oppressed*, Freire (1970) discussed the contradiction between the oppressor and the oppressed as well as the need to develop a mutual process between each to achieve liberation for both. He drew parallels between the power dynamic that exists in systems of oppression, often playing out quite visibly in politics, and the contradiction that exists between teachers and students in educational settings. Freire noted that most oppressed people are unaware of the systems that perpetuate their own condition and that educational systems are utilized by the oppressors to perpetuate those circumstances. Freire (1970) proposed educational methods that can potentially transform this dynamic to one that can support liberation. He also later noted that "knowledge emerges only through invention and re-invention, through the restless, impatient, continuing, hopeful inquiry human beings pursue in the world, with the world, and with each other" (Freire 2008, 244). In thinking of Freire's socioemancipatory lens in which learning fundamentally changes how one sees oneself in the world in which one lives (Freire 1970), we can identify rap and Hip Hop as tools to engage liberating educational processes. In this process, Islam and its relationship to Black ancestral spiritual identity and cultural aesthetic intersect through rap and Hip Hop, and provide a process of liberating pedagogical practices.

In recent years, there has been emergent research on Hip Hop culture as both pedagogy and critical pedagogy. Scholars such as Antwi Akom (2009), who draws from Freire (1970), argue that liberatory praxis can be achieved through Hip Hop culture. Other scholars, including Marc Lamont Hill (2009), focus on classroom pedagogy and Hip Hop. However, very little scholarship has focused on the out-of-classroom learning experiences of individuals who engage Hip Hop culture. Merriam, Caffarella, and Baumgartner (2007, 35) noted that informal environments are often a site of learning for adults that are "embedded . . . in our everyday activities" and are also impacted by technology, particularly the Internet.

In any learning setting, one's experience is a significant factor in how knowledge is acquired, learned, and integrated into one's life. David Kolb (1984) argued that learning is an ongoing process rooted in one's human experience in which a person constantly creates and tests knowledge experientially. However, many theorists do not account for contextual factors in experiential learning. Tara Fenwick (2001, 79) noted that we must account for "the social relations and political cultural dimensions of the community, . . . the nature of the task, . . . the vocabulary and cultural beliefs through which the individual makes meaning of the whole situation, and the historical, temporal, and spatial location of the situations." In doing so, learners are permitted to bring their whole self into the learning situation. Hip Hop can create learning environments that connect experiential learning, globalization, technology, and learning in formal and informal settings in a manner that allows individuals to be their whole self in learning situations.

Mejai Bola Avoseh (2008) argued that learning is a lifelong process in indigenous modes of education. Furthermore, Avoseh (2011) added that much of indigenous learning occurs in informal settings in Africa. Such conceptions of education validate nondominant perspectives and deepen the validation of informal settings as sites of educational learning and practice. Given that Hip Hop culture draws from African aesthetics of culture, ritual, and communication of ideas, knowledge, and wisdom, one can infer that similar types of learning experiences are occurring for those engaged in it. More specifically, participants in rap music engage the oral tradition as a mode of disseminating knowledge in a manner that is similar to African forms of oral pedagogical practices.

Islamic Rap as Transformational Learning and Liberatory Praxis

Most academic research on Hip Hop pedagogy focuses on formal learning environments, emphasizing integration into curricula, lesson plans, classroom environments, and learning experiences in formal learning spaces. Marcella Runell and Martha Diaz (2007) compiled Hip Hop pedagogical methods that specifically focused on K-12 classrooms. Hill (2009) introduced an anthropological approach into Hip Hop pedagogy with a critical perspective through ethnographic study of a South Philadelphia high school. Hill and Emery Petchauer (2013) offered an edited collection that articulated numerous examples of how Hip Hop can be integrated into curricular circumstances in various formal educational contexts (K-12, college, and so on). Finally, Petchauer (2012) examined Hip Hop culture in the lives of college students, looking at both curricular and cocurricular dynamics while drawing from higher education student development concepts like self-authorship (Baxter Magolda 2008).

Hill (2009) and Noguera (2008) identified Hip Hop pedagogy with a social justice lens as one of the few areas of potential for liberation of learners from marginalized identities. This is particularly true and significant given dramatic failures as well as the stagnation that persists in educational systems throughout the United States. Given the existing research, there is little doubt that in formal and informal settings, Hip Hop pedagogy can have effective learning outcomes on marginalized student populations in classroom environments.

Despite this research on formal learning settings, Hip Hop critical pedagogy often occurs outside classroom settings in informal learning environments. It is in these settings that transformative learning experiences, grounded in sociocultural emancipatory learning experiences, are translated into liberatory praxis. Islamic rap music is a specific vehicle within broader Hip Hop culture in which this pedagogy and praxis are enacted. As this chapter has shown, Islamic rap music engages indigenous West African aesthetics, such as improvisation and oral tradition, to communicate and convey complex messages and ideas drawn from ancestral wisdom, knowledge, spirituality, and ritual.

Critical theoretical lenses offer less Eurocentric and more contextually based perspectives and account for a fuller range of experiences.

Coupled with Freire's (1970) ideas of more dialogic, student-driven learning processes, these perspectives can inform methods and practices that allow learners to identify injustices and seek to take action to address them. Contextually based, non-Eurocentric pedagogy creates opportunities to develop inclusive actions for social justice.

Recommendations

As noted earlier, I have been utilizing Hip Hop as a tool for education, resistance, and liberation for most of my adult life in numerous contexts. This section presents strategies that educators, activists, community leaders, and others can consider in order to operationalize the insights offered in this chapter. Drawing from Marcia B. Baxter Magolda's (2008) notion of self-authorship, Hip Hop as liberatory praxis is most possible when learners create and generate knowledge from their own beliefs and values. Islamic-based ideologies are not the only beliefs, values, or identities that can be integral to learners utilizing Hip Hop as liberatory praxis. These recommendations encompass the use of Hip Hop to empower and inform liberation across a myriad of marginalized identities and their intersections.

- Formal learning environments, particularly in higher educational settings, can encourage and support learners to draw from marginalized, intersectional identities when expressing and engaging Hip Hop in cocurricular learning settings. For example, diversity offices can advise, fund, and support student programming that utilizes Hip Hop as a tool for equity, inclusion, and social/racial justice. Events and practices can include student-led Hip Hop summits with workshops, performances, and sessions with artistic expression as well as topical issues relevant to marginalized, intersectional identities.
- Nonprofit organizations and youth centers (e.g., Boys and Girls Clubs, YMCAs, etc.) working with young people can utilize Hip Hop as a tool for artistic expression, empowerment, and social justice. In these programs, learners can be encouraged to draw from their personal cultural backgrounds, aesthetics, and other social identities.
- Foundations providing funding for programs, community centers, and faith-based organizations can earmark or prioritize money for events that

utilize Hip Hop as a tool of empowerment and social justice in communities. Organizations like Inner-City Muslim Action Network in Chicago and 1Hood Media in Pittsburgh are struggling to find foundations that will fund such efforts despite consistent demonstrated impact on marginalized youth and broader challenges in marginalized communities. Meanwhile, organizations with far less meaningful impact are often receiving funding. This highlights the need for foundations to learn, understand, and prioritize the implications of relevant cultural dimensions and expressions for young people.
- Faith-based organizations like mosques, churches, and others can embrace Hip Hop as a tool of expression and empowerment for marginalized youth. Hip Hop can also be used to teach religious/spiritual concepts and ideas.

Closing Thoughts

Hip Hop and Islam have been tremendously influential resources in my life journey as a person, a scholar, and an educator. My experiences, relationships, and research have taught me that Islam and Hip Hop are powerful forces in Black America that are part of a broader historical continuum of resistance to oppression and yearning for liberation. The resourcefulness of Black people to draw from spirit and culture, even when denied material resources and basic human rights, is not a new attribute, but one that was evident and that has evolved across centuries of oppression. In recent years, Hip Hop has been used as a tool in classroom settings in an attempt to create culturally relevant pedagogy for learners. What is rarely discussed, however, is how Hip Hop, in and of itself, is a form of liberatory praxis that empowers and reflects learning for people historically marginalized across numerous intersections. As individuals tap in to their culture, their spirit, and their ancestry, they redefine their identity and experience, transform art and ways of knowing, and create ways of addressing systemic oppression.

REFERENCES

Abdul Kabeer, Su'ad. 2016. *Muslim Cool: Race, Religion, and Hip Hop in the United States*. New York: New York University Press.

Akom, Antwi A. 2009. "Critical Hip Hop Pedagogy as a Form of Liberatory Praxis." *Equity and Excellence in Education* 42, no. 1: 52–66.

Alexander, Michelle. 2010. *The New Jim Crow: Mass Incarceration in the Age of Colorblindness.* New York: New Press.

Alim, H. Samy. 2006. *Roc the Mic Right: The Language of Hip Hop Culture.* New York: Routledge.

Anderson, Benedict. 1991. *Imagined Communities: Reflections on the Origin and Spread of Nationalism.* Rev. ed. New York: Verso.

Arnold, Eric K. 2005. "Rhythm Nation of Islam: Spinning through a Cipher of Muslim Rap with the Bishop of Hip-Hop." *East Bay Express,* January 19. www.eastbayexpress.com.

Avoseh, Mejai B. M. 2008. "A Comparative Review of Lifelong Learning in Traditional African and Native American Indigenous Education." In *Comparative Adult Education 2008: Experiences and Examples,* edited by Jost Reischmann and Michal Bron Jr., 191–202. New York: Peter Lang.

———. 2011. "Informal Community Learning in Traditional Africa." In *Innovations in Lifelong Learning: Critical Perspectives on Diversity, Participation and Vocational Learning,* edited by Sue Jackson, 34–48. New York: Routledge.

Baxter Magolda, Marcia B. 2008. "Three Elements of Self-Authorship." *Journal of College Student Development* 49, no. 4 (July): 269–84.

Chang, Jeff. 2005. *Can't Stop Won't Stop: A History of the Hip-Hop Generation.* New York: Picador.

Daulatzai, Sohail. 2012. *Black Star, Crescent Moon: The Muslim International and Black Freedom beyond America.* Minneapolis: University of Minnesota Press.

Dirks, Nicholas B. 1994. "Ritual and Resistance: Subversion as a Social Fact." In *Culture/Power/History: A Reader in Contemporary Social Theory,* edited by Nicholas B. Dirks, Geoff Eley, and Sherry B. Ortner, 483–503. Princeton: Princeton University Press.

Fenwick, Tara J. 2001. *Experiential Learning: A Theoretical Critique from Five Perspectives.* Information Series No. 385. Columbus: ERIC Clearinghouse on Adult, Career, and Vocational Education, Center on Education and Training for Employment.

Floyd-Thomas, Juan M. 2003. "A Jihad of Words: The Evolution of African American Islam and Contemporary Hip-Hop." In *Noise and Spirit: The Religious and Spiritual Sensibilities of Rap Music,* edited by Anthony B. Pinn, 49–72. New York: New York University Press.

Freire, Paulo. 1970. *Pedagogy of the Oppressed.* New York: Herder and Herder.

———. 2008. "The 'Banking' Concept of Education." In *Ways of Reading,* 8th ed., edited by David Bartholomae and Anthony Petrosky, 242–54. Boston: Bedford-St. Martin's.

Gomez, Michael A. 2005. *Black Crescent: The Experience and Legacy of African Muslims in the Americas.* New York: Cambridge University Press.

Hill, Marc Lamont. 2009. *Beats, Rhymes, and Classroom Life: Hip-Hop Pedagogy and the Politics of Identity.* New York: Teachers College Press.

Hill, Marc Lamont, and Emery Petchauer. 2013. *Schooling Hip-Hop: Expanding Hip-Hop Based Education across the Curriculum.* New York: Teachers College Press.

Kolb, David. 1984. *Experiential Learning: Experience as the Source of Learning and Development*. Englewood Cliffs: Prentice-Hall.
Levine, Lawrence W. 1977. *Black Culture and Black Consciousness: Afro-American Folk Thought from Slavery to Freedom*. New York: Oxford University Press.
Lusane, Clarence. 2004. "Rap, Race and Politics." In *That's the Joint: The Hip-Hop Studies Reader*, edited by Murray Forman and Mark Anthony Neal, 351–62. New York: Routledge.
Maultsby, Portia. 1991. "Africanisms in African-American Music." In *Africanisms in American Culture*, edited by Joseph E. Holloway, 326–55. Bloomington: Indiana University Press.
McCloud, Aminah Beverly. 1995. *African American Islam*. New York: Routledge.
Merriam, Sharan B., Rosemary S. Caffarella, and Lisa M. Baumgartner. 2007. *Learning in Adulthood: A Comprehensive Guide*. 3rd ed. San Francisco: Jossey-Bass.
Mitchell-Kernan, Claudia. 1990. "Signifying." In *Mother Wit from the Laughing Barrel: Readings in the Interpretation of Afro-American Folklore*, edited by Alan Dundes, 310–28. New York: Garland.
Mubashshir, Debra Washington. 2001. "A Fruitful Labor: African American Formulations of Islam, 1928–1942." Doctoral dissertation, Northwestern University.
Noguera, Pedro A. 2008. *The Trouble with Black Boys: . . . And Other Reflections on Race, Equity, and the Future of Public Education*. San Francisco: Jossey-Bass.
Perkins, William Eric, ed. 1996. *Droppin' Science: Critical Essays on Rap Music and Hip Hop Culture*. Philadelphia: Temple University Press.
Perry, Imani. 2004. *Prophets of the Hood: Politics and Poetics in Hip Hop*. Durham: Duke University Press.
Petchauer, Emery. 2012. *Hip-Hop Culture in College Students' Lives: Elements, Embodiment, and Higher Edutainment*. New York: Routledge.
Poor Righteous Teachers. 1990. "Rock This Funky Joint." *Holy Intellect*, Profile/Arista Records, 01515-11289.
Rose, Tricia. 1994. *Black Noise: Rap Music and Black Culture in Contemporary America*. Hanover: Wesleyan University Press.
Runell, Marcella, and Martha Diaz. 2007. *The Hip-Hop Education Guidebook*. Vol. 1. New York: Hip-Hop Association.
Scott, James C. 1985. *Weapons of the Weak: Everyday Forms of Peasant Resistance*. New Haven: Yale University Press.
———. 1990. *Domination and the Art of Resistance: Hidden Transcripts*. New Haven: Yale University Press.
Swedenburg, Ted. 2001. "Islamic Hip-Hop versus Islamophobia." In *Global Noise: Rap and Hip Hop outside the USA*, edited by Tony Mitchell, 57–85. Middletown: Wesleyan University Press.
Turner, Richard Brent. 1997. *Islam in the African American Experience*. Bloomington: Indiana University Press.

10

Understanding and Responding to Resistance When Intersectionality Is Utilized to Address Race, Racism, and Racial Justice Work

CHARMAINE L. WIJEYESINGHE

"Intersectionality" is a term that appears increasingly often in discussions of identity, diversity, inequality, and social justice movements. As the use of intersectionality as a tool of critical inquiry and critical practice (Collins 2019; Collins and Bilge 2016) increases, so do questions and challenges concerning the framework's more complex, multifaceted approach to social identities and systems of inequality. For example, authors have offered varied perspectives on how the centrality of Black women's experiences to intersectionality should be recognized and maintained (Carbado 2013; Collins 2015, 2019; Grzanka 2020; Nash 2008, 2019). Others question the extent that intersectionality informs identity at the individual level (Cho, Crenshaw, and McCall 2013; Collins and Bilge 2016; Wijeyesinghe 2019; Wijeyesinghe and Jones 2019). Even the most basic question, "What counts as intersectionality?" (Collins and Bilge 2016, 190), remains contested. These issues and questions reveal "tension points" (Wijeyesinghe and Jones 2019, 8) that can fuel resistance to intersectionality as a theoretical and practical tool. However, these tension points can also direct reflection that increases our understanding of resistance and our ability to address it.

This chapter examines aspects of resistance to intersectionality when the framework is used to examine race, racism, and racial justice. It includes an overview of central tenets of intersectionality, specific examples of resistance and tension points drawn from the experiences of the author and the literature on intersectionality, and reflections on how reframing resistance to intersectionality provides the challenges and momentum needed to guide future scholarship and work.

Central Themes of Intersectionality

Intersectionality is deeply rooted in the experiences of Black women and their activism against racial injustice across centuries (see Hancock 2016 for an excellent overview of the historical underpinnings of intersectionality). In acknowledging the long history of what we have come to recognize as intersectional themes, Jennifer Nash (2019, 6) described intersectionality as "part of a cohort of terms that black feminists created in order to analyze the interconnectedness of structures of domination." Even as it is considered a "social theory in the making" (Collins 2019, 51), intersectionality's foundation reflects several enduring tenets (Collins 2015, 2019; Dill and Zambrana 2009; Weber 2010). A summary of these interrelated tenets is presented next, organized by the six central themes offered by Patricia Hill Collins and Sirma Bilge (2016): relationality, social context, power relations, social inequality, social justice, and complexity.

Relationality

Intersectionality addresses "the connections among entities *that had been seen as separate and often oppositional*" (Collins and Bilge 2016, 194, emphasis added). Rather than approaching socially constructed categories such as race, gender, and sexual orientation as individual, discrete characteristics, intersectionality highlights that "social identities which serve as organizing features of social relations, mutually constitute, reinforce, and naturalize each other" (Shields 2008, 302). This orientation "shifts focus away from the essential qualities that seemingly lie in the center of categories and toward the relational processes that connect them" (Collins 2019, 45). An intersectional perspective fosters a "both/and" versus an "either/or" way of understanding how people experience the world and how systems operate to sustain oppression (Collins and Bilge 2016; Wijeyesinghe and Jones 2019). Therefore, an individual is not defined by race in one situation, gender in another, and nationality in yet another. All of the categories, together, frame how a person experiences the world and is treated by others in all situations. When an intersectional perspective is applied beyond the personal level, social concerns, such as housing insecurity and inequality, are understood through *interrelated lenses and relationships* of positionalities and systems based on economics, race, gender, sexual orientation, disability status, and more. By connecting this complex understanding of social issues with efforts to address them, intersectionality reinforces the relationship between critical inquiry and praxis.

Social Context

Collins (2015, 14) noted that "because social formations of complex social inequalities are historically contingent and cross culturally specific, unequal material realities and social experiences vary across time and space." In intersectionality, the meaning and expression of social identities, social locations, and systems of inequality are fluid and reflect the dynamic nature of social, cultural, and historical environments. For example, the labels attached to social groups have changed over time, seen in the different racial designations offered on various years of the census (see López, this volume) and the addition of *T* and *Q* to include transgender and queer or questioning people in the acronym GLBTQ. The prevailing social narratives about members of social groups, created and reinforced by dominant social forces, are also influenced by contexts. Thus, for example, the migration of people from one country to another is framed and addressed differently when social, economic, and political dynamics of a particular period are considered along with the dominant narratives associated with the diverse social positions (such as race, nationality, and faith) of the people seeking entry into a country. Attention to context enables efforts to enact change, such as the Black Lives Matter and #MeToo movements, to be relevant to the pressing social issues of their time. Context also informs the interpretation and uses of intersectionality, illuminating similarities and differences when the framework is situated in social movements, academic arenas, or various fields.

Power Relations and Social Inequality

In intersectionality, social identities and systems of inequality gain meaning because they are formed by and manifested within systems of power (Dill and Zambrana 2009; Hancock 2016; Weber 2010).

Analyzing social identities through the lens of power relationships distinguishes between how people are treated based on multiple identities (which we all have) versus their multiple locations in relation to systems of power that influence their access to benefits and privileges within various forms of oppression (Holvino 2012; Wijeyesinghe and Jones 2019; Yuval-Davis 2006). Thus, race and racial categories, for example, are not benign descriptors or identities experienced solely at the individual level but socially constructed groupings that support White supremacy across multiple systems and multiple generations. In these systems, individuals are positioned in locations of privilege and access or locations of marginalization and oppression.

Collins and Bilge (2016) described power as organized within and across four domains: interpersonal, disciplinary, cultural, and structural. In the interpersonal domain, a person's various social locations in relation to power "work together and influence one another to shape each individual biography" (8). Social and institutional rules that affect which options are available to individuals are reflected in the disciplinary domain of power. The cultural domain encompasses larger messages about systems and groups of people that a society wishes to convey, such as the ability of anyone to succeed and the lack of capability or motivation of those people who do not. Social norms, rules, and messages about social groups are adopted into various institutions and organizations that represent the structural domain of power. Power relations are manifested in forms of social inequality that provide the contexts where individuals understand and make meaning of self, other people and groups, social issues, history, and culture. As Nash (2015, 14) noted, "To put it simply, 'who people are' can never be understood apart from 'the way things work.'" Intersectionality highlights that even as they are often treated as distinct and independent, systems of inequality work because they are intertwined, and created and maintained within multiple levels of power.

Social Justice

Engagement in social justice is not a requirement of intersectionality; however, the framework is often used by people committed to social change. Because it centers the experiences of people overlooked or left out of dominant social norms, processes, and structures, intersectionality engages and empowers new voices to define social problems and direct their solutions (Dill and Zambrana 2009). Therefore, People of Color, women, GLBTQ people, immigrants, and people with disabilities, for example, move from being objects named by dominant systems to subjects whose experiences are validated and used to create social change (Collins 2019). The emancipatory potential of social justice work that addresses interconnected forms of oppression was captured by the Combahee River Collective (1977, 215) when they declared, "We might use our position at the bottom, however, to make a clear leap into revolutionary action. If Black women were free, it would mean that everyone else would have to be free since our freedom would necessitate the destruction of all systems of oppression." However, Collins and Bilge (2016, 202) cautioned that "intersectionality is not a simple substitute for social justice" in that adopting an intersectional lens to examine issues does not automatically further critical practice to eradicate inequality. Like Paulo Freire's (1994, 68) analysis of dialogue and change, reflection *and* action informed by intersectionality are needed to "transform the world."

Complexity

Complexity is evident throughout intersectionality. Attending to multiple identities means that examining, for example, racism and how it affects Indigenous people of the Americas requires also considering the differences Indigenous people hold across other social locations, such as gender, sexual orientation, tribal and national affiliation, and age. The fluidity of social, political, and cultural contexts affects how categories of, for example, race and gender identity are labelled and understood, raising challenges for transposing knowledge about social groups across space and time. Considering social identities and systems of power as interconnected highlights that most people embody social locations of marginality and of privilege (Collins and Bilge 2016; Kendall and Wijeyesinghe 2017; Wijeyesinghe and Jones 2019). In addition, the intersections between systems of inequality necessitate that efforts to eradicate one consider the influence of all of the others.

The complexities embedded in intersectionality can feed questions and tension points about the content and use of the framework. Rather than positioning these issues as challenges to contest or avoid, I view them as opportunities to reflect on the core tenets reviewed previously and how this exploration might broaden, not curtail, the use of intersectionality. This analysis can lead to a greater understanding of how individuals experience life based on their multiple social locations (which often reflect both privileged and marginalized positions); how systems of oppression work together to create social norms, policies, and structures; and how social justice work can be informed by interwoven issues at a specific moment in time.

Core Tenets and Resistance

In more than a dozen years of exploring intersectionality through teaching, writing, and consulting, I have mostly encountered positive receptions to intersectionality and its central themes. However, I have also had interactions that conveyed skepticism, distrust, and dismissal of intersectionality's content and orientation to social systems and social justice. For example, people have expressed concern that intersectionality allows some White people to deflect attention from their racial privilege because some of their other social locations reflect positions of marginalization. In other instances, people represented intersectionality (through their words and the material they utilized) as a framework mostly about individual identity and advanced the position that "everyone is intersectional." In the next sections I share episodes where I encountered questions or resistance, by others and on my own, when intersectionality is used to address race, racism, White privilege, and racial justice; and discuss how the core tenets can address larger issues that often underlie these questions and concerns.

Five Brief Stories
There May Be Multiple Identities but Race Is at the Top of the List

While in an airport catching a flight back from a national conference related to race, I was approached by an African American woman who had attended a conference session I co-facilitated on intersectionality. After a brief greeting, the woman told me that although she found intersectionality interesting, she didn't think it was an effective tool to address race and racism. She went on to say that racism was the most pressing issue of inequality in America and that bringing other issues like heterosexism and classism into discussions of racism and racial justice took attention away from how race affected the lives of Black people every day. Drawing on her own experiences, the woman said that her color did not afford her the ability to hide from racism, and that people and society as a whole would always see and treat her as a Black woman. After moving further along toward my boarding gate, I was approached by an African American man who had attended the same seminar. Although our interaction was much shorter, he expressed concerns similar to the ones offered in my first conversation—that intersectionality watered down the primacy of race and urgency to address racism in America.

I Am Not Privileged Like Those Other White People

During a training seminar on cultural competence for mental health professionals that I led with a White co-facilitator, a White male participant repeatedly noted that he did not experience White privilege because he grew up in an economically disadvantaged household. At times this participant became emotional when he recounted going without basic necessities during his early years. He believed that any benefits that race conferred to him as an adult were different from the privileges afforded to other White people, and that even though his economic circumstances had changed, he would always feel the stigma of being disadvantaged earlier in his life. Whenever the discussion turned to White privilege, this man interjected that it did not apply to him, and by the final time he spoke he was crying.

What's Power Got to Do with It?

While participating in a program planning meeting for a national conference, I joined colleagues from around the country to brainstorm session topics related to intersectionality. From the outset, the group's discussion became bogged down by debates over what constituted intersectionality and, thus, what topics should be represented in conference sessions. Half of the group felt that sessions should address any topic related to multiple identities. The other half adamantly believed that intersectional programs had to highlight issues of power and privilege. After much time and energy was expended, we could not resolve our differences, and thus the group chose to develop two topic lists—intersectional identities and intersectional systems of power.

Never Forget That Intersectionality Reflects the Labor of Black Women

During a panel presentation on intersectionality, a fellow panelist spoke strongly against intersectionality being co-opted through the misappropriation of Black women's experience that defined the framework. He noted that people using intersectionality needed to prominently cite the work of Kimberlé Crenshaw and other critical Black women authors, and always discuss intersectionality as reflecting Black feminist standpoints. From his perspective, omitting attention to these areas negated intersectionality's roots and fundamental relevance to Black women's lives. While facilitating a different session on intersectionality at the same conference, my co-presenter and I were asked by an attendee to stop our presentation and explain why Crenshaw's name did not appear as a reference on one of our slides.

Let's Make a Model Based on It

Colleagues and I have used intersectionality to inform our identity models that include varying levels of attention to multiple social identities and larger social systems. At the time when I developed the Intersectional Model of Multiracial Identity (IMMI) (Wijeyesinghe 2012), my goal was to use the complexity of intersectionality to better capture the interaction of factors influencing racial identity in Multiracial people that emerged from my earlier work (Wijeyesinghe 1992). With the passage of several years during which I've read, discussed, mulled, and been challenged by intersectionality, I now view the IMMI and the models offered by most of my colleagues as inspired by intersectionality without truly being intersectional. As I've shared in more recent presentations and publications (Wijeyesinghe 2019; Wijeyesinghe and Jones 2019), I believe that intersectionality has little relevance to my (or anyone else's) experience as an individual. Thus, it's not (personally) about me.

Synthesis

These five short stories reflect my experiences and, where relevant, my recollection of events. At first glance, aspects of intersectionality seem to be at the heart of the matters raised in the vignettes, inspiring questions such as, If individuals embody all of their social identities, why can't some be experienced as more important or relevant than others? Do people's marginalized social positions draw down the amount of benefit they receive based on locations that convey privilege? Can intersectionality be applied to populations beyond Black women whose voices and histories gave rise to the framework? These valid questions and other points of tension can feed resistance to intersectionality's content and application. I now turn to a more focused discussion of resistance to intersectionality in relation to race, racism, racial privilege, and racial justice work.

Resistance to Intersectionality

What constitutes resistance to intersectionality is open for discussion. What one person considers a point of tension or intense debate can be thought of as a welcome invitation for dialogue by someone else. There may be a myriad of places and subjects where resistance can be encountered. Given the stories and material shared thus far, this section explores resistance to intersectionality across four areas: individual experiences and social locations related to race, racism in relation to other systems of oppression, foundations and ownership of intersectionality's content, and challenges of moving from theoretical analysis to racial justice efforts. In each area, examples of resistance and tension points are explored first, followed by a discussion of how core tenets of intersectionality can inform relevant strategies to address or lower resistance.

Resistance and Relevance in Relation to Identity, Social Location, and Experience

Building a sense of identity on categories such as race, gender, nationality, faith, or sexual orientation may be an experience familiar to most people. Even though they are socially constructed, these categories are so normalized that Lynn Weber (2010, 119) described them as "so fundamental that to be without them would be like being without an identity at all." Tension around intersectionality can be raised when one category or a select group of categories feels more fundamental in a person's life than all of the rest. For example, some people may feel that race is the most salient aspect of their lives, and/or see it as singular and distinct from their other social identities. This may be especially true if they are members of groups targeted by racism (since racism renders Whiteness and White privilege invisible or "the norm" in general society). A Black or Brown person is always seen as Black or Brown, even if the people doing the observing believe that they "don't see color." Because of the invisibility of Whiteness to Whites (see Foste, this volume), White people may not identify with their Whiteness and the privileges they receive based on race, or may downplay their race and feel that other identities, such as gender, class, or disability, form the pillars of their identity. Such experiences can appear to contest a framework that posits race as *inextricably linked* to all of a person's other social identities.

Because intersectionality has often been discussed in relation to identity and what scholars refer to as identity politics (Collins 2019; Collins and Bilge 2016; Nash 2008), it is not surprising that people apply it to their individual experiences. However, engaging people in debates about whether they experience race more urgently or frequently, or experience race daily at all, will not lessen resistance to intersectionality or promote greater understanding of how the framework relates to race and racism. However, clarifying the focus and intent of intersectionality can lead to dialogue that might ultimately lessen tensions related to intersectionality and the lived experiences of race and identity.

Intersectionality does not address how individuals feel about their identity or the salience they attribute to a single identity or set of identities at a given time or circumstance (Nash 2008; Wijeyesinghe and Jones 2019). By focusing on the experiences of socially constructed groups that are *formed by and employed within systems of power*, intersectionality shifts the discussion from the level of personal identities to the level of social locations (Cho, Crenshaw, and McCall 2013; Kendall and Wijeyesinghe 2017; Weber 2010). Wijeyesinghe and Jones (2019, 9, emphasis added) noted that tension can arise due to "the *perceived* gaps between the lived experiences of identity salience by the individuals . . . and the perspective that all identities are at play at all times." Exploring the gaps in how and why individuals recognize some social identities and locations in discussions of race while ignoring others can foster critical and sometimes difficult discussions of privilege and agency. For example, because social locations, together, influence how people are treated, White women or White GLBTQ people, for example, can be seen as getting a "pass" on racism since they are targeted by other forms of oppression. However, intersectionality is not an equation based on the total "points" or privileges that remain when all of a person's targeted locations are subtracted from their locations that afford privilege—as Lisa Bowleg (2008) so aptly captured in the title and content of her paper "When Black + Lesbian + Woman ≠ Black Lesbian Woman." Likewise, intersectionality does not detract from the reality that "*everyone* is racialized according to a hierarchy of advantage and disadvantage, and . . . other identity categories do not neutralize that fact" (Luft 2009, 111). Applying an intersectional lens to race does highlight how White racial privilege may be experienced differently (versus "less") by White women compared to White men, White affluent people compared to people who are White and poor, or White Christians compared to White Jews or White Muslims. Relatedly, intersectionality provides a lens for People of Color to examine how their sites of privilege based on, for example, being able-bodied, heterosexual, or Christian, influence their experiences of race and racism. Commenting on Collins's conceptualization of the matrix of domination (2000), where racism is positioned alongside other forms of inequality, Patrick Grzanka (2020, 4) noted that "the matrix is not a comfortable place of diversity and inclusion, but one that demands discomforting introspective and critical analysis of subject positions that would otherwise be left un-interrogated."

People working for racial justice can use this broader, more nuanced representation of privilege in work involving coalitions (Carbado 2013;

Kendall and Wijeyesinghe 2017). For example, if a Latinx man is willing to explore how he may enact heterosexual and gender privilege in interactions, he may be better able to engage with GLBTQ people and women working with him on antiracist projects. If a White woman is aware of how her Whiteness conveys benefits to her, as she engages in racial justice work, she may be less likely to enact racism when interacting with People of Color or reinforce racism when working with other Whites.

In addition to informing privilege and agency, intersectionality highlights the diverse subjectivities within particular socially constructed racial groups that are oftentimes seen as monolithic (Dill and Zambrana 2009; Luft 2009). From an intersectional perspective, there is no one "Black experience" or "Asian experience" under racism, since people presumed to be members of a single racial category reflect great diversity based on other social categories that may influence how they experience and perceive race and racism. For example, some of the ways racism is experienced by an elderly, heterosexual Japanese man living in Ohio will differ from those of a young, Chinese, cisgender lesbian living in California. Intersectionality disrupts the dominant narrative of singularity of experience of socially constructed groups. Thus, communities formed around race and other social identities can engage in the work described by Crenshaw (1991, 1299):

> With identity thus reconceptualized, it may be easier to understand the need for and to summon the courage to challenge groups that are after all, in one sense, "home" to us, in the name of the parts of us that are not made at home. This takes a great deal of energy and arouses intense anxiety. The most one could expect is that we will dare to speak against internal exclusions and marginalizations, that might call attention to how the identity of "the group" has been centered on the identities of the few.

Considering how multiple, intertwined social locations influence how race is experienced by individuals and members of racial groups adds levels of complexity to personal reflections, collective dialogue, and scholarly debates. As the words of Crenshaw and other authors cited in this section illustrated, this work is difficult, essential, and liberating.

Resistance and Relevance in Relation to Multiple Interrelated Systems

Audre Lorde (1983) offered the often-quoted position that there is no hierarchy of oppression. However, many people feel that their lives are constrained by a particular form of inequality and that certain oppressions are more prevalent, pertinent, and pressing to address. In the context of over four centuries of violence, inequity, discrimination, and denial of basic rights, and many more recent and vivid examples of systemic racism, race can be positioned as the primary issue of inequality in the United States. Dominant narratives and constructions of race create markers that, while problematic in many ways, identify who is oppressed and who is the oppressor within systems of racism. The centrality of race and racism in politics, culture, intergroup dynamics, and lived experiences can seem to set racism apart from other forms of oppression. In many cases, identifying and eradicating racism are literally matters of life and death, and can motivate national movements for change. Thus, it is not surprising that a framework that positions racism as inextricably linked with other oppressions can be seen as diluting the prominence of race in national and global landscapes and the urgent need to address racism, first and foremost, in all its forms.

Intersectionality provides few resources for addressing whether or not racism is the most pervasive or extreme form of oppression. Quite simply, constructing a hierarchy is not relevant to the framework, so forcing intersectionality as an educational tool with people who insist there is a ranking of oppression is counterproductive. However, as with issues of identity, core tenets can promote dialogue on how positioning race as intertwined with other systems enhances, not diminishes, the understanding of how race touches so many aspects of people's lives. For example, stereotypes of Black men and Asian men differ because of the dynamics of sexism, genderism, heterosexism, and ableism. A more comprehensive picture of racial disparities in health care services is gained when services specific to, for example, women of color and disabled people of color are included in statistical analyses. Addressing the systemic issues revealed through the Black Lives Matter movement requires recognizing how racial violence may be experienced differently by GLBTQ Black people, Black women, Black veterans, Black men,

Black nonbinary individuals, Black youth, and Black elders. Attending to the relationships between and across systems renders a more nuanced and complex understanding of how diverse people experience racism when systems of inequality targeting, for example, their gender, economic standing, disability, or age are also considered.

Addressing systems of inequality as interwoven and mutually supportive does not erase issues that are unique within each (Hancock 2016; Luft 2009). When Collins and Bilge (2016, 27) stated that "within intersectional frameworks, there is no pure racism or sexism. Rather, power relations of racism and sexism gain meaning in relation to each other," they weren't saying that these two systems of oppression were the same. There are exceptional aspects of various manifestations of inequality, many of them fed by forces that support oppression. For example, dominant cultural and social norms construct social groups based on certain characteristics. Some social groups are deemed essential or determined at birth, while others are posited as choices. Some can change over time, while others are seen as more stable. The norms, messages, and values conveyed about each group and form of oppression through the dominant culture change over time and space.

Intersectionality is a tool to explore the experiences and perceptions of social locations within interconnected, mutually supporting systems of inequality. For example, the perspective that race is visible and therefore inescapable emphasized the role that appearance plays in the ascription of (presumed) racial group membership. Visibility takes on different meaning when considered from the perspective of GLBTQ people, and fosters different presumptions about their experiences and management of visibility and invisibility. Visibility is connected to social norms, expectations, and stereotypes, so that a person is recognized, for example, as a woman because she fits the image of what a woman looks like rendered by the dominant culture. People who contest this image or appear more fluid can be questioned and targeted. Using intersectionality "strategically and differentially" (Luft 2009, 100) fosters understanding and dialogue about the diversity in how categories and forms of inequality are experienced.

When communities targeted by oppression are positioned as separate and even in opposition, inequality in all its forms and at all levels is maintained. As Crenshaw (1989, 166–67) noted, "Failure to embrace the complexities of correspondedness is not simply a matter of political will, but is also due to the influences of a way of thinking about discrimination which structures politics so that struggles are categorized as singular issues. Moreover, this structure imports a descriptive and normative view of society that reinforces the status quo." Framing locations and forms of oppression as distinct and isolated perpetuates dominant narratives and the status quo, feeds division, obscures connectivity of systems of oppression, and challenges coalitions. Instead of "flattening" differences in experiences (Luft 2009, 100), intersectionality counters the compartmentalizing of marginalized groups and allows perceived, assumed, and real differences to foster critical dialogues that we don't often engage in and even avoid.

Resistance and Relevance Related to History, Ownership, and Inclusion

Commenting on intersectionality's deep roots in Black women's lives and Black feminist thinking, Antonio Duran and Romeo Jackson (2019, 43, emphasis added) noted that "theories come with rich intellectual and activist histories that scholars *must* engage with in order to *appropriately* apply them to their work." The fact that the experiences, words, and analysis of generations of Black women formulated the core of the framework is not disputed in most settings. However, the extent to which these contributions are acknowledged and reinforced, in ways deemed appropriate (a standard that varies across scholars and practitioners), and through the citing of a certain number of specified texts, can feed tension points summarized by questions such as, Whose experiences underlie intersectionality? Where does the history of intersectionality begin? Are there names and citations that must be included in discussions of the framework's content or application, or, as Collins (2019, 123) posed, "Who gets to tell intersectionality's story?" And thus, if we include other groups in addition to Black women in the telling of intersectionality's story, does that detract from the contributions of Black women to the framework? Rather than analyzing the various positions or wading into the historical origins aspect of what Nash referred to as "the intersectionality wars" (2017, 117), discussion of intersectionality's roots and credentials offered here takes a "both/and" approach to recognizing the contributions of Black women and other women of color to intersectionality, while noting the relevance of the framework to other groups marginalized by systems of oppression.

The experiences of Black women, told in their own voices and from their own standpoints, provided critical counternarratives (Dill and Zambrana 2009) that contribute to the analytical content and power of intersectionality. In social contexts formed by intersecting systems of power, retaining interpretive power over individual and group experience constitutes a "form of epistemic resistance" (Collins 2019, 139). The complexities and interconnections inherent in how Black women, Latinas, and other women of color experience their lives inject meaning into the core themes of intersectionality, such as relationality, social power, and social justice. Grounding intersectionality within the lived experiences of women of color over centuries allows these voices to remain central to the framework even while its core tenets are extended to other groups and analyses of systems of inequality (Cooper 2016; Collins 2015). However, relying on what Nash referred to as "close reading" of and "textual fidelity" (2019, 62) to selected works obscures the fact that many women who wrote about the complexities of multiple positions and multiple systems of oppression did not make it onto the reading list (Collins 2019) or that "multiple genealogies" of intersectionality exist based on the positions of different scholars or critics (Nash 2019, 6). Relatedly, Collins and Bilge (2016) and Hancock (2016) noted that core tenets of intersectionality were in wide usage within and beyond the United States prior to the publication of Crenshaw's (1989, 1991) foundational works.

Scholars, researchers, students, and practitioners studying and applying intersectionality might be guided by the insight offered by Nash (2019, 69) when she stated that "*all* readings are interpretive." Strategies for unveiling the level and effect of such interpretations include challenging personal and disciplinary values related to textual fidelity, connections or lack thereof to the diversity of intersectional publications (including those that might be considered more obscure and less cited), and motivation for designating certain works as essential and others not. What each person takes away from whichever works they choose for their personal base related to intersectionality, and how they acknowledge the role of Black women and other women of color in framing, applying, critiquing, and expanding intersectionality must also be analyzed. As Barbara Tomlinson (2013, 994) reminds us, "Reading, writing, and arguing are material social practices laced with ideologies of legitimacy and propriety so powerful and pervasive that we presuppose their value rather than examining their effects."

In discussing intersectionality's relevance to identity, social systems, and social justice work, Wijeyesinghe (2019, 26) noted that "employing intersectionality within the same evolving systems of power that it centers in the analysis of these areas can result in fundamental aspects of the framework being ignored or overlooked and the muddying of intersectionality's definition and intent." Systems such as racism, sexism, and heterosexism will always be deployed to erase and discount the critical role that Black women, other women of color, and lesbians of color played and continue to play in intersectionality's herstory and future evolution. However, intersectionality is not a static knowledge project (Collins 2015, 2019; Collins and Bilge 2016; Hancock 2016). As intersectionality continues to evolve, to be that theory in the making, the challenge might be for us "to remain open *both* to the fact that analytics transform, move, wane, develop, and morph, *and* to the fact that analytics' movements are political and institutional questions" (Nash 2015, 16). Instead of holding fast to positions that *either* Black women's experiences and certain citations are included *or* discussions of intersectionality are not valid or complete, perhaps we can use our energies to investigate how the lives of women of color inform theory and social justice related to other groups. As Sumi Cho, Kimberlé Crenshaw, and Leslie McCall (2013, 795) noted,

> If intersectionality is an analytic disposition, a way of thinking about and conducting analyses, then what makes an analysis intersectional is not its use of the term "intersectionality," nor its being situated in a familiar genealogy, nor its drawing on lists of standard citations. Rather, what makes an analysis intersectional—whatever terms it deploys, whatever its iteration, whatever its field or discipline—is its adoption of an intersectional way of thinking about the problem of sameness and difference and its relation to power.

As with debates over hierarchies of oppression or the implications of similarities and differences of social groups, forces of power benefit when intersectionality gets derailed by debates related to origins, ownership, and credentialing. As intersectionality moves, in terms of time and space, further from its foundational origins, perhaps the vision of "stewardship" offered by Hancock (2016, 200) can guide scholars and practitioners of intersectionality in "drawing some boundaries while simultaneously relaxing into the ambiguities of newer formulations."

Resistance and Relevance Related to Moving from Theory to Practice

Intersectionality foregrounds how systems of inequality gain meaning through relationships with each other, multiple evolving contexts, and the lived experiences of marginalized people. However, Susan Jones and Elisa Abes (2013, 136) noted that operationalizing intersectionality through social justice movements "may prove daunting when trying to apply this approach to everyday life." Because intersectionality is applied within the very systems of power that it critiques (Collins 2015; Collins and Bilge 2016; Wijeyesinghe 2017), forms of intersectional practice will always have to consider and contest forces that seek to lessen their impact and relevance. For example, dominant narratives and practices often position communities and the systematic inequality they face as discrete and isolated subjects, perspectives that can be internalized by people even as they engage in social justice work. In the context of efforts to eradicate racism, incorporating attention to the interrelations of systems of inequality may appear to decenter the importance of race as the "issue at hand" or to deflect limited resources and energy away from racism in order to attend to a myriad of nonracial social locations and issues.

At the larger level of groups and the causes they embrace, Bonnie Thornton Dill, Amy McLaughlin, and Angel Nieves (2007, 635) observed that "every single social justice movement has had a problem of essentialism, giving primacy to some aspects of their identity while ignoring others that intersect with and re-form that primary identity." Thus divided, communities may be less inclined to explore the complexities of racism and, as described earlier, the range of its effects on People of Color who differ by age, race, ability status, gender, sexual orientation, veteran status, faith, and so on. Thus divided, they may knowingly or unknowingly silence voices that could provide essential perspectives and ideas, or that could assist in structuring racial justice efforts so they avoid perpetuating sexism, heterosexism, Christian hegemony, various forms of disability oppression, and classism. Thus divided, systems of oppression and the groups who benefit from them are ultimately served.

Intersectionality provides a tool to disrupt dominant representations and systems, and reveals the ways that these forces constrain social justice efforts by artificially fracturing communities and dividing social justice efforts. By positioning efforts to combat sexism, heterosexism, ableism, nationalism, classism, and other systems *as integral to antiracism work*, intersectionality again contests the ranking of oppressions. As Lorde (1983, 9) stated, "I simply do not believe that one aspect of myself can possibly profit from the oppression of any other part of my identity. I know that my people cannot possibly profit from the oppression of any other group which seeks the right to peaceful existence." The relationships among systems of oppression are relevant to antiracism work because heterosexism affects how GLBTQ and heterosexual People of Color experience racism, sexism affects how women and men of color experience racism, and ageism affects how youth, middle-aged people, and elders experience racism. Some people working for racial justice will embrace this interrelated perspective, and others may not.

By highlighting the interrelated nature of systems of oppression, and the linking of experiences under oppression, intersectionality disrupts dominant goals of fracturing communities and their social justice efforts. Through an intersectional lens, differences in the experiences of diverse communities move from being obstacles to sites of connections. As Jennifer Chun, George Lipsitz, and Young Shin (2013, 923) noted, "Intersectionality can be used strategically to take inventory of differences, to identify potential contradictions and conflicts, and to recognize split and conflicting identities not as obstacles to solidarity but as valuable evidence about problems unsolved and as new coalitions that need to be formed." By promoting connection through perceived or real differences, core tenets of intersectionality provide tools for developing and maintaining coalitions (Carastathis 2013; Collins and Bilge 2016; Kendall and Wijeyesinghe 2017). Coalitions informed by intersectionality provide more nuanced strategies for addressing racism since multiple voices are recruited, respected, and included in all aspects of racial justice work. Strategies for investigating and managing privilege revealed by intersectionality can be used to do the difficult work of self-reflection. Unveiling how systems of oppression construct and support each other allows individuals and groups to realize how they benefit from addressing multiple forms of oppression as they pursue racial justice. As intersectionality moves across disciplines and spectrums of practice, new sites of coalitions and collaboration will be identified. With the adoption of intersectional practice in a fuller range of areas, Collins (2019, 276) noted that "the challenge that intersectionality now faces is to figure out how to accommodate the heterogeneity of the perspectives and practices of its current practitioners."

Closing Thoughts

In drawing this chapter to a close, I am inspired and challenged by the words offered by Cris Mayo (2015, 251):

> When we reach toward intersectionality, we may come to think that we're finally addressing complexity. The simplest point is that we're not there yet. There is as yet only the tentative connection and the troubled subject. That might at least be our partial, as yet incomplete gesture toward a method, one that leaves us to stumble together over the difficulties of there being no there there yet.

When wrestling with the relationship between intersectionality and resistance related to race, racism, and racial justice work, I know that I am learning as much from the questions and tension points as I have from texts, analyses, and presentations. I am still learning to seek out and engage questions such as, What does attending to multiple social locations and social systems offer for understanding just one aspect of these concepts (in the case of this chapter, race and racism)? To what extent do the experiences of individuals under a specific form of oppression, such as racism, inform experiences of people under others? Are there aspects of some systems of oppression that make them more immediate, primary, or essential to address? Does one form of inequality truly underlie all the rest? Do any of the questions posed here contradict the perspective offered within core tenets of intersectionality in ways that render the framework irrelevant or even harmful?

I have moments where my grasp of intersectionality seems firm, but then I encounter another topic or example that joggles that grasp loose, and requires that I wrestle with the complexities, questions, and tension points again. Even as I accept Mayo's perspective that "I/we are not there yet," I believe that intersectionality can inform understanding of race, racism, racial justice efforts, and the resistance to applying the framework to any of these topics. Alone, each of these areas is complex; applying intersectionality to all of them—in this moment—reveals complexity that I sometimes struggle to capture in my head and in my words. It is in those moments of confusion or doubt that I embrace the image provided to me by mentor and colleague Bailey Jackson, to whom this volume is dedicated. He told me decades ago that we can only offer "a snapshot of a moving picture" when investigating social inequality and social justice, because systems, cultures, histories, and politics are always changing and, thus, the topics they inform will change too. Bailey's words are so worthy of remembering as issues of race, racism, and racial justice continue to evolve in interrelated ways, such that, for example, the murder of George Floyd has engaged the Black Lives Matter movement and the possibility of social change in ways that could not have been predicted or imagined. No one knows how future injustices and future movements will be affected by intersectionality, and in turn, how they might affect the content and use of the framework.

So what I believe about intersectionality today has been formed by discussions I've had, books I've read, questions I've asked and that I've answered, and presentations I've attended. I may believe something else about how intersectionality can be applied to race, racism, and racial justice work in the years to come. I find an odd sense of peace in the challenge and uncertainty that lie ahead. Through writing this chapter I became more aware that advancing understanding of intersectionality as a tool of knowledge and practice, in relation to race and to other topics, doesn't require that all questions and tension points be answered. Like the approach offered by intersectionality, emerging topics like resistance present opportunities to adopt a "both/and" orientation. People can question and push back on intersectionality *and* still find it useful and relevant to their work. As the framework continues to travel across time, disciplines, and situations, all immersed in power, I believe that Collins and Bilge (2016, 204) summed it up best when they stated, "The central challenge facing intersectionality is to move into the politics of the not yet."

Intersectionality, race, racism, and racial justice are evolving concepts affected by changing contexts. Understandings of the framework and its applicability to a range of social justice areas will increase, be challenged, and be revised. Resistance to intersectionality will also evolve, as it should, to reflect the pressing questions and points of tension that will become evident in the future. Core tenets of intersectionality can provide guideposts on the paths we stumble on together as we further our understanding of intersectionality and employ its emancipatory potential in the world.

REFERENCES

Bowleg, Lisa. 2008. "When Black + Lesbian + Woman ≠ Black Lesbian Woman: The Methodological Challenges of Qualitative and Quantitative Intersectionality Research." *Sex Roles* 59, nos. 5–6 (March): 312–25.

Carastathis, Anna. 2013. "Identity Categories as Potential Coalitions." *Signs: Journal of Women in Culture and Society* 38, no. 4 (Summer): 941–65.

Carbado, Devon. 2013. "Colorblind Intersectionality." *Signs: Journal of Women in Culture and Society* 38, no. 4 (Summer): 811–45.

Cho, Sumi K., Kimberlé Williams Crenshaw, and Leslie McCall. 2013. "Toward a Field of Intersectionality Studies: Theory, Applications, and Praxis." *Signs: Journal of Women in Culture and Society* 38, no. 4 (Summer): 785–810.

Chun, Jennifer Jihye, George Lipsitz, and Young Shin. 2013. "Intersectionality as a Social Movement Strategy: Asian Immigrant Women Advocates." *Signs: Journal of Women in Culture and Society* 38, no. 4 (Summer): 917–66.

Collins, Patricia Hill. 2000. *Black Feminist Thought: Knowledge, Consciousness, and the Politics of Empowerment*. 2nd ed. New York: Routledge.

———. 2015. "Intersectionality's Definitional Dilemmas." *Annual Review of Sociology* 41, no. 1 (July): 1–20.

———. 2019. *Intersectionality as Critical Social Theory*. Durham: Duke University Press.

Collins, Patricia Hill, and Sirma Bilge. 2016. *Intersectionality*. Malden: Polity.

Combahee River Collective. 1977. "A Black Feminist Statement." In *All the Women Are White, All the Blacks Are Men, but Some of Us Are Brave*, edited by Gloria T. Hull, Patricia Bell Scott, and Barbara Smith, 13–22. New York: Feminist Press.

Cooper, Brittney. 2016. "Intersectionality." In *The Oxford Handbook of Feminist Theory*, edited by Lisa Disch and Mary Hawkesworth, 385–401. New York: Oxford University Press.

Crenshaw, Kimberlé Williams. 1989. "Demarginalizing the Intersection of Race and Sex: A Black Feminist Critique of Antidiscrimination Doctrine, Feminist Theory and Antiracist Politics." *University of Chicago Legal Forum* 140, Article 8: 139–67.

———. 1991. "Mapping the Margins: Intersectionality, Identity Politics, and Violence against Women of Color." *Stanford Law Review* 43, no. 6 (July): 1241–99.

Dill, Bonnie Thornton, Amy E. McLaughlin, and Angel David Nieves. 2007. "Future Directions of Feminist Research: Intersectionality." In *Handbook of Feminist Research: Theory and Praxis*, edited by Sharlene Nagy Hesse-Biber, 629–37. Thousand Oaks: Sage.

Dill, Bonnie Thornton, and Ruth Enid Zambrana, eds. 2009. *Emerging Intersections: Race, Class, and Gender in Theory, Policy, and Practice*. New Brunswick: Rutgers University Press.

Duran, Antonio, and Romeo Jackson. 2019. "Thinking Theoretically with and Beyond Intersectionality: Frameworks to Center Queer and Trans People of Color Experiences." In *Intersectionality and Higher Education: Theory, Research, and Praxis*, 2nd ed., edited by Donald Mitchell, Jakia Marie, and Tiffany L. Steele, 41–50. New York: Peter Lang.

Freire, Paulo. 1994. *Pedagogy of the Oppressed*. 20th anniversary ed. New York: Continuum.

Grzanka, Patrick R. 2020. "From Buzzword to Critical Psychology: An Invitation to Take Intersectionality Seriously." *Women & Therapy* 43, nos. 3–4. doi: 10.1080/02703149.2020.1729473.

Hancock, Ange-Marie. 2016. *Intersectionality: An Intellectual History*. New York: Oxford University Press.

Holvino, Evangelina. 2012. "The 'Simultaneity' of Identities: Models and Skills for the Twenty-First Century." In *New Perspectives on Racial Identity Development: Integrating Emerging Frameworks*, 2nd ed., edited by Charmaine L. Wijeyesinghe and Bailey W. Jackson III, 161–91. New York: New York University Press.

Jones, Susan R., and Elisa S. Abes. 2013. *Identity Development of College Students: Advancing Frameworks for Multiple Dimensions of Identity*. San Francisco: Jossey-Bass.

Kendall, Frances E., and Charmaine L. Wijeyesinghe. 2017. "Advancing Social Justice Work at the Intersections of Multiple Privileged Identities." In *Enacting Intersectionality in Student Affairs: New Directions for Student Services*, number 157, edited by Charmaine L. Wijeyesinghe, 91–100. San Francisco: Jossey-Bass.

Lorde, Audre. 1983. "There Is No Hierarchy of Oppressions." *Council on Interracial Books for Children Bulletin*, 14, nos. 3–4: 9.

Luft, Rachel E. 2009. "Intersectionality and the Risk of Flattening Difference: Gender and Race Logics, and the Strategic Use of Antiracist Singularity." In *The Intersectional Approach: Transforming the Academy through Race, Class, and Gender*, edited by Michele Tracy Berger and Kathleen Guidroz, 100–117. Chapel Hill: University of North Carolina Press.

Mayo, Cris. 2015. "Unexpected Generosity and Inevitable Trespass: Rethinking Intersectionality." *Educational Studies* 51, no. 3: 244–51.

Nash, Jennifer C. 2008. "Re-Thinking Intersectionality." *Feminist Review* 89, no. 1 (June): 1–15.

———. 2015. "Feminist Originalism: Intersectionality and the Politics of Reading." *Feminist Theory* 17, no. 1 (December): 1–18. DOI: 10.1177/1464700115620864.

———. 2017. "Intersectionality and Its Discontents." *American Quarterly* 69, no. 1 (March): 117–29.

———. 2019. *Black Feminism Reimagined after Intersectionality*. Durham: Duke University Press.

Shields, Stephanie A. 2008. "Gender: An Intersectional Perspective." *Sex Roles* 59, no. 5 (January): 301–11.

Tomlinson, Barbara. 2013. "To Tell the Truth and Not Get Trapped: Desire, Distance, and Intersectionality at the Scene of Argument." *Signs: Journal of Women in Culture and Society* 38, no. 4 (Summer): 993–1017.

Weber, Lynn. 2010. *Understanding Race, Class, Gender, and Sexuality: A Conceptual Framework*. 2nd ed. New York: Oxford University Press.

Wijeyesinghe, Charmaine L. 1992. "Towards an Understanding of the Racial Identity of Bi-Racial People: The Experience of Racial Self-Identification of African-American/Euro-American Adults and the Factors Affecting their Choices of Racial Identity." Doctoral dissertation, University of Massachusetts, Amherst.

———. 2012. "The Intersectional Model of Multiracial Identity: Integrating Multiracial Identity Theories and Intersectional Perspectives on Social Identity." In *New Perspectives on Racial Identity Development: Integrating Emerging Frameworks*, 2nd ed., edited by Charmaine L. Wijeyesinghe and Bailey W. Jackson III, 81–107. New York: New York University Press.

———. 2017. "Editor's Notes." In *Enacting Intersectionality in Student Affairs: New Directions for Student Services*, number 157, edited by Charmaine L. Wijeyesinghe, 5–13. San Francisco: Jossey-Bass.

———. 2019. "Intersectionality and Student Development: Centering Power in the Process." In *Rethinking College Student Development Using Critical Frameworks*, edited by Elisa S. Abes, Susan R. Jones, and D-L Stewart, 26–34. Sterling, VA: Stylus.

Wijeyesinghe, Charmaine L., and Susan R. Jones. 2019. "Intersectionality, Identity, and Systems of Power and Inequality." In *Intersectionality and Higher Education: Theory, Research, and Praxis*, 2nd ed., edited by Donald Mitchell, Jakia Marie, and Tiffany L. Steele, 3–14. New York: Peter Lang.

Yuval-Davis, Nira. 2006. "Intersectionality and Feminist Politics." *European Journal of Women's Studies* 13, no. 3 (August): 93–209.

11

Embracing the Complexities of Race, Racism, and Social Justice in Changing Times

RAECHELE L. POPE, AMY L. REYNOLDS, AND
CHAZZ ROBINSON

If ever there was a time we needed to scrutinize, excavate, and complicate our understanding of race, racism, and social justice, now is that time. Globalization has created a shrinking world where connections among countries are heightened and overlapping in new and challenging ways. Events in one part of the world reverberate and influence what happens in other parts. The COVID pandemic spread across this planet like wildfire, highlighting inequities in health care and incompetence in governing. Shifts in worldview and politics are happening more quickly than ever before. For example, public sentiment against marriage equality and equal rights for Queer and Trans individuals was long-standing in our public discourse and yet, seemingly overnight, public opinion and constitutional law have forever changed. Similarly, rapid changes in perceptions and attitudes toward the Black Lives Matter movement have occurred during the past decade and will continue to evolve with heightened scrutiny of police brutality and ongoing public response and protests across the country and the globe (Sawyer and Gampa 2018). While, in some ways, these current and emerging social dynamics affect, complicate, and obscure our understanding of race, racism, and social justice work, they also amplify and expand our perspectives. This continual change and uncertainty have birthed fresh perspectives, new and evolving theories, and diverse and expansive social justice strategies, actions, and social movements.

We are experiencing a compelling time, as we have in the past and will in the future, in the evolution of theory and praxis where the ways we conceptualize and contextualize race, racial identity, and racism are expanding and our efforts to subvert, uproot, and dismantle racism, white supremacy, and interlocking forms of oppression are quickly adapting and creating new forms of protest, action, and change. The purpose of this chapter is to use a critical lens to examine these changes in our theories and understanding and their implications for our social justice efforts during such uncertainty.

Before we explore how to conceptualize and engage in social justice work, it is important to highlight how our understanding of race, racial identity, and racism has evolved and grown. Moving beyond simplistic discussions of racial identity that do not take multiracial identity, intersectionality, transracial adoption, acculturation, sovereignty, and privilege into account is essential if we truly want to combat racism at individual, group, and institutional levels. During times of uncertainty and chaos, as well as significant bias, discrimination, and violence, it is essential that we continually educate ourselves and each other. Our openness to changing ideas, theories, strategies, and practices will ensure that we understand the ground that is often shifting beneath us. This need for openness is evident in the constantly evolving language around gender and the profound ways the gender binary is reified in everything we do when, in fact, it is based on inconsistent and incomplete science (Hyde et al. 2019). Another example is the ongoing conversation about the merits of focusing on racism versus anti-Blackness. This dialogue is happening more frequently because of questions about how attention to the broader issue of racism can sometimes obscure and minimize the unique ways that anti-Blackness is core to this country and even centered in our antiracism efforts (Dumas 2016).

As is true in these examples and many others, it is often our limited worldview that prevents us from fully absorbing and understanding the complexity of many ever-changing issues. Transformative, intersectional, and liberatory literature offered by visionaries such as Frantz Fanon (1967), Paulo Freire (1970), Combahee River Collective (1977), Cherríe Moraga and Gloria Anzaldúa (1981), Kimberlé Crenshaw (1991), Ignacio Martín-Baró (1991), Gloria Ladson-Billings and William Tate (1995), and Patricia Hill Collins (2000) challenges us to consider new lenses and frameworks to more deeply grasp this complexity and how to best intervene and create lasting structural change. Raechele Pope, Amy Reynolds, and John Mueller (2019) call for a paradigm shift, moving from a dichotomous to a diunital lens to facilitate deeper and more nuanced discussions that truly center and embrace the complexities of race and racism in our social justice work. A dichotomous mindset is based in either/or thinking, where one perceives the world in hierarchical (up/down) ways; however, a diunital mindset spurs both/and thinking and allows for the possibility that "seemingly contradictory or incompatible ideas exist simultaneously" (Pope, Reynolds, and Mueller 2019, 661). Further, diunital reasoning encourages more complex and complicated reflection and understanding, which hopefully leads to more nuanced responses and solutions. Returning to the previous example of anti-Blackness and racism, a dichotomous mindset assumes that focusing on anti-Blackness makes other forms of racism irrelevant and less important, when in fact the complexity of racism, in terms of its origins and unique manifestations, particularly in the United States, demands that we carefully consider the intricate, contradictory, and unique manifestations of racism for various racial groups. According to kihana ross (2020, 1), "Anti-blackness is one way some black scholars have articulated what it means to be marked as black in an anti-black world. It's more than just 'racism against black people.' That oversimplifies and defangs it. It's a theoretical framework that illuminates society's inability to recognize our humanity—the disdain, disregard and disgust for our existence."

This book and this specific chapter aim to push the reader toward a more diunital, nuanced, and multifaceted understanding of race, racial identity, racism, and social justice work through the exploration of many complex issues such as multiracial identity, intersectionality, whiteness and wokeness, transracial adoption, and sovereignty and indigeneity. Through examination of the fluidity of race and racial identity, the challenges of addressing multiple and interlocking forms of oppression simultaneously, and the difficulty of engaging self and community amidst the dehumanizing force known as racism, the chapters in this book provide unique conceptualizations that ultimately illuminate a path forward to dismantling racism and anti-Blackness in new and transformative ways.

Complicating Our Understanding of Race and Racism

This book features core themes and constructs worth highlighting before we move toward reexamining, resituating, and transforming our social justice efforts and actions. Our understanding of race and racism has always been informed and enhanced through an examination of racial identity. Robert Carter (1995) suggested that given the social construction of race, it is actually our racial identity, or the meaning or significance that our racial group membership holds for us, that profoundly affects how we make sense of ourselves, others, and the world around us. Our collective understanding of racial identity as a theory has evolved from the very beginning with important works by Carter (1995); William Cross (1971, 1991); and Janet Helms (1984, 1990, 2020), and many others to embrace more complex and intersectional realities such as multiracial identity (Johnston-Guerrero, this volume; Root 1992; Wijeyesinghe 2001) and intersectional identities (Blockett and Renn, this volume; Pope and Reynolds 2017; Rashad and Stewart, this volume; Reynolds and Pope 1991; Wijeyesinghe and Jones 2019). The themes offered by the thoughtful and stimulating chapters in this book encourage readers to reconsider their understanding of race and racial identity and how they are influenced by racism and the many social structures that shape us. This personal work allows individuals to become more aware of the biases, assumptions, and beliefs about race and identity that they carry with them when they engage in social or racial justice work. Three themes with which this book has engaged are (1) how racial identity is determined and influenced by individual, group, and social structures; (2) how institutions and governments affect our identity as well as our sense of belonging and community; and (3) how intersectionality influences how individuals experience their racial and other identities and social locations in the world.

Racial Identity

The first theme has suggested that racial identity is continually determined and influenced by various individual, group, and social structures that sometimes work separately and sometimes simultaneously. The type of racial exposure and socialization experienced greatly shapes and forms the racial identity for individuals of any race (Thomas and Speight 1999). Racial socialization can be affected by where and how we are raised, our generation, and the values of our parents (Tatum 2000). Social structures, such as our family or community, can profoundly shape how individuals perceive and respond to their racial identity, as detailed by JaeRan Kim in her discussion of transracial adoption of children of color in white families. How transracially adopted individuals experience their own race as well as how others in their life perceive the race of those transracially adopted people is greatly influenced by how prevalent discussions of race were in their home. Similarly, Zak Foste shared that salience also affects white individuals who are typically raised in families where issues of race are rarely addressed, so their ability to form a racial identity is largely delayed or denied. Marc Johnston-Guerrero discussed how individuals may use ancestry searches and DNA tests to shape how they self-identify and disclose their racial identity. However, as Johnston-Guerrero pointed out, how we present publicly may ultimately affect whether we have the privilege of choosing our own racial identity or not.

It is important to acknowledge how these various individual, group, and social structures, particularly families and communities, shape if, how, when, and where we engage in social justice work. Growing up in families and communities that openly discuss the significance of social justice work and demonstrate its importance in their actions increases the likelihood that we will become advocates for others. Such influence can also occur later in life due to exposure and experiences that may encourage us to reconsider our stance or engagement in social justice work. For example, an event that happens within our community or our country can awaken individuals to the experiences of others and motivate them to get involved in new and more active ways.

Institutions and Governments

The second theme has highlighted how, in addition to the impact of socialization within the family, community, and larger society, the institutions we participate in and the governments that shape our lives may also define and confine our identities, access to power, and where we belong. From the founding of this country we call the United States, the government has taken an active role in determining identity, nation, citizenship, community, power, and privilege through laws, treaties, and everyday practices. This reality cannot help but affect everything from how we individually identify to how our government identifies or classifies us. The United States government, through enactments such as the

Constitution and census, has dictated who gets to identify as a citizen and who has value. Such actions have been based in racism from the beginning of this country, affecting how Native Americans and enslaved Africans and their descendants were, and continue to be, viewed and treated. This is also currently true in the treatment of undocumented immigrants in the United States. Robert Keith Collins shared the interconnected and often complex relationships between enslaved Africans and Native Americans that influenced their identities and how their cultures and behaviors were linked. Nancy López highlights how "conflating race, nation, citizenship, and belonging affects the lives of individuals and groups marginalized by racism in the United States every day." While using the lens of race and racism is vital in understanding the influence of our institutions and governments on determining who belongs and has value, it is important to acknowledge that not all racial groups view our institutions or the government in the same way. Often when we discuss citizenship it is in the context of immigrants rather than the original peoples of this land. We are able to do this because of our collective amnesia regarding the sovereignty of Native American people and their land. According to Jeanette Writer (2010, 70), "The reality of tribal nationhood and the dual citizenship that Native Americans carry in their tribal nations and the United States significantly expands the definition and parameters of citizen." The lens offered by López incorporates critical race theory, settler colonialism, and intersectionality to further our ability to complicate our understanding of race, sovereignty, and belonging. The complexity and possibilities offered by these conversations, as evidenced in explorations of the Cherokee Freedmen (Sturm 2014), while challenging, create opportunities to deepen and complicate our understanding of race, power, and place.

In addition to our personal awareness, different levels of government and institutions significantly frame our view of social justice issues. These frames, which may pass as neutral or bureaucratic, are in fact based on unspoken values and assumptions that shape the role of government and other institutions in defining, regulating, and determining power, identity, and community. Unless we interrogate and challenge those frames, our social justice work is likely to recreate those same values, assumptions, and structures. For example, many institutions embrace a color-blind frame centered in an individualistic mindset, which causes them to minimize race and racism and not attend to the collective nature of many communities of Color. Unless individuals are able to deconstruct these assumptions and provide counter-stories, it is likely that their social justice work will recreate and reify such beliefs, thus decreasing the likelihood of transformative change.

Intersectionality

The final theme has focused on how other social identities (such as gender, sexual orientation, faith, and class) and intersectionality influence how individuals experience their race, their identity, and their place in the world. The analysis offered by Charmaine Wijeyesinghe urges us to center intersectionality in our understandings of race, identity, and racism. The framework of intersectionality makes it easier to identify, correct, and challenge systems of oppression by providing a lens that considers oppression in all of its forms. By focusing on how power and interlocking systems of oppression support, validate, and actually co-construct each other, intersectionality cultivates a more complex and dynamic understanding of racism and how it operates in the world. This is particularly important in the United States, given our unique history with race and racism. As profoundly shared in chapters by Reginald Blockett and Kristen Renn and by Kameelah Rashad and D-L Stewart, until we are able to fully embrace the complex ways that intersecting identities and interlocking oppressions affect how individuals express themselves and how they experience racism and other forms of oppression, our understanding will be diminished and incomplete. The groups these authors examined, Queer and Trans People of Color and religiously minoritized People of Color, highlight the limitations of old models of identity and encourage more expansive and fluid frameworks for identity. The power of these identities, born out of the unique ways that oppression, erasure, and dichotomous thinking shape our worldview, creates forms of worldmaking and resistance that can be used as models for combatting and subverting oppression.

Given that much of social justice work does not adequately adopt an intersectional lens, the experiences and lives of BIPOC (Black and Indigenous People of Color) individuals and communities with other marginalized identities are often erased, diminished, and even denied as relevant. And while some, like Rachel Luft (2009), have highlighted the value of strategic antiracist singularity, where focus on specific individual identities in a nonintersectional way can have short-term value, as a long-term approach to social justice work, this single-issue focus diminishes the interactive nature of all oppressions and weakens opportunities for collaborative movements. Social justice work that is intersectional in nature provides the opportunity for a nexus of movements challenging institutions and other structures based in racism and other forms of oppression. For example, climate change advocacy must be done with a lens that includes race and social class, since true environmental justice cannot occur in a vacuum given that the worst environmental disasters and crises occur in communities and areas with marginalized individuals. Systemic oppression operates in ways that create barriers among marginalized individuals and various social justice movements so they are less able to join together to collectively combat inequity, bias, and discrimination.

Critical Theories as a Lens

Scholars utilize a variety of lenses and theories, such as intersectionality, critical race theory, Crip theory, and Queer theory, to make sense of how race is constructed in individual, social, and organizational settings. Further, in social justice work, it is paramount to utilize these transformational theoretical perspectives to understand the role of race in combatting racial inequities and creating social change.

Critical Race Theory

Critical race theory (CRT) reminds us that any examination of race must occur in tandem with the discussion of racism (Delgado and Stefancic 2001). CRT was developed to complicate and deepen our understanding of the role of race and racism in creating social inequalities between marginalized and dominant groups (DeCuir and Dixson 2004; Ladson-Billings 1998; Ladson-Billings and Tate 1995). CRT has five basic elements that have been applied in a variety of professions, such as law and education, to examine the role of race and racism: (1) counter-storytelling; (2) the permanence of racism; (3) whiteness as property; (4) interest convergence; and (5) critiquing liberalism (DeCuir and Dixson 2004; Ladson-Billings 1998).

Counter-storytelling is a framework that centers the experiences of marginalized groups and allows for counternarratives to be legitimized (DeCuir and Dixson 2004; Ladson-Billings 1998). It encourages members of marginalized groups to share their own experiences instead of relying on narratives being told about them. The *permanence of racism* explains how racism is embedded in the political, social, and economic realms of US society. In CRT, racism is viewed as giving privilege to white individuals over others in multiple arenas, including education (DeCuir and Dixson 2004; Delgado 1995; Ladson-Billings 1998; Ladson-Billings and Tate 1995). Due to the history of racism, the third tenet of CRT emphasizes *whiteness as property* (DeCuir and Dixson 2004). Basic rights are given to white individuals that are not given to other groups, such as the right to exclude others (DeCuir and Dixson 2004; Ladson-Billings and Tate 1995; Ladson-Billings 1998). For example, since the United States was founded on the belief that whiteness was superior, society was formed to privilege those who were/are white; therefore, special property rights are indeed inherited based on race. The fourth tenet, *interest convergence*, acknowledges how white people are actually the main inheritors of civil rights legislation (Cross, this volume; DeCuir and Dixson 2004; Ladson-Billings 1998). The fifth, and final, tenet of CRT, *critique of liberalism*, thoroughly examines the tenets of liberalism and the assumption and limitation of liberty for all people (DeCuir and Dixson 2004).

Social justice work that is centered in critical theory, particularly CRT, has the potential to make institutional racism foundational to all social justice work. If social justice work was actually based in counter-storytelling, then it would focus on the issues that were important to the community rather than the frequent, and often biased, narratives that exist about the needs of a particular racial group. If a CRT lens is used to deconstruct every system that is the focus of social justice work, such as education, homelessness, or interpersonal violence, then the actions will be focused on the underlying and reinforcing causes of inequities rather than the more superficial concerns that receive disproportional attention.

Queer Theory and Crip Theory

Since the initial development of CRT there have been a variety of related theories formulated from the perspective of other marginalized and oppressed groups, such as Queer and Trans individuals and those living with disabilities. Queer theory, since its creation in 1991, is aimed at addressing the systemic notions of heteronormative structures within society (Berlant and Warner 1998). Crip theory, some argue, grew out of Queer theory. Crip theory views disability as an integral part of one's identity and also recognizes the importance of the intersections of other identities, particularly marginalized identities (McRuer 2006). Both of these critical lenses are crucial to understanding the impact of intersectionality when discussing social justice work in any context.

Queer critical theory (QueerCrit) initially was established with three main tenets: rejecting heteronormativity in society, dismissing the idea that lesbian and gay studies were the same, and emphasizing how race impacts sexual bias (De Lauretis 1991). Heteronormativity sets heterosexuality as the norm or standard in society, which has led to the development of structures, worldviews, and practices that, by their very nature, oppress those who identify as Queer (Berlant and Warner 1998). This understanding helps to explain why resistance to heteronormativity is a necessity in the same way that CRT rejects whiteness as the norm. Queer theory challenges our understanding of sexuality and sexual orientation, and includes intersectionality at its core since sexuality cannot be separated from other identities.

Crip theory is positioned similarly to QueerCrit, but through the unique lens of disability. Crip theory, first named by Carrie Sandahl (2003), is an interdisciplinary approach formed through Queer theory, feminist theory, and other theories of oppressed communities. Though critiqued by some like Kirstin Bone (2017), Crip theory contends that the historical system that has led to the oppression of Queer identities is the same system that produces and stigmatizes disabilities (McRuer 2006). Examination of the structures created to determine what is normal is pervasive in all critical theories, since the concept of "normal" was constructed by a small group of people who determined what "normal" (typically rooted in white supremacy, neoliberalism, and heterosexism) is and benefited from that definition (Delgado 1995; De Lauretis 1991; McRuer 2006).

These theories and others that overlap with the tenets of CRT fit well with intersectionality. Queer and Crip theory both take intersectional approaches and recognize that individuals hold multiple identities and are shaped by interlocking forms of oppression. CRT makes the case that race and racism drive the formation of structures that oppress a multitude of identities. Carried over to Queer and Crip theories, this belief informs positions that one cannot dismantle the systems of heterosexism and ableism without also dismantling the system of racism. Theories and practices that lack an intersectional approach will ultimately limit our understanding of the totality of the human experience and the systems of power that often continue to contribute to and fortify inequalities within society. Crenshaw (1991) repeatedly underscores how the interlocking forms of oppression reinforce how oppression manifests in unique ways across groups and are parts of a greater system that requires that we view identity and combat racism in unified and collaborative ways.

One area that both intersectionality and CRT have in common is the belief that understanding race and racism must be a focal point for analyzing theories and systems and determining actions. Additionally, intersectionality and CRT are interdisciplinary in nature and are increasingly being incorporated across areas such as government, law, education, and public health. For example, in the context of higher education, Lori Patton et al. (2007) challenged educational leaders to use critical race perspectives to examine the disadvantages that educational systems have when addressing racism, and how they reproduce social inequality. Given how fundamental race and racism are to the fabric of the United States, it is essential that we use these theories to increase our understanding of not only how racism operates here but also how we must combat racism and create racial justice.

How to Understand, Prepare for, and Engage in Social Justice Work

Lee Anne Bell (2007, 3) offers one of the most frequently used definitions of how social justice shows up as "a society in which the distribution of resources is equitable and all members are physically and psychologically safe and secure." Robert Reason and Tracy Davis (2005) added depth to that common understanding by distinguishing between distributive and procedural justice. According to Pope, Reynolds, and Mueller (2019, 4–5), "Distributive justice focuses on how the limited goods and resources in society are distributed based on need, fairness, or equality, whereas procedural justice is about which members of society or groups are able to have influence and input in any decision-making process." We need social justice work because there are endless examples of how societal resources are distributed inequitably and how various groups are mistreated and harmed by the very infrastructure of our society and government. Such inequities exist because power differences are rooted in discrimination and various forms of oppression so those with power have the money and resources to ensure that resources are not adequately or equally distributed to those with less power and privilege. As noted by Bell (2007), this unequal distribution leads to harmful and negative health, psychological, and spiritual effects with generational consequences. If we do not eradicate these inequities, we inevitably maintain and reinforce oppressive systems and structures that ensure that equality and equity cannot be achieved.

The purpose of social justice, as suggested by Jennifer Caldwell and Elizabeth Vera (2010, 164), is to "work for the common good by transforming the social organizations and processes that contribute to power inequalities, oppression, and marginalization." Social justice work is inherently centered in change, resistance, and transformation and, therefore, has always occurred within rapidly changing, complex environments. While there are too many examples of social inequities in the United States to mention, some of the most obvious and compelling include the lack of adequate health care for the poor and those people without insurance; the educational disparities and inequities in urban, rural, and tribal settings; and the racial inequities in every aspect of the criminal justice system, particularly for Black and Brown individuals.

It is important to acknowledge that social justice work has limitations as well. As Kathleen Manning (2009, 17) offered, "Just as diversity became a catch-all phrase for all practice related to difference, social justice is unfortunately becoming the generic phrase for the same. Yet without an understanding of oppression, action related to transformation change, and passion for equitable sharing of power, claims of social justice may be another perspective in disguise." Social justice work is more than being inclusive; it is about redistributing power and resources. D-L Stewart (2017) further warned that social justice efforts are often co-opted by leaders who may use the language of social justice but ultimately center their outcomes on appeasement rather than transformation. Finally, some argue that broadening our language to social justice rather than racial justice allows individuals, groups, and institutions to avoid addressing racism. For example, Afeni Cobham and Tara Parker (2007) made a case for inserting race back into campus diversity initiatives after years of erasure. As Michael Omi and Howard Winant (1994) have suggested, when race and racism become just one part of an ever-expanding diversity umbrella, it is hard to fully appreciate and understand the profound historical, economic, social, and political impact of race on every aspect of life. There are times when it is right to focus more broadly on social justice and times when it is necessary to be more precise and focused on racial justice, just as there are reasons and times to specifically focus on anti-Blackness instead of general antiracism work. Being well-versed in the literature, attentive to the zeitgeist of the time, and engaged in the real-life work of community activists and advocates can assist in determining what type of justice is most needed in the moment.

Paths toward Justice

There are many ways social justice and racial justice may be enacted and implemented. Justice can be integrated and centered in everything and everywhere, in the policies or practices that take place at the private or public level or in our work roles or personal relationships. It can be in the work we do and/or how we choose to live our life. We can enter social justice work with intention and planning or we can become someone who, accidentally or without intention, becomes a social justice advocate. If it isn't clear yet, there is no one path and no one way to engage in social justice work.

Doing social justice work may require specific competencies, but it does not require a college degree or certification. However, there is an increased marketing of opportunities for individuals interested in doing social justice work. There are common paths to social justice work through community organizing, education, nonprofit work, law, advocacy, government, human rights, lobbying, and others. Beth Thorne (n.d.) suggests,

> Countless occupations exist for people who want to fight inequality. Some people become activists positioned at picket lines. Others work with those from disadvantaged groups as career counselors, teachers in underserved communities or public defenders. Still others attempt to bring about high-level change by running for public office or informing policy decisions with research. Anyone with a passion for fighting inequality can find their niche in the field: there are fulfilling careers out there for high school graduates and PhD holders alike.

Forms of Social Justice

Beth Thorne (n.d.) further highlighted six ways to fight inequality depending on how individuals want to focus their efforts: (1) providing immediate support (social worker, interpreter, psychologist); (2) improving education (teacher, school counselor, health educator); (3) changing policy and interpreting the law (politician, public defender, civil rights attorney); (4) spreading the word (journalist, documentary filmmaker, activist); (5) informing policy and the public (sociologist, political scientist, economist); and (6) improving career prospects (career counselor or adult literacy and high school equivalency teacher). However, it is important to underscore that there is not a job that exists where social justice issues are not relevant and cannot be addressed. It is simply a matter of creativity, will, and commitment to creating systems and supports to ensure equity and justice through proactive and prevention-oriented work.

Challenges to Social Justice Work

Whatever paths individuals pursue to engage in social justice work, there will be challenges, barriers, and resistance, particularly in the complex environments and uncertain times we are currently experiencing and will face in the future. These barriers and challenges exist individually and institutionally. They also vary based on our positionality and how much power and privilege we are afforded based on our intersectional identities and social locations. Self-doubt, insecurities, limited self-awareness, poor skill sets, knowledge deficits, and limited social support and personal resources are just a few of the barriers facing individuals, particularly those with power and privilege, such as white people. Many white individuals engaged in social justice work have not done extensive personal work that fully interrogated their own privilege and how it affects their work and their life. Such personal work requires that white individuals allow themselves to be uncomfortable and challenged. Involvement in social justice work, while fulfilling, is not meant to reduce guilt or hopelessness but instead is meant to produce cooperative efforts that eradicate racism. Additionally, whites often undervalue the importance of doing antiracism work with other white people and do not set up essential accountability networks and relationships with Black, Indigenous, and other People of Color (BIPOC), which limits the effectiveness and meaningfulness of their work.

Of course, those from marginalized groups, such as BIPOC, Queer and Trans individuals, and Queer and Trans People of Color, also face individual barriers, but their investment in uprooting discrimination and oppression is often more accessible and ready for action. Such readiness is valuable, but also may limit critical analysis of group and intersectional needs within social movements that ultimately create barriers to essential coalitions. For example, if Queer and Trans individuals who are Black are not fully integrated into Black Lives Matter community movements and other actions to address systematic violence and oppression against Black people, then the power and reach of those efforts will be diminished. Examination of one's identity and social location is essential for all who fight for social justice. Ultimately, social identities, particularly racial identity, are a major factor in determining whether any individuals become motivated to do social justice work (Edwards 2006).

In addition to individual barriers to social justice work, institutional barriers and resistance exist in every setting and at every possible level. Many institutions become invested in maintaining the status quo and are resistant to change (Prochaska, Prochaska, and Levesque 2001). Barbara Rose (2017) highlighted the desire to maintain privilege as a major barrier, while Janice Prochaska, James Prochaska, and Deborah Levesque focused on limited readiness for change. Patton et al. (2019), Pope,

Reynolds, and Mueller (2014, 2019), and others highlighted key reasons that multicultural interventions fail in higher education. These reasons include limited resources of time and money; inadequate levels of sustained and consistent support and commitment from senior leadership; no sustained evaluation, feedback, and accountability efforts; and no meaningful infrastructure to support long-term change. Although originally framed within higher education contexts, these reasons for failure of social change efforts are applicable to other contexts. Being cognizant of and planning for these barriers will allow social justice and change advocates to anticipate and counteract the resistance they know will occur. Additionally, centering one's work in cutting-edge theory and praxis will ensure the accessibility of new tools, strategies, and approaches and create new opportunities for transformative social justice work.

New Directions and Approaches for Social Justice Work

In this time of uncertainty and constant change, we need new ways of envisioning how to create meaningful and lasting change in the systems that continue to harm and disadvantage some while privileging and rewarding others. While social justice work, antiracism efforts, and movements against anti-Blackness have existed for many decades if not centuries, how we understand and work toward change has evolved over time. There are always new theories, strategies, tactics, and movements that have taken hold during any given moment whose roots are often ancient, communal, and liberatory. It is vital that we take the time to learn from and heed these new ideas, approaches, and actions in order to benefit from and be nourished by these efforts that are more capable of integrating a nuanced and ever-changing definition of race, racial identity, racism, and intersectionality into social justice work. These complex and evolving models and frameworks can assist educators, advocates, and activists in their efforts to explicate and effectively tackle race and racism in more meaningful and constructive ways. While in-depth examination and application of these approaches and movements are not possible in this limited space, we will endeavor to expose, highlight, and amplify their power and possibility by focusing briefly on four: (1) liberatory practices; (2) emergent strategy; (3) advocacy efforts; and (4) the Black Lives Matter movement.

Liberatory Practice

The roots of liberatory practice largely grew out of the liberation psychology and theology that challenged the ability of Western mindsets and theories to truly benefit the poor and oppressed in Latin America (Tate et al. 2013). Much of the liberation movement has been traced back to the work of Martín-Baró (1991), a Jesuit priest doing social justice work in El Salvador. Tom Chavez et al. (2016) highlighted some of the key principles of liberation psychology, including recovering historical memory; denaturalization, or the critical exploration of underlying assumptions and values, virtues, and strengths of oppressed people; and conscientization and praxis, which is taking critical consciousness and turning it into action. Bobbi Harro (2000) operationalized the principles of liberation into the Cycle of Liberation, which offered a model for conceptualizing and enacting liberatory social change. Beginning with a focus on waking up and readiness, Harro provided a blueprint for reaching out, building community, coalescing, creating change, and maintaining through self-awareness and interpersonal change as a means for creating meaningful and lasting social change. At the core of this cycle are self-love, hope, balance, joy, and authentic love of others, which provides fuel for every step of the process. Liberation as a basis for social change is about healing, which is essential because as Freire (1970), another contributor to the foundation of liberation theory, has suggested, one cannot live in an oppressive system without internalizing the harm. This liberatory and healing influence is increasingly visible in social justice movements that highlight the importance of self-compassion but in a radical and political way, as advocated for by Audre Lorde (1988, 228) who stated, "Caring for myself is not self-indulgence, it is self-preservation, and that is an act of political warfare." Liberatory principles provide a sustainable mindset and praxis that can be used to fuel any social change effort.

Emergent Strategy

Emergent strategy, a framework for understanding complex systems and patterns, has been championed by adrienne maree brown (2017, 14) as a method for creating social change in a world that is continually changing and in ways that are more natural and organic. She believes that "emergence shows us that adaptation and evolution depend more upon critical, deep, and authentic connections, a thread that can be tugged for support and resilience." This deep and thoughtful work by brown is not designed to offer a step-by-step guide for change, but rather a liberatory and natural process that encourages us to be aware of the systems that operate around and through us. By highlighting the ways that change occurs in the natural world around us—such as how cells split, viruses mutate, and birds flock and move—brown offers a different perspective on change. Her core principles are both simple and profound, and they create a foundation for process-oriented and organic change and practice: (1) Small is good, small is all; (2) Change is constant; (3) There is always enough time for the right work; (4) There is a conversation in the room that only these people at this moment can have. Find it; (5) Never a failure, always a lesson; (6) Trust the people; (7) Move at the speed of trust; (8) Less prep, more presence; and (9) What you pay attention to grows. Emergent strategies offer more than a paradigm shift; through the incorporation of these principles, advocates and activists can create new and different tools and strategies to work with the natural systems around us. According to brown (2017, 214), emergent strategy, as a tool for social justice, is focused on "facilitation as a practice and a toolset, a way of being with each other, and in community in the world." While personal assessment to explore one's strategy at a given moment is essential, emergent strategy is mostly interpersonal and process-oriented. With an emphasis on goal and intention setting, along with collaborative and living agendas, the focus turns to creating a learning community and building consensus as a means to create transformative justice.

Advocacy Efforts

Advocacy efforts, which have largely been shaped by and grown out of the social work, counseling, and counseling psychology professions, are often focused on methods, strategies, and approaches to creating social change. For example, the American Counseling Association Advocacy Competencies emphasize action on behalf of, or in collaboration with, clients and systems on the individual, community, and public arena level

(Toporek and Daniels 2018). In addition to considering level of client involvement, this competencies framework focuses on the level of advocacy intervention from the micro (individual) to the macro (systemic), which provides advocates with a plan for when and how to intervene in systems to create change. According to Marian Lee, Tammy Smith, and Ryan Henry (2013), advocacy can be case-oriented or cause-oriented. Case advocacy is typically focused on helping individuals and families address oppressive structures and focuses on empowerment. Cause advocacy is often oriented toward ameliorating underlying structural issues and barriers that are harmful and oppressive. Lee, Smith, and Henry (2013, 72) believe that "understanding the strategic components of power politics is necessary to be effective in all areas of advocacy to achieve goals for tuning, incremental and/or structural change." Advocacy can incorporate activism with a focus on direct action to create social and political change through expert testimony/policy research, policy formation and evaluation, lobbying for policy change, and organizing to change the status quo. Rebecca Toporek and Muninder Ahluwalia (2020) offer a framework and step-by-step guide for taking action to mitigate harm and create positive social change. Through the use of four key principles of strength, solidarity, strategy, and sustainability, Toporek and Ahluwalia (2020) advance a model that can be used by individuals and groups to better understand themselves, build meaningful coalitions, develop effective strategies, and create sustainable movements toward change.

Black Lives Matter Movement/Movement for Black Lives

Finally, the Black Lives Matter movement, through its principles and practices, has created a roadmap for successful change efforts that are both activist and advocacy-oriented, and offer new ways to organize, agitate, and activate change. Candice Hargons et al. (2017) describe Black Lives Matter (BLM) and the Movement for Black Lives (MBL) as being oriented toward intervention and affirmation. Interventions are focused on interrupting, uprooting, and ending anti-Black racism, while affirmations are centered in the celebration and honoring of Black lives and culture. The BLM and MBL movements are oriented toward four principles: (1) all Black lives matter; (2) love and self-love are signposts of success; (3) 360-degree vision guides the work and honors both Black elders and future generations through the creation of community or extended family; and (4) training and leadership development are constant. These principles guide BLM efforts, with their empowering and community-based approach centered in *leaderfull* leadership and spontaneity (Hargons et al. 2017). A leaderfull approach prioritizes and prizes multiple leaders rather than a hierarchical leadership structure with one primary spokesperson. Through application of work by David Snow and Dana Moss (2014), Hargons et al. (2017) provide insight into the unique components of BLM/MBL that have contributed to changing public attitudes and created capacity for change. Through the building of nonhierarchical organizations and movements, BLM/MBL have been able to be spontaneous and responsive rather than rigid and reactive. The ongoing focus on police brutality targeting Black lives and violence against Black Trans women has allowed for spontaneous reactions and outcries in real time, leading to activism and action in the streets at unprecedented levels. The localization of the movement also has built capacity because of the creation of ongoing relationships and connections that encourage engagement and action. The lessons learned and strategies enacted by BLM/MBL provide communities with powerful, organic, and sustainable approaches to creating social change.

Synthesis

These four unique approaches to creating social change (liberatory practices, emergent strategy, advocacy efforts, and BLM/MBL) provide social justice advocates and activists with far-reaching and diverse tools to fuel their efforts and movements. In addition to broadening our understanding of how to conceptualize and enact change, we must also consider specific strategies for translating and shaping our actions as change agents who are committed to doing social justice work in our institutions and communities in novel, engaging, and transformative ways. SaVonne Anderson (2016) highlights the importance of self-education in order to determine where to focus one's energy. Such education involves personal work, centered in accountability, as well as external engagement with local social justice efforts and movements. By researching local groups, attending demonstrations, volunteering time, and donating resources, social justice activists, advocates, and their allies can contribute to important work and progress in their own communities. Given that our personal resources, comfort and commitment levels, and social justice experience can vary significantly, we need to begin in the place that makes sense for us as individuals. For those considering how to engage in this work, Anderson recommends beginning with issues where there is a natural affinity or passion. In these uncertain times, more than ever, many individuals want to get involved, speak out, and take action.

As Anderson suggests, educating ourselves about how to get involved and support social justice efforts is an important first step. Nina Flores (2015) offered additional ways to contribute to social movements, create momentum, and engage in long-term social justice work. Creating social change, as the frameworks previously discussed show, requires sustained and multifaceted engagement. According to Flores, some ways to get involved include (1) organize; (2) show solidarity; (3) hone your allyship; (4) see the connections; (5) take risks; (6) look closer at language; (7) deepen your critiques; (8) get to know your communities; (9) asset mapping for action; (10) in-person presence matters; (11) online presence matters; (12) run for office; (13) pay attention to policy; (14) share your story; (15) share your skills; (16) use your talents; and (17) stay loud. Every single day.

Applying these suggestions for social justice work to the complexities of addressing racism in this moment and into the future requires that we commit ourselves to deepening our understanding of race, racial identity, and racism locally and globally. In these uncertain times when globalization is continually shrinking the world and its impact on us, we can likely make the biggest impact in our own backyard. Complicating our understanding of race and racism in our community from both historical and current perspectives is an essential first step. Increasing awareness of our own racial identity and how it influences our assumptions and actions is key to our effectiveness as an advocate, ally, or activist. Exposing ourselves to some of these new and evolving theories and the unique social justice strategies, actions, and movements we have shared can provide a roadmap for engagement in social justice efforts. And guiding us through these complex and uncertain times are the words of bell hooks (1996, 192), who called for "a paradigm, a practical model for social change that includes an understanding of the ways to transform consciousness that are linked to efforts to transform structures."

Summary

Embracing the complexities of race, racism, and social justice in unclear and uncharted times is no easy task. Deepening our understanding of race, racial identity, and racism is essential, and this chapter and this book provide the depth and range of knowledge needed to begin that process. Our knowledge of ourselves, others, and the world around us must never be static. Social justice work is inherently centered in change, resistance, and transformation and therefore has always occurred in rapidly changing, complex environments. Through the unique theories, approaches, and movements offered here, activists can build a complex understanding and the capacity to fully engage in meaningful, effective, and lasting social justice work.

REFERENCES

Anderson, SaVonne. 2016. "8 Ways to Meaningfully Support Social Justice Movements." Mashable, March 26. https://mashable.com.

Bell, Lee Anne. 2007. "Theoretical Foundations for Social Justice Education." In *Teaching for Diversity and Social Justice*, 2nd ed., edited by Maurianne Adams, Lee Anne Bell, and Pat Griffin, 1–14. New York: Routledge/Taylor & Francis.

Berlant, Lauren, and Michael Warner. 1998. "Sex in Public." *Critical Inquiry* 24, no. 2 (Winter): 547–66. doi:10.1086/448884.

Bone, Kirstin Marie. 2017. "Trapped behind the Glass: Crip Theory and Disability Identity." *Disability & Society* 32, no. 9 (April): 1297–1314. doi:10.1080/09687599.2017.1313722.

brown, adrienne maree. 2017. *Emergent Strategy*. Chico: AK Press.

Caldwell, Jennifer C., and Elizabeth M. Vera. 2010. "Critical Incidents in Counseling Psychology Professionals' and Trainees' Social Justice Orientation Development." *Training & Education in Professional Psychology* 4, no 3 (August): 163–76. doi:10.1037/a0019093.

Carter, Robert T. 1995. *The Influence of Race and Racial Identity in Psychotherapy: Toward a Racially Inclusive Model*. Wiley Series on Personality Processes. Oxford: Wiley.

Chavez, Tom A., Ivelisse Torres Fernandez, Carlos P. Hipolito Delgado, and Edil Torres Rivera. 2016. "Unifying Liberation Psychology and Humanistic Values to Promote Social Justice in Counseling." *Journal of Humanistic Counseling* 55, no. 3 (October): 166–82. doi:10.1002/johc.12032.

Cobham, B. Afeni, and Tara L. Parker. 2007. "Resituating Race into the Movement toward Multiculturalism and Social Justice." *New Directions for Student Services*, no. 120 (December): 85–93. doi:10.1002/ss.260.

Collins, Patricia Hill. 2000. *Black Feminist Thought: Knowledge, Consciousness, and the Politics of Empowerment*. Rev. 10th anniversary ed. New York: Routledge.

Combahee River Collective. 1977. "The Combahee River Collective Statement." Boston: Combahee River Collective.

Crenshaw, Kimberlé. 1991. "Mapping the Margins: Intersectionality, Identity Politics, and Violence against Women of Color." *Stanford Law Review* 43, no. 6 (July): 1241–99. doi:10.2307/1229039.

Cross, William E., Jr. 1971. "The Negro-to-Black Conversion Experience." *Black World* 20, no. 9 (July): 13–27.

———. 1991. *Shades of Black: Diversity in African-American Identity*. Philadelphia: Temple University Press.

DeCuir, Jessica T., and Adrienne D. Dixson. 2004. "'So When It Comes Out, They Aren't That Surprised That It Is There': Using Critical Race Theory as a Tool of Analysis of Race and Racism in Education." *Educational Researcher* 33, no. 5 (June): 26–31. doi:10.3102/0013189X033005026.

De Lauretis, Teresa. 1991. *Queer Theory: Lesbian and Gay Sexualities*. Bloomington: Indiana University Press.

Delgado, Richard. 1995. *Critical Race Theory: The Cutting Edge*. Philadelphia: Temple University Press.

Delgado, Richard, and Jean Stefancic. 2001. *Critical Race Theory: An Introduction*. New York: New York University Press.

Dumas, Michael J. 2016. "Against the Dark: Antiblackness in Education Policy and Discourse." *Theory into Practice* 55, no. 1 (December): 11–19. doi:10.1080/00405841.2016.1116852.

Edwards, Keith E. 2006. "Aspiring Social Justice Ally Identity Development: A Conceptual Model." *NASPA Journal* 43, no. 4: 39–60.

Fanon, Frantz. 1967. *Black Skin, White Masks*. New York: Grove.

Flores, Nina. 2015. "17 Ways You Can Work for Social Justice." *Yes! Magazine*, July 8. www.yesmagazine.org.

Freire, Paulo. 1970. *Pedagogy of the Oppressed*. New York: Continuum.

Hargons, Candice, Della Mosley, Jameca Falconer, Reuben Faloughi, Anneliese Singh, Danelle Stevens-Watkins, and Kevin Cokley. 2017. "Black Lives Matter: A Call to Action for Counseling Psychology Leaders." *Counseling Psychologist* 45, no. 6 (August): 873–901. doi:10.1177/0011000017733048.

Harro, Bobbie. 2000. "The Cycle of Liberation." In *Readings for Diversity and Social Justice*, edited by Maurianne Adams, Warren J. Blumenfeld, Rosie Casteñeda, Heather W. Hackman, Madeline L. Peters, and Ximena Zuniga, 463–70. New York: Routledge.

Helms, Janet E. 1984. "Toward a Theoretical Explanation of the Effects of Race on Counseling: A Black and White Model." *Counseling Psychologist* 12, nos. 3–4 (December): 153–65. doi:10.1177/0011000084124013.

———, ed. 1990. *Black and White Racial Identity: Theory, Research, and Practice.* New York: Greenwood.

———. 2020. *A Race Is a Nice Thing to Have: A Guide to Being a White Person or Understanding the White Persons in Your Life.* San Diego: Cognella.

hooks, bell. 1996. *Killing Rage: Ending Racism.* New York: Henry Holt.

Hyde, Janet Shibley, Rebecca S. Bigler, Daphna Joel, Charlotte Chucky Tate, and Sari M. van Anders. 2019. "The Future of Sex and Gender in Psychology: Five Challenges to the Gender Binary." *American Psychologist* 74, no. 2 (July): 171–93. doi:10.1037/amp0000307.

Ladson-Billings, Gloria. 1998. "Just What Is Critical Race Theory and What's It Doing in a Nice Field Like Education?" *International Journal of Qualitative Studies in Education* 11, no. 1 (January): 7–24.

Ladson-Billings, Gloria, and William F. Tate IV. 1995. "Toward a Critical Race Theory of Education." *Teachers College Record* 97, no. 1: 47.

Lee, Marian A., Tammy Jorgensen Smith, and Ryan G. Henry. 2013. "Power Politics: Advocacy to Activism in Social Justice Counseling." *Journal for Social Action in Counseling & Psychology* 5, no. 3 (September): 70–94.

Lorde, Audre. 1988. *A Burst of Light: Essays.* New York: Firebrand.

Luft, Rachel E. 2009. "Intersectionality and the Risk of Flattening Difference: Gender and Race Logics, and the Strategic Use of Antiracist Singularity." In *The Intersectional Approach: Transforming the Academy through Race, Class, and Gender*, edited by Michele Tracy Berger and Kathleen Guidroz, 100–117. Chapel Hill: University of North Carolina Press.

Manning, Kathleen. 2009. "Philosophical Underpinnings of Student Affairs Work on Difference." *About Campus* 14, no. 2 (May): 11–17.

Martín-Baró, Ignacio. 1991. "Developing a Critical Consciousness through the University Curriculum." In *Towards a Society That Serves Its People: The Intellectual Contributions of El Salvador's Murdered Jesuits*, edited by John Hassett and Hugh Lacey, 220–44. Washington, DC: Georgetown University Press.

McRuer, Robert. 2006. *Crip Theory: Cultural Signs of Queerness and Disability.* New York: New York University Press.

Moraga, Cherríe, and Gloria Anzaldúa. 1981. *This Bridge Called My Back: Writings by Radical Women of Color.* London: Persephone.

Omi, Michael, and Howard Winant. 1994. *Racial Formation in the United States: From the 1960s to the 1990s.* New York: Routledge.

Patton, Lori D., Marylu McEwen, Laura Rendón, and Mary F. Howard-Hamilton. 2007. "Critical Race Perspectives on Theory in Student Affairs." *New Directions for Student Services*, no. 120 (Winter): 39–53. doi:10.1002/ss.256.

Patton, Lori D., Berenice Sánchez, Jacqueline Mac, and D-L Stewart. 2019. "An Inconvenient Truth about 'Progress': An Analysis of the Promises and Perils of Research on Campus Diversity Initiatives." *Review of Higher Education* 42, no. 5 (Supplement) (January): 173–98.

Pope, Raechele L., and Amy L. Reynolds. 2017. "Multidimensional Identity Model Revisited: Implications for Student Affairs." In *Enacting Intersectionality in Student Affairs: New Directions for Student Services*, number 157, edited by Charmaine L. Wijeyesinghe, 5–24. San Francisco: Jossey-Bass.

Pope, Raechele L., Amy L. Reynolds, and John A. Mueller. 2014. *Creating Multicultural Change on Campus*. San Francisco: Jossey-Bass.

———. 2019. "'A Change Is Gonna Come': Paradigm Shifts to Dismantle Oppressive Structures." *Journal of College Student Development* 60, no. 6 (January): 659–73.

Prochaska, Janice M., James O. Prochaska, and Deborah A. Levesque. 2001. "A Transtheoretical Approach to Changing Organizations." *Administration and Policy in Mental Health and Mental Health Services Research* 28, no. 4 (March): 247–61.

Reason, Robert D., and Tracy L. Davis. 2005. "Antecedents, Precursors, and Concurrent Concepts in the Development of Social Justice Attitudes and Actions." *New Directions for Student Services*, no. 110 (June): 5–15. doi:10.1002/ss.161.

Reynolds, Amy L., and Raechele L. Pope. 1991. "The Complexities of Diversity: Exploring Multiple Oppressions." *Journal of Counseling & Development* 70, no. 1 (September): 174–80.

Root, Maria P. P., ed. 1992. *Racially Mixed People in America*. Newbury Park: Sage.

Rose, Barbara. 2017. "Moving from Chasm to Convergence: Benefits and Barriers to Academic Activism for Social Justice and Equity." *Brock Education: A Journal of Educational Research and Practice* 27, no. 1 (December): 67–78.

ross, kihana miraya. 2020. "Call It What It Is: Anti-Blackness." *New York Times*, June 4.

Sandahl, Carrie. 2003. "Queering the Crip or Cripping the Queer? Intersections of Queer and Crip Identities in Solo Autobiographical Performance." *GLQ: A Journal of Lesbian & Gay Studies* 9, nos. 1–2 (January): 25–56. doi:10.1215/10642684-9-1-2-25.

Sawyer, Jeremy, and Anup Gampa. 2018. "Implicit and Explicit Racial Attitudes Changed during Black Lives Matter." *Personality & Social Psychology Bulletin* 44, no. 4 (March): 1039–59. doi:10.1177/0146167218757454.

Snow, David A., and Dana M. Moss. 2014. "Protest on the Fly: Toward a Theory of Spontaneity in the Dynamics of Protest and Social Movements." *American Sociological Review* 79, no. 6 (December): 1122–43. doi:10.1177/0003122414554081.

Stewart, Dafina-Lazarus. 2017. "Language of Appeasement." *Inside Higher Ed*, March 30. www.insidehighered.com.

Sturm, Circe. 2014. "Race, Sovereignty, and Civil Rights: Understanding the Cherokee Freedmen Controversy." *Cultural Anthropology* 29, no. 3 (August): 575–98. doi:10.14506/ca29.3.07.

Tate, Kevin A., Edil Torres Rivera, Eric Brown, and Leslie Skaistis. 2013. "Foundations for Liberation: Social Justice, Liberation Psychology, and Counseling." *Interamerican Journal of Psychology* 47, no. 3 (January): 373–82.

Tatum, Beverly Daniel. 2000. *Assimilation Blues: Black Families in White Communities: Who Succeeds and Why?* New York: Basic Books.

Thomas, Anita Jones, and Suzette L. Speight. 1999. "Racial Identity and Racial Socialization Attitudes of African American Parents." *Journal of Black Psychology* 25, no. 2 (May): 152–70. doi:10.1177/0095798499025002002.

Thorne, Beth. n.d. "College Degrees for Social Justice." Affordable Colleges Online. www.affordablecollegesonline.org. Accessed July 22, 2020.

Toporek, Rebecca, and Muninder Kaur Ahluwalia. 2020. *Taking Action: Creating Social Change through Strength, Solidarity, Strategy and Sustainability*. San Diego: Cognella.

Toporek, Rebecca L., and Judy Daniels. 2018. "American Counseling Association Advocacy Competencies." www.counseling.org.

Wijeyesinghe, Charmaine L. 2001. "Racial Identity in Multiracial People: An Alternative Paradigm." In *New Perspectives on Racial Identity Development: A Theoretical and Practical Anthology*, edited by Charmaine L. Wijeyesinghe and Bailey W. Jackson III, 129–52. New York: New York University Press.

Wijeyesinghe, Charmaine L., and Susan R. Jones. 2019. "Intersectionality, Identity, and Systems of Power and Inequality." In *Intersectionality and Higher Education: Theory, Research, and Praxis*, 2nd ed., edited by Donald Mitchell Jr. with Jakia Marie and Tiffany L. Steele, 9–19. New York: Peter Lang.

Writer, Jeanette Haynes. 2010. "Broadening the Meaning of Citizenship Education: Native Americans and Tribal Nationhood." *Action in Teacher Education* 32, no. 2: 70–81. https://doi.org/10.1080/01626620.2010.10463551.

ACKNOWLEDGMENTS

This book was made possible through the knowledge, skill, persistence, and support of many people. First, I wish to acknowledge the contributing authors, whose words provide critical analyses of race, racism, and movements for racial justice in America. Together we formed a *community* of writers and thinkers, and the book benefited from our collective energy, wisdom, and purpose. I thank the people in the authors' professional and personal circles who provided them with care and encouragement as they completed the chapters for this book.

I acknowledge Jennifer Hammer at New York University Press, with deep gratitude and respect. From our early communication about the focus and orientation of this book to the final discussions of its production, Jennifer offered attentive and responsive guidance that enabled this book to reach its full potential. I value the relationship she and I have built over nearly twenty-five years and three volumes. In addition, I thank New York University Press staff members Veronica Knutson for providing critical technical assistance, and Alexia Traganas for shepherding the manuscript through the production process.

I was extremely fortunate to have Michael Cooper join me in the various phases of manuscript production. Mike's skills in copyediting, formatting, and organizing the material for submission were invaluable. Simply said, I could not have done this project without him, and I am grateful for our partnership.

While I worked on this book, I was also serving as coeditor for another volume. The projects ran neck and neck, and it was sometimes challenging for me to balance the needs and demands of each one. I would be remiss if I did not acknowledge my coeditor for the other book, Marc Johnston-Guerrero, who showed patience and understanding as I juggled everything and got the two projects across the line.

Lastly, I wish to acknowledge the people in my life who came on this journey with me. My spouse, Christian Lietzau, and our children, Andreas Wijeyesinghe Lietzau and Rebecca Wijeyesinghe Lietzau, allowed me the time and space needed to develop this book, write chapters, and work with the authors. Our spirited discussions about race, identity, and issues of social justice across the years gave me much to think about, so your wisdom and insights appear by proxy in some of these pages. In addition, I have been blessed with a special group of colleagues and friends who have offered me invaluable support and feedback, including Diane Goodman, Susan Jones, Jim Bonilla, Sharon Washington, Francie Kendall, Mary Wilson-Hyde, Georgia Fishburn, and Justin Lincks. Thank you for guiding me in work, scholarship, and life.

ABOUT THE EDITOR

CHARMAINE L. WIJEYESINGHE is a consultant with over thirty-five years of experience working with colleges, universities, and organizations on issues of social justice, racial and social identity, intersectionality, and conflict resolution. Her professional background includes positions as Staff Associate to the Vice Chancellor of Student Affairs and Assistant Ombudsperson at the University of Massachusetts/Amherst, Dean of Students at Mount Holyoke College, and National Program Consultant for the National Conference for Christians and Jews. Her work focuses on social identities and systems of oppression, Multiracial identity, and intersectionality, and she was co-editor (with Bailey W. Jackson III) of two editions of *New Perspectives on Racial Identity Development*, editor of *Enacting Intersectionality in Students Affairs: New Directions for Student Services*, and co-editor (with Marc Johnston-Guerrero) of *Multiracial Experiences in Higher Education: Contesting Knowledge, Honoring Voice, and Innovating Practice*. Wijeyesinghe served on the editorial board of the *Journal Committed to Social Change on Race and Ethnicity* and was the inaugural recipient of the NCORE Social Justice Award for Scholarship in 2017. Wijeyesinghe has presented over 125 programs at national-level conferences on topics such as Multiracial identity, racial identity and conflict resolution, intersectionality, and writing for social justice. Most recently, Wijeyesinghe's contributions to enhancing Multiracial scholarship and education were recognized by the ACPA-College Student Educators International Multiracial Network when she was named co-recipient (with Marc Johnston-Guerrero) of the 2021 Innovation Award, and chosen to serve as the Multiracial Network's scholar in residence for the 2021–2022 academic year.

ABOUT THE CONTRIBUTORS

AMER F. AHMED is the Founder and CEO of AFA Diversity Consulting, LLC, a consulting practice dedicated to enhancing the development of organizations through leadership, professional development, assessment, and strategic change. In addition, he is the Vice Provost for Diversity, Equity, and Inclusion at the University of Vermont and Chief Diversity Officer at Dickinson College and is a member of SpeakOut: Institute for Democratic Education. Ahmed's approach is grounded in social justice and commitment to community. He is the host of *The Eclectic Inclusion Podcast* and has been featured in media such as MSNBC, documentary film, and other national press outlets. He also has keynoted prominent conferences including the National Conference on Race and Ethnicity (NCORE) in Higher Education, the Global Engagement in the Liberal Arts Conference, and the Society for Intercultural Education (SIETAR) Conference.

REGINALD A. BLOCKETT is Assistant Professor of Higher Education at Grand Valley State University. He teaches courses on theories and intervention strategies for college student development; college campus environments; and race, gender, and sexuality in higher education. His research centers on the sociocultural experiences of lesbian, gay, bisexual, trans*, and queer collegians of color, Black sexual cultures in postsecondary contexts, and queer of color worldmaking in college and beyond. His scholarship has been published in *Higher Education: Handbook of Theory and Research*, *International Journal of Qualitative Studies in Education*, *Western Journal of Black Studies*, and *Urban Education*. Blockett is a proud native of Detroit, Michigan, where he first learned the values of family, community, education, and social justice.

ROBERT KEITH COLLINS is four-field trained anthropologist and Associate Professor of American Indian Studies at San Francisco

State University. Using a person-centered ethnographic approach, his research explores American Indian cultural changes and African and Native American interactions in North, Central, and South America. His recent academic efforts include being a co-curator on the Smithsonian's traveling banner exhibit *IndiVisible: African-Native American Lives in the Americas*, the edited volume *African and Native American Contact in the US: Anthropological and Historical Perspectives*, a special edition edited volume for the *American Indian Culture and Research Journal* at UCLA, *Reducing Barriers to Native American Student Success*, the forthcoming edited volume *Studying African-Native Americans: Problems, Perspectives, and Prospects*, and the forthcoming edited volume *Native American Populations and Colonial Diseases*.

WILLIAM E. CROSS JR. holds Professor Emeritus status at the University of Denver in the College of Education, with a joint appointment in Counseling Psychology and Higher Education. Graduating from Princeton University with a PhD in social psychology, Cross spent his first twenty years at Cornell University in Africana studies, and thereafter affirmed the academic status of Africana scholar, fusing the disciplines of Africana and social psychology. His seminal 1971 article on black identity change ("The Negro-to-Black Conversion Experience") as well as his 1991 book, *Shades of Black*, are considered foundational readings in the discourse on the psychology of the African American experience. His new text, *Black Identity Viewed from the Barber's Chair*, revisits Nigrescence Theory, presents a devastating critique of the deficit perspective on black families, and shows that former slaves exited slavery with more positive psychological attributes than previously understood.

ZAK FOSTE is Assistant Professor of Higher Education Administration at the University of Kansas. His research critically explores whiteness in American higher education. This work examines both how whiteness functions to underwrite racially hostile and unwelcoming campus climates for students of color and the ways white college students understand their relationship to race and whiteness. His most recent work has examined how whiteness structures students' experiences in campus residence halls. Foste received his bachelor's degree in sociology and political science from Western Illinois University, his master's degree in student affairs in higher education from Miami University, and his PhD in higher education and student affairs from the Ohio State University.

MARC P. JOHNSTON-GUERRERO serves as Associate Chair of the Department of Educational Studies at the Ohio State University, where he is also Associate Professor in the Higher Education and Student Affairs Program. He completed a PhD in education (with an emphasis in higher education and organizational change) from the University of California, Los Angeles. Johnston-Guerrero's research interests focus on diversity and social justice issues in higher education and student affairs, with specific attention to college students making meaning of race and racism and multiracial/mixed-race issues. He is co-editor of *Multiracial Experiences in Higher Education: Contesting Knowledge, Honoring Voice, and Innovating Practice* (with Charmaine L. Wijeyesinghe). He serves on the Governing Board of the American College Personnel Association (ACPA) as Member-at-Large, Faculty, and previously served as an Associate Editor of the *Journal of Higher Education*.

JAERAN KIM, PhD, MSW (she/hers) is Associate Professor in the School of Social Work and Criminal Justice at the University of Washington at Tacoma. She was a Title IV-E Doctoral Fellow and a Leadership Education in Neurodevelopmental Disabilities (LEND) Fellow at the University of Minnesota. Prior to completing her doctoral degree, Kim worked with foster and adopted children and families and with adults with disabilities in residential care. Her research is focused on the intersection of adoption and disabilities, in particular exploring disability, race, and transnational experiences for adoptees. As a public scholar, Kim is passionate about engaging in community-based projects; her blog, *Harlow's Monkey*, which focuses on the transracial/transnational adoptee experience, is one of the longest-running transracial adoption blogs in the United States.

NANCY LÓPEZ is Professor of Sociology at the University of New Mexico; she co-founded and directs the Institute for the Study of "Race" and Social Justice. Her scholarship and teaching are guided by the insights of intersectionality—the *simultaneity* of tribal status/settler colonialism, race/structural racism, gender/heteropatriarchy, class/capitalism, ethnicity/nativism, and sexuality/heterosexism as systems of oppression/resistance across a variety of social outcomes (education, health, employment, and housing), and the importance of developing contextualized solutions that advance justice. Her books include *Hopeful Girls, Troubled Boys: Race and Gender Disparity in Urban Education* and *Mapping "Race": Critical Approaches to Health Disparities Research*. She co-edited a special issue of the journal *Race, Ethnicity and Education* on quantitative methods and critical race theory. She is also known for developing the concept of "street race."

RAECHELE L. POPE is the Associate Dean for Faculty and Student Affairs and the Chief Diversity Officer for the Graduate School of Education at the University at Buffalo as well as an Associate Professor in the Department of Education, Leadership, and Policy. She earned her doctorate in organization development from the University of Massachusetts at Amherst and her MA in student personnel administration from Indiana University of Pennsylvania. Her principal teaching, research, publication, and consultation interests have focused on multicultural competence, the creation of multicultural campus environments, and multicultural organization development for the past forty years. She is a co-author or co-editor of three books: *Multicultural Competence in Student Affairs, Creating Multicultural Change on Campus*, and *Why Aren't We There Yet? Taking Personal Responsibility for Creating an Inclusive Campus*.

KAMEELAH MU'MIN RASHAD is the Founder and President of the Muslim Wellness Foundation (MWF), a nonprofit organization dedicated to promoting healing and emotional well-being in the American Muslim community. Through the Muslim Wellness Foundation, Rashad has established the annual Black Muslim Psychology Conference and the Deeply Rooted Emerging Leaders Fellowship for Black Muslim young adults. Rashad is a Visiting Assistant Professor in Psychology and Muslim Studies at Bayan Islamic Graduate School and Chicago Theological Seminary (CTS) and CTS's Director for the InterAct on Race Project: Engaging Diverse Faith Communities in Anti-Racist Work. Rashad graduated from the University of Pennsylvania with a BA in psychology and an MEd in psychological services; earned a second master's in restorative practices and youth counseling (MRP) from the International Institute for Restorative Practices, and completed her doctorate in clinical psychology at Chestnut Hill College in Philadelphia.

KRISTEN A. RENN is Professor of Higher, Adult, and Lifelong Education and serves as Associate Dean of Undergraduate Studies for Student Success Research at Michigan State University. Her research focuses on the learning, development, and success of minoritized students in higher education, with particular focus on mixed-race students and LGBTQ+ students. As a faculty member, Renn teaches courses on student development theory, college students in the United States, and research methods. In her administrative role she develops research-informed practices and practice-informed research on student success policies and programs. She is author or co-author of nine books about higher education, including *Student Development in College: Theory, Research, and Practice* and *College Students in the United States: Characteristics, Experiences, and Outcomes*.

AMY L. REYNOLDS is Professor in the Department of Counseling, School, and Educational Psychology at the University at Buffalo. She received her master's degree in student personnel work and her doctorate in counseling psychology from Ohio State University. Her work as a scholar, teacher, and consultant for the past thirty-five years has focused on multicultural competence and training in counseling and student affairs as well as college mental health issues. Reynolds has published over fifty journal articles and book chapters and made over eighty presentations at regional or national conferences or on college campuses. She is one of the co-authors of *Multicultural Competence in Student Affairs* and *Creating Multicultural Change on Campus*, and is the author of *Helping College Students: Developing Essential Skills for Student Affairs Practice*.

CHAZZ ROBINSON is currently an Arthur A. Schomburg Fellow and third-year doctoral student in the Higher Education Program at the University at Buffalo. He received his BA in psychology from Saint Mary's University of Minnesota and his EdM in higher education administration from the University at Buffalo. His research interests include race and racial identity formation of college students and how they inform the creation of multicultural college campus environments. Prior to his doctoral journey, Robinson worked in a variety of functional areas in higher education, including residential life, admissions, and college access and transitional programs. He serves as the Coordinator for Recruitment for the Graduate Students and New Professional Community of Practice within ACPA-College Student Educators International (ACPA). He is also a proud native of Milwaukee, Wisconsin.

D-L STEWART is Chair of the Department of Higher Education at Morgridge College of Education at the University of Denver. Their scholarship focuses on higher education's history and philosophy, as well as institutional systems and structures that affect the postsecondary experiences, learning, growth, and becoming of minoritized students across a range of identities. They examine these topics through intersectional, critical, and poststructural frameworks that incorporate ableism, religious hegemony, and classism alongside racism, patriarchy, and queer/trans-antagonism. They are the author of *Experiences of Black Collegians in US Northern Private Colleges: A Narrative History, 1945–1965*, and the editor or co-editor of three other volumes.

INDEX

Abes, Elisa, 89, 233
ableism, 2, 228, 234, 250
acculturation, 128
ACS. *See* American Community Survey
activism, 258; Hip Hop, 194, 195–96; political, 166; social, 3
adoptees, transracial, 115–16, 117, 119
adoption: agencies, 113, 114; census on, 121; context of, 104, 105–6; fees, 114; same-race matching in, 108–10
adoption, transnational, 105, 106, 109, 121, 122
adoption, transracial, 8; adoptee impact, 115–16, 117; as civil right, 111–12; historical eras of, 106–12; intercountry, 106; justice, 116–17, 118, 119, 120, 121; racist policies in, 104–5, 112–21, 122; scholars on, 122; after World War II, 109
adoptive parents, 104, 105
advocacy efforts, 257–58
affirmations, 206, 258
affirmative action programs, 66–67
African-Native Americans, 133, 136–41
Africans, cultural change of, 127, 128–32; literature on, 132–33; Native American racism and, 133–35
Afrika Bambaataa, 199–200
agencies, adoption, 113, 114
agency, intellectual, 92
Ahluwalia, Muninder, 258
Ahmed, Amer F., 9
alienation, 6, 9, 22–23
Allah, 203
American Community Survey (ACS), 74–75

American Counseling Association Advocacy Competencies, 257–58
American iconography, 156
American Psychological Association, 86
ancestry, 40, 41, 44, 74
Anderson, SaVonne, 259, 260
anti-Blackness, 57, 59, 133–34, 241, 242
antiracism work, 234, 254
apartheid, residential, 20, 22
Applebaum, Barbara, 182
applications, college, 44
Arnold, Eric, 202
art, assimilation of, 18
ascription, racial, 39
assessment-driven culture, 181–82
assimilation, 128; of art, 18; mass child placement and, 107–8; same-race matching and, 108–10
assumptions, 5, 165, 166
asylums, 106
at-risk students, 71–72
attitudes: contemporary, 144; white Christian, 154–55
autoethnographic moments, 57–61
Avoseh, Mejai Bola, 210

Baldwin, James, 30–31, 184, 185, 187
Bangladeshi American Muslims, 155–56
barriers, 253–55
baseline assumptions, 165, 166
beatboxing, 201
beliefs, racial, 40
Bell, Derrick, 25, 33, 151
Bell, Joyce, 179

277

Bell, Lee Anne, 250–51
belonging: of African-Native Americans, 136–41; boundaries of, 57–61; conceptualizations of, 62–63, 63; definitions of, 126, 127; domains of, 58; in higher education, 66–70; political landscapes of, 77–79
Berrey, Ellen, 179
best interest of the child, 8, 107, 112, 113, 121
Between the World and Me (Coates), 175
biases, 105, 134, 243
Bibles, Della, 134
Bilge, Sirma, 217, 219, 229, 236–37
"Bill of Rights for Racially Mixed People" (Root), 36
biology, 45, 46
BIPOC. *See* Black, Indigenous, and other People of Color
birth certificates, 106
Black, Indigenous, and other People of Color (BIPOC), 246, 254
Black Americans, 38, 42, 192, 196–97, 198; resistance, 9; struggles of, 208; violence experienced by, 160; world of, 184
Blackburn, Mollie, 96–97
Black children, in foster care, 111–12
Black culture, 197–98
Black disposability, 27
blackface, digital, 49
Black feminists, 223
Black-ish, 43
Black Lives Matter movement (BLM), 2, 13, 228–29, 236, 240, 254; intersectionality of, 25; principles of, 258–59
Black Muslims, 149, 152–53, 158, 195
Black Nationalism, 199–202, 204
Black queer vernacular, 96, 97, 98
Black religion, 192–93
Black Star, Crescent Moon (Daulatzai), 207–8
Black women, 217, 220, 222, 223, 231–32

Blair, Sam, 22
Bliuc, Ana-Maria, 47
BLM. *See* Black Lives Matter movement
Blockett, Reginald A., 7, 92, 246
Blood Politics (Sturm), 135
blues, 17–18, 24
boarding schools, Native American, 107–8
Boellstorff, Tom, 95–96
Bonilla-Silva, Eduardo, 74
Boston, Massachusetts, 58–59
both/and framework, 117, 217, 230–31, 232, 236
boundaries, of race and belonging, 57–61
The Boundaries of Blackness (Cohen), 94
Bowleg, Lisa, 162, 226
Brace, Charles Loring, 108
Brandt, Joseph, 130
Brockenbrough, Edward, 92
brown, adrienne maree, 256–57
Brunsma, David, 39
brutality, police, 3, 13, 30, 32–33
Buchanan, Lucile, 15
Bush, George H. W., 23
business, of DNA testing, 45–46

Caldwell, Jennifer, 251
capitalism, 14, 23, 95; modifying, 29; racial, 20, 64, 187; regulated, 27, 30
Case, Anna, 26–27, 30
case advocacy, 258
Cass, Vivienne, 86–87
caste, 14, 17, 24
Castells, Manuel, 48
categories, racial, 39, 56
CDC. *See* Centers for Disease Control and Prevention
census, 1, 42, 49, 61, 70, 131; on adoption, 121; designers, 72, 74, 75; questions, 73; recommendations for, 75–77
Census Bureau, US, 38, 42, 74, 131
Centers for Disease Control and Prevention (CDC), 94

certainty, 178; of goodness, 177; of knowledge, 172, 176, 183–84, 188–89; uncertainty, 176, 188, 189, 190, 255
Chamberlain, Alexander Francis, 128, 132–33
change, 220; climate, 247; strategies for, 164; substantive, 29–33
Cherokee Freedmen, 245
Cherokee Nation, 114, 140–41, 143
Chicago Race Riot, 19
children: as adoptable, 118; of immigrants, 59, 108; mass placement of, 107–8
Child Welfare League of America, 109, 111
child welfare services, 105, 106–7, 109, 111
Cho, Sumi, 232
Choctaw Nation, 138–39, 141, 143
choice: forcing, 43; legitimacy of, 45; questions of, 50, 51; race as, 6–7, 36–37, 39–41
Christian hegemony, 150, 159, 160–61, 166–67
Christianity, 149, 150, 153–54
Christians, white: attitudes and interactions of, 154–55; RMPOC interactions with, 155–58
Christonormativity, 154
cipher, 201–2
citizenship, 16, 58, 59–60, 135, 245
civilization, 153–54
civil rights, 76; enforcement, 74, 75, 77; movement, 110; transracial adoption as, 111–12
Civil War, 139, 140
class, 68; indicators of, 70; race and, 6, 14; social, 30; underclass, 25–26
climate change, 247
Clinton, Bill, 23
Clinton, Hillary, 48
coalitions, 2, 9, 226–27; building, 77, 86; challenging, 6, 230; intersectionality informing, 234, 235
Coates, Ta-Nehisi, 175
Cobb, W. Montague, 142

code switching, 115–16
Cohen, Cathy J., 94
Cole, Jefferson, 138–39, 143
college applications, 44
College Board, 68
Collins, Patricia Hill, 56, 63, 89, 93–94, 236–37; on heterogeneity, 235; on intersectionality themes, 217; on power, 219, 229
Collins, Robert Keith, 8, 245
collusion, 16, 160–61
colonialism, settler, 62–66, 95, 151, 152, 153–54
color-blind racism, 65, 68, 74
colorism, 7, 8, 160, 162, 165, 168
color line, 75, 76
Combahee River Collective, 220, 241
commentary, social, 202–7
communities, 2, 149, 244; faith, 164–65, 213; fracturing, 233, 234; of origin, 119–20; RMPOC, 163–64; vulnerable, 76
community college, 67
community service, 174–76
competency: cultural, 183, 184; frameworks for, 258
complexity, of intersectionality, 220–21, 235–36
complicity, 172
conceptualizations: of belonging, 62–63, 63; racial, 40; of social justice, 241
conferences, 222–23
consciousness, 160, 197, 261
consequences, of racial innocence, 183–86
contexts, 3, 4; social, 47–48, 218; of US adoption, 104, 105–6
convergence, interest, 248
conversations, 167–68
counternarratives, 231, 248
counterpublics, 90, 91–92, 98, 99
counter-storytelling, 248
COVID-19 pandemic, 1, 13, 14, 28, 64, 77, 240

Creek Nation, 139–40
Crenshaw, Kimberlé, 152, 165, 223, 227, 229–30, 232, 250
criminality, 24
Crip theory, 249–50
critical engagement, 187
critical pedagogy, 193, 194, 209–10, 211
critical race theory (CRT), 57, 62–66, 247–48
critical reflexivity, 61–62
Cross, William E., Jr., 3, 6, 243, 248
CRT. *See* critical race theory
Cuban Counterpoint (Ortiz), 128
cultural change, of Africans, 127, 128–32; literature on, 132–33; Native American racism and, 133–35
cultural competency, 183, 184
cultural genocide, 118
cultural sociopathy, 23
culture, 5; assessment-driven, 181–82; Black, 197–98; dominant, 229; drive-by, 119; keeping, 117
cyber-racism, 47
Cycle of Liberation, 163, 256

Dakota Access Pipeline, 65
The Dangerous Classes of New York (Brace), 108
Dartmouth College, 154
Darwinism, social, 17
D'Augelli, Anthony, 87
Daulatzai, Sohail, 200, 207–8
Davis, Ada, 134
Davis, Louisa, 139, 145
deaths, of despair, 14, 26–27, 28, 29
Deaton, Angus, 26–27, 30
dehumanization, 22–23, 93
deindustrialization, 23–27, 29–30
Delgado, Daniel, 39
depression, 24
designers, census, 72, 74, 75
despair, deaths of, 14, 26–27, 28, 29
DeVega, Chauncey, 44

development: phases of, 120; racial identity and sexual orientation, 85–87, 88
dialogue, 163, 166, 225
dichotomous mindset, 241–42
digital blackface, 49
Dillon, Frank, 88
disabilities, 249
discrimination: with GI Bill, 20; with transracial adoptees, 119
disidentification, 90, 91
disposability, 13–14, 27
diunital mindset, 241–42
diversity, 177, 227, 252; framing, 179–80, 181; religious, 148; student, 44; in terminology, 6; training, 183–84
DNA Discussion Project, 45
DNA testing, 7, 37, 40; business of, 45–46; popularity of, 45–47; research on, 45; reveals, 47
Dolezal, Rachel, 36–37, 40, 48, 49
domains: of belonging, 58; of power, 219
dominant culture, 229
domination, matrix of, 226
Domination and the Art of Resistance (Scott), 193
Dominican Republic, 58, 79
Dowling, Julie, 60–61
Du Bois, W. E. B., 76, 187
Duran, Antonio, 230
Dyson, Michael Eric, 178

Eck, Diana, 148, 166–67
ecological models, for QTPOC identity, 87–88, 99
economy: depression-like, 24; mixed, 28
ecumenism, 149
education, 241; city, 18–19; critical pedagogy in, 209–10; K-12, 15, 17, 31, 211; postsecondary, 99; prisons and, 32; self-education, 259–60; social movement for, 15; support for, 31. *See also* higher education
educators, 99

emancipation, 15–16
emergent strategy, 256–57
empiricism, 83, 90–91
enforcement, civil rights, 74, 75
engagement: critical, 187; RMPOC self-perception and, 159–63
Enlightenment Narrative, 184
epistemic violence, 60
equity lifts, 67
Erikson, Erik, 137
essentialism, 42, 233
ethnic fraud, 36
eugenics, 83
exclusion, 59, 60, 67
experiences, 4, 5, 56; community service, 174–76; filtering, 48; lived, 138–41, 145; of privilege, 226; resistance to intersectionality and, 225–27; of RMPOC, 150
expression, 201

Facebook, 48–49, 116
Factor Model of Multiracial Identity (FMMI) (Wijeyesinghe), 36, 41
faith communities, 164–65, 213
family, 8, 64–65, 104–5, 115, 244
Farrakhan, Louis, 198, 199, 200, 204
Feagin, Joe, 182
Federal Housing Association (FHA), 126
feminists, Black, 223
Fenwick, Tara, 210
FHA. *See* Federal Housing Association
Filipino Americans, 38, 41
filter, social media as, 48–49
financial aid, federal, 69–70
Finding Your Roots, 47
Fisher v. University of Texas, 44
Five Civilized Tribes, 127
Five Percenters, 203–4
flexible solidarity, 77
Flores, Nina, 260
Floyd, George, 1, 13, 14, 23, 28, 236
Floyd-Thomas, Juan M., 198, 206–7

FMMI. *See* Factor Model of Multiracial Identity
forms, "race question" on, 43
Foste, Zak, 9, 244
Foster, Laurence, 129, 132, 134–35, 136, 144
foster care, 105–6, 110, 111–13
framing: diversity, 179–80, 181; minimization of racism, 74; oppression, 151–54; social justice, 245–46
Frankenberg, Ruth, 60
fraud, ethnic, 36
freestyling, 201
Friere, Paulo, 193, 209, 212, 220, 256
funding, higher education, 71–72

gangs, 24
gaps: perceived, 226; race-gender-class, 70; in wealth, 20–22, 21
Gates, Henry Louis, Jr., 186–87
gaybonics, 96–97
Genetic Ancestry Project, 45
genetics, 45. *See also* DNA testing
genocide, 95, 118
GI Bill, 14, 19–20, 28, 32, 126
globalization, 240, 260
GOA. *See* Government Office of Accountability, US
goals, 257
goodness: certainty of, 177; moral, 173, 175; performative spectacles of, 156–57
Government Office of Accountability, US (GOA), 76
governments, 244–46
graduations, 68–69, 69
Grande, Sandy, 36
Grayson, Mary, 139, 145
groups, social, 218, 229
Grutter v. Bollinger, 66
Grzanka, Patrick, 226

Hallberg, Emma, 49
Hallowell, A. Irving, 129, 142
Harlem Renaissance, 18, 25

Harro, Bobbie, 163, 166, 256
Hartmann, Douglas, 179
Harvard University, 154
healing, 163, 164–65, 256
health care, 27, 28, 31
hegemony: Christian, 150–52, 159, 160–61, 166–67; narratives of, 66–70
heterocisnormativity, 84, 85, 90, 98
heterogeneity, 37, 235
heteronormativity, 249
heteropatriarchy, 7, 84–85; pillars of, 95; QTPOC racialized, 93–95
heterosexism, 250
hierarchy, of oppression, 228
higher education, 31–32, 44, 255; belonging in, 66–70; federal financial aid in, 69–70; funding formulas, 71–72; graduations, 68–69, 69
Hip Hop, 9, 24, 25, 193; activism, 194, 195–96; as critical pedagogy, 209–10, 211; as global, 207–9; Islam and Black Nationalism intersecting with, 199–202; Islamic-based ideologies in, 195, 198–99; as male-dominated, 205; as oral tradition, 196–98; signifying in, 202–4; as social commentary, 202–7; Sunni Islam in, 206–7; as transformational learning, 211–13
history: intersectionality and, 230–33; reinventing, 204, 205; of slavery, 15; of transracial adoption, 106–12; US, 6; of white supremacy, 186–87, 190
History of the Negro Race in America (Williams), 130–31
HIV/AIDs epidemic, 93–94
Homel, Michael, 19
homonationalism, 84
homosexuality, 83–84, 86
hooks, bell, 97–98, 175, 178–79, 260–61
houseboy, 139, 143
humility, 175, 176, 182, 188, 189, 190
Hutchinson, Darren, 94
hypodescent, laws of, 38

IAP. *See* Indian Adoption Project
iconography, American, 156
ICWA. *See* Indian Child Welfare Act
identification, racial, 39
identities, 246–47; integration of, 161–63; mixed race, 41; multiple, 220, 223; politics of, 225; racially ambiguous, 41; resistance to intersectionality and, 225–27; situational, 36; social, 2, 5, 217, 254; Utopian African, 205; variations in, 16–18
identity, racial, 3, 39, 243–44; choice and, 2, 6–7, 36–37; development, 85–87, 88; intersectionality of, 50–51; questions about, 37–38
identity models, QTPOC: ecological approaches to, 87–88, 99; multidimensional and intersectional, 88–90, 99; single-category, 85–87. *See also specific models*
IEPA. *See* Interethnic Provisions Act
illness, mental, 86
IMAN. *See* Inner-City Muslim Action Network
IMMDI. *See* Intersectional Model of Multiple Dimensions of Identity
IMMI. *See* Intersectional Model of Multiracial Identity
immigrants, children of, 59, 108
immigration, 59, 150
imperialism, 208
impression management, 155–57, 162
incarceration, 32, 200, 206
inclusion, 230–33
income, graduation rates and, 68–69, 69
Indian Adoption Project (IAP), 110, 111, 115
Indian Child Welfare Act (ICWA), 111, 114
Indianization, 129, 142, 143, 144
individualism, 174, 186
IndiVisible (Smithsonian exhibit), 127, 138
inequality, 1, 76; influence of, 4; occupations fighting, 253; social, 30, 218–19;

systems of, 2, 5, 216, 233; Thorne on fighting, 253
inequities, 251
infrastructure, 31
Inner-City Muslim Action Network (IMAN), 196, 213
innocence, proving, 156–57. See also racial innocence
institutionalized racism, 126
institutions, 244–46, 254–55
insulation, racial, 178–79, 187
integration, identity, 161–63
intellectual agency, 92
interactions: RMPOC and white Christian, 155–58; strategies for, 156; white Christian, 154–55
intercountry adoption. See transnational adoption
interest convergence, 248
Interethnic Provisions Act (IEPA), 112, 113, 114
intergenerational families, 64–65
intermarriage, 131, 141
internalized oppression, 160–61
interpersonal congruency theory, 86–87
intersectional identity models, QTPOC, 88–90, 99
intersectionality, 4, 9–10, 57, 62–66, 216, 246–47; and Black women, 216, 217, 223, 224, 230–32; of BLM, 25; coalitions informed by, 234, 235; complexity of, 220–21, 235–36; core tenets of, 217–20, 221, 231, 237; Crip theory, QueerCrit and, 249; on power and social inequality, 218–19; of racial identity, 50–51; relationality within, 217–18; social context and, 218; social justice and, 219–20; stories about, 221–24; themes of, 217–21
intersectionality, resistance to, 224–35, 237; history, ownership, and inclusion in, 230–33; identity, social location and experience in, 225–27; multiple inter-related systems and, 228–30; theory and practice in, 233–35
intersectional microaggressions, 158
Intersectional Model of Multiple Dimensions of Identity (IMMDI) (Jones and Abes), 89–90
Intersectional Model of Multiracial Identity (IMMI), 223
intersectional oppression, 148, 152–53, 159, 162–63, 167
interviews, 26, 158, 177, 179, 183–84
Islam, 149, 158, 160, 166; Hip Hop and, 195, 198–99, 206–7; Hip Hop and Black Nationalism intersecting with, 199–202; Hip Hop and global, 207–9; orthodox, 206; as resistance, 192; as social commentary, 202–7

Jackson, Bailey W., 2, 3, 236
Jackson, Romeo, 230
Jacobs, Margaret, 107
Jacobson, Heather, 117
Jefferson, Thomas, 131
Jews, 18, 126, 163, 226
jihad (struggle), 198
"*jihad* of words," 198, 208
jobs, 31
Johnson, Guy, 16
Johnson, Patrick, 96, 97
Johnston-Guerrero, Marc P., 6–7, 244
Jones, Susan, 89, 233
Jourian, T. J., 91
justice: procedural, 251; racial, 2, 3, 8, 226–27; strategies for, 164; transracial adoption, 116–17, 118, 119, 120, 121. See also social justice

Katznelson, Ira, 19–20
Kendi, Ibram, 4, 119, 153, 154, 165, 185
Khan, Khizr, 157
Kim, JaeRan, 8, 244
King, Martin Luther, Jr., 28, 30–31
kinship, 137, 141–42, 145

Kivel, Paul, 162–63
knowledge, 4, 261; certainty of, 172, 176, 183–84, 188–89; resistance to, 5
Koreans, 109–10
Krug, Jessica, 37
Ku Klux Klan, 16–17

language, 5–6, 135, 241, 252
The Language of Blood (Trenka), 115
The Last Poets, 198, 199
Latinas and Latinos of Mixed Ancestry (LOMA), 49
laws: of hypodescent, 38; miscegenation, 1
leadership, 177, 188, 252, 259
Leap, William, 95–96
learning, 235, 255; informal, 209–10; transformational, 211–13
legibility, QTPOC sexual language and, 95–98
legitimacy: of choice, 45; presidential, 66
lenses, 1, 247–50
Leonardo, Zeus, 180
Leong, Nancy, 187
Levine, Lawrence, 197
liberalism, 248
liberation, 163, 209, 212, 213, 256
liberatory practice, 256
lifeways, 133, 137
Lincoln, Abraham, 16
Lindsey, Felix, 140, 142
lived experiences, 138–41, 145
logic, 72, 74
LOMA. *See* Latinas and Latinos of Mixed Ancestry
López, Nancy, 7, 245
Lopez, Thomas, 49
Lorde, Audre, 161–62, 228, 234, 256
Loving v. Virginia, 109
Luft, Rachel, 37, 226, 229, 230, 247
lynching, 22, 23

Magolda, Marcia B. Baxter, 212
Malcolm X, 200–201, 204, 206, 208
Manning, Kathleen, 251–52
manufacturing, 23
marginalization, 201, 208
Markle, Meghan, 42–43
Martin, Trayvon, 117
MASC. *See* Multiracial Americans of Southern California
masculinities, 18, 25, 92
mass child placement, 107–8
matching, same-race, 108–10
matrix, of domination, 226
Maultsby, Portia, 197
Mayo, Cris, 235, 236
MBL. *See* Movement for Black Lives
McCall, Leslie, 232
McCready, Lance, 92
McEwen, Marylu, 89
McLaren, Peter, 185
McNair, Chaney, 140–41, 143
meaning, intersubjective, 96
meaning-making, 161
media. *See* social media
membership recognition, 97
mental illness, 86
MEPA. *See* Multiethnic Placement Act
Metzenbaum, Howard, 112
Mexican Americans, 61
microaggressions, 157–58, 162
mindsets, dichotomous and diunital, 241–42
minimization of racism frame, 74
minimum wage, 14, 21, 32
Mir, Pedro, 58
miscegenation laws, 1
misogyny, 25
misrecognition, 157–58, 162
Mitchell-Kernan, Claudia, 202–3
mixed economy, 28
mixed heritage, 36, 41, 44, 89
Mixed-ish (2019), 43–44
mixed race, 36, 41, 44, 60, 61, 75, 109, 142
models, stage-based, 86–87. *See also* identity models, QTPOC

Mohawk Nation, 130
Moradi, Bonnie, 88
moral goodness, 173, 175
Morrison, Toni, 180–81
Mos Def, 206–7
Movement for Black Lives (MBL), 258–59
Mubashshir, Debra Washington, 192–93
multidimensional identity models, QTPOC, 88–90, 99
Multiethnic Placement Act (MEPA), 112, 113–14
multiple identities, 220, 223
multiple systems, 228–30
Multiracial Americans of Southern California (MASC), 49
multiracial individuals, 36, 41–45
multiracial students, 44
Muñoz, José E., 83, 90, 91
Muslims: Bangladeshi American, 155–56; Black, 149, 152–53, 158, 195; IMAN, 196, 213; South Asian American, 194; Third World, 207, 208

NABSW. *See* National Association of Black Social Workers
Nanticoke Nation, 135
Narragansett Nation, 135
narratives, 4; counternarratives, 231, 248; Enlightenment Narrative, 184; hegemonic, 66–70; personal, 194–96; WPA slave, 132, 133, 134, 138–41
Nash, Jennifer C., 219, 231
National Association of Black Social Workers (NABSW), 110–11
National Sikh Campaign (NSC), 156
National Urban League/African American Pulse, 113
Nation of Islam, 204
Native Americans, 8, 127, 245; African cultural change and racism of, 133–35; African-Native American being/belonging and racism of, 136–41; Africans contacting with, 129–30; boarding schools for, 107–8; contemporary attitudes of, 144; populations of, 130; racism of, 136–41. *See also specific nations*
Navajo Nation, 64–65
New Negro, 18, 25
New Perspectives on Racial Identity Development (Wijeyesinghe and Jackson, B.), 2
new racism, 93
New York Times, 3–4, 20, 29, 46, 157
nihilism, 26
non-citizens, 74–75
nonprofit organizations, 212
"nonracist white," 177
Notes on the State of Virginia (Jefferson), 131
NSC. *See* National Sikh Campaign

Obama, Barack, 2, 42, 65–66
Ocampo, Anthony, 38
occupations, 253
Ocklbary, Julia Grimes Jones, 141, 142
Office of Management and Budget, US (OMB), 74, 75
one-drop rule, 38
openness, 241
oppression, 4, 87, 89, 119, 250; framing, 151–54; hierarchy of, 228; internalized, 160–61; intersectional, 148, 152–53, 159, 162–63, 167; systems of, 221, 233, 234, 235
oral tradition, 196–98, 199, 205
origins, 56, 72, 74, 119–20
orphanage, 106
orphan trains, 107–8
orthodox Islam, 206
Ortiz, Fernando, 128
otherness, 7, 26, 60, 155, 157

pandemic, 1, 13, 14, 64, 240
paradigms, 241–42, 257
the past, 5

paternalism, 105–6
Patton, Lori, 92, 250
Patton, Stacey, 93
pedagogy, critical, 193, 194, 209–10, 211
Pedagogy of the Oppressed (Freire), 209
performative spectacles, of goodness, 156–57
Perkins, William Eric, 198–99, 204
permanence, of racism, 25, 33, 248
Perry, Imani, 201–2, 203
personal narratives, 194–96
perspectives, 2, 10, 240
Peter (interviewee), 59–60
Pew Research Center, 166
Pickens, William, 15
plantations, 15–16
pluralism, religious, 150
poetry, 195, 200
poets, 198–99
police brutality, 3, 13, 30, 32–33
political activism, 166
politics, 240; of belonging, 77–79; identity, 225; QTPOC sexual, 93–95
Poor People's March on Washington, 28
Poor Righteous Teachers, 204–5
Pope, Raechele L., 10
populations, 130, 131
Pose, 91
power, 8, 38, 46, 229; domains of, 219; in family making, 104–5; global dynamics of, 56; intersectionality on, 218–19; relational, 5; structures, 1; systemic, 4
practice: of intersectionality, 233–35; liberatory, 256
praxis, 193, 211–13, 240
presidential elections, US, 48, 66
prisons, 32, 200, 206
private adoption, 106
privilege, 8, 87, 89, 180–81, 185, 222, 226. *See also* white privilege
procedural justice, 251
professionalism, 166
Progressive Era, 106, 108

property, whiteness as, 248
protests, 1, 2, 65
proximity, relational, 120
Puar, Jasbir, 84
public adoptions, 105–6
Public Enemy, 204
public transcripts, 193

queer and trans* people of color (QTPOC), 7, 83, 254; separatism of, 84; sexual language and legibility of, 95–98; sexual politics and racialized heteropatriarchy, 93–95. *See also* identity models, QTPOC
Queer critical theory (QueerCrit), 249–50
Queering the Color Line (Somerville), 83
Queer of Color Worldmaking, 7, 85, 90–92, 98–99
Quinn, Naomi, 136

race: belonging and boundaries of, 57–61; as choice, 6–7, 36–37, 39–41; class and, 6, 14; complicating, 242–47, 260; lens of, 1; rules of, 37–39, 50. *See also specific topics*
racial ascription, 39
racial beliefs, 40
racial capitalism, 20, 64, 187
racial categories, 39, 56
racial conceptualizations, 40
racial essentialism, 42
racial fluidity, 42
racial identification, 39
racial identity. *See* identity, racial
racial innocence, white, 9, 172, 190; conditions of, 177–82; consequences of, 183–86; guarding against, 186–89; investment in, 173–76
racial insulation, 178–79, 187
racialization: of everyone, 226; of religion, 155
racialized heteropatriarchy, QTPOC, 93–95

racial justice, 2, 3, 8, 226–27
racial literacy skills, 119
racially ambiguous individuals, 41–45
racial purity, 46
racial socialization, 119, 243
racism, 151, 152, 178, 228; anti-Blackness and, 242; Christianity, colonialism and, 153–54; color-blind, 65, 68, 74; complicating, 242–47, 260; cyber-racism, 47; institutionalized, 126; as lens, 1; naming, 172; Native American, 133–41; new, 93; permanence of, 25, 33, 248; reverse, 112; scientific, 83–84; social class inequities and, 30; in transracial adoption, 104–5, 112–21, 122; urgency of, 222
Rainey, Ma, 18
rapping, 9, 198, 199, 200
Rashad, Kameelah Mu'Min, 8–9, 246
readability, 41
readiness, 254
reading, 231–32
recognition: membership, 97; misrecognition, 157–58, 162
Reconceptualized Model of Multiple Dimensions of Identity (RMMDI) (Abes, Jones and McEwen), 89, 90
reconstruction, 16, 135, 181, 187
Red Table Talk, 116
reflexivity, 61–62, 78
Refugee Relief Act, 109
regulated capitalism, 27, 30
relationality, 217–18
relational power, 5
relational proximity, 120
religion, 8–9; Black, 192–93; diversity of, 148; racialization of, 155; redefinitions of, 193. *See also specific topics*
religious hegemony, 151, 152. *See also* Christian hegemony
Religiously Minoritized People of Color (RMPOC), 8–9, 148, 154, 167–68; burden of, 152; experiences of, 150;

microaggressions towards, 157–58; self-perception and engagement among, 159–63; strategies for, 163–64; white Christian interactions with, 155–58
religious pluralism, 150
Renn, Kristen A., 7, 88, 246
reparations, 30–31
residential apartheid, 20, 22
resistance, 167, 216; Black Americans, 9; everyday, 193; to intersectionality, 224–35; Islam as, 192; to knowledge, 5
reverse racism, 112
Reynolds, Amy L., 10
ritual, 201
RMMDI. *See* Reconceptualized Model of Multiple Dimensions of Identity
RMPOC. *See* Religiously Minoritized People of Color
Robinson, Chazz, 10
Robinson, William, 83–84
Rockquemore, Kerry Ann, 39
roles, social, 144–45
Roosevelt, Franklin, 20
Roosevelt, Theodore, 83
Root, Maria, 36, 88
Roque, Frank, 158
Rose, Tricia, 196, 205
ross, kihana, 242
rules: naming, 50; of race, 37–39, 50; rethinking, 50–51
Rust Belt, 25

Sacks, Karen Brodkin, 126–27, 142
safety nets, social, 27–28, 30, 33
Sandahl, Carrie, 249
SAT. *See* Scholastic Aptitude Test
Scholastic Aptitude Test (SAT), 68
science, social, 72, 74, 137
scientific racism, 83–84
Scott, James C., 193
segregation, 48, 134
self-authorship, 211, 212

self-education, 259–60
self-perception, 152, 159–63
self-reflexivity, 78
self-understanding, 137–38
self-work, 185, 254
Seminoles, 132, 134
separatism, QTPOC, 84
service, community, 174–76
settler colonialism, 62–66, 95, 151, 152, 153–54
sexism, 250
sexuality, 17, 25, 83–84, 86
sexual language, QTPOC legibility and, 95–98
sexual orientation, 7, 85–87, 88
sexual politics, QTPOC, 93–95
signifying, 202–4
Sikh Americans, 156, 157–58
Silva, Jennifer, 26, 28, 31
simultaneity, 62–63
single-category identity models, QTPOC, 85–87
singularity, strategic, 37
Sioux Nation, 65
situational identities, 36
slaveholders, 132, 136
slavery, 15, 93, 95, 127, 129–30
slaves, WPA narratives of, 132, 133, 134, 138–41
Slave Theatre, 149
Smith, Andrea, 37, 95
Smith, Bessie, 18
social activism, 3
social class, 30
social commentary, 202–7
social concerns, 217–18
social context, 47–48, 218
social Darwinism, 17
social groups, 218, 229
social identities, 2, 5, 217, 254
social inequality, 30, 218–19
socialization, 136, 137; mechanisms, 166; racial, 119, 243

social justice, 10, 51, 211, 219–20, 233–34; advocacy efforts for, 257–58; challenges to, 253–55; conceptualizing, 241; CRT and, 248; emergent strategy for, 256–57; Flores on, 260; forms of, 253; institutions and governments framing, 245–46; liberatory practice for, 256; limitations of, 251–52; new directions for, 255–61; paths toward, 252–53; understanding, 250–51
social location, 225–27
social media, 1–2, 3; curating, 49–50; DNA testing reveals on, 47; as filter, 48–49; pervasiveness, 47–50; social contexts collapsed by, 47–48
social movements, 15, 16
social roles, 144–45
social safety nets, 27–28, 30, 33
social sciences, 72, 74, 137
social statuses, 63, 70
social structures, 243–44
social work, 108, 113
society, US, 165–66
sociopathy, cultural, 23
Sodhi, Balbi Singh, 158
solidarity, 63, 77, 160
Somé, Malidoma Patrice, 161
Somerville, Siobhan B., 83
South Asian Muslim Americans, 194
Spanish, 57
Speaking in Queer Tongues (Leap and Boellstorff), 95–96
Speck, Frank, 129, 135
sports, 22
stage-based models, 86–87
Standards for Adoption Service (manual), 109
Statement on Race and Race Prejudice, UN, 78
status, social, 63, 70
stereotypes, 115, 117, 119, 157, 228
stewardship, 233
Stewart, D-L, 8–9, 246, 252

stigmatized solidarity, 160
Stony the Road (Gates), 186–87
stories, 221–24
strategic singularity, 37
strategies, 231, 234; for change and justice, 164; emergent, 256–57; for faith communities, 164–65; for RMPOC, 163–64; for US society, 165–66
street life, 24, 29
street race, 61–62, 75, 77
stress, 26, 29, 155
structures: infrastructure, 31; power, 1; social, 243–44
struggle (*jihad*), 198
students: defining at-risk, 71–72; diversity, 44
Sturm, Circe, 135
subjectivities, 227
substantive change, 29–33
Sullivan, Shannon, 184
Sunni Islam, 149
Sunni Muslims, 206–7
support, for education, 31
Supreme Alphabet, 203
Supreme Mathematics, 203
surveys, 74–75, 113
systems, 232; of inequality, 2, 5, 216, 233; intersectionality and multiple, 228–30; of oppression, 221, 233, 234, 235; of power, 4

Tachine, Amanda, 46
talking back, 98
teachers, 78
Tears We Cannot Stop (Dyson), 178
technology, 2, 17, 208, 210
tenets, of intersectionality, 221, 231, 237
tensions, 10, 216, 224
tenure, 67
terminology, 6, 85
Third World, Muslim, 207, 208
Thompson, Audrey, 176
Thorne, Beth, 253

tolerance, 157
Tomlinson, Barbara, 232
tools, for social justice, 259–61
Toporek, Rebecca, 258
traditions: non-static nature of, 197; oral, 196–98, 199, 205
trans*. *See* queer and trans* people of color
transaction, adoption as, 104
transcripts, 193
transculturalization, 129, 138, 142–43, 145–46
transculturation, 128–29
transformational learning, 211–13
transnational adoption, 105, 106, 109, 121, 122
transracial adoptees, 115–16, 117, 119
transracial adoption. *See* adoption, transracial
Trenka, Jane Jeong, 115
TribalCrit, 65
A Tribe Called Quest, 206, 207
Trump, Donald, 1, 2, 26, 28, 48, 159
Tucker, Angela, 116
Tulsa Massacre, 17
Turner, Richard Brent, 198
Tuskegee syphilis study, 22

UN. *See* United Nations
uncertainty, 176, 188, 189, 190, 255
underclass, 25–26
United Nations (UN), 7, 77–79
United States (US), 244–45; adoption in, 105–6; Census Bureau, 38, 42, 74, 131; citizenship, 58, 59–60; GOA, 76; history, 6; OMB, 74, 75; presidential elections, 48, 66; settler colonialism, 151
urban, becoming, 16–18
Utopian African identity, 205

Vera, Elizabeth, 251
vernacular, Black queer, 96, 97, 98
violence, 60, 160

visibility, 148, 229
Vitolo-Haddad, CV, 37
vulnerable communities, 76

wage, minimum, 32
Warner, Michael, 91
wealth, gaps in, 20–22, 21
Weapons of the Weak (Scott), 193
welfare, 105, 106–7, 109, 111
white Christians. *See* Christians, white
White Hawk, Sandy, 116
white innocence. *See* racial innocence
"White Man's Guilt" (Baldwin), 184
whiteness, 158, 173, 178–79, 181, 185, 187–90, 248
white people, 172–73, 178–79
white privilege, 180–81, 185, 222; measures of, 21; proximal, 115, 121
white supremacists, 46
white supremacy, 90, 151, 174; history of, 186–87, 190; pillars of, 95
Who Do You Think You Are?, 47

Wijeyesinghe, Charmaine, 2, 9–10, 36, 39–40, 88, 246
Williams, George Washington, 130–31
Wilson, Woodrow, 16
wokeness, 28
women, Black, 217, 220, 222, 223, 231–32
Works Progress Administration (WPA), 127, 132, 133, 134, 138–41
worldmaking, 7, 84, 85, 90–92, 96–97, 98–99
worldviews, 182, 240, 241
World War II, 19–20, 77, 78, 109, 126
Worthington, Roger, 88
WPA. *See* Works Progress Administration
Writer, Jeanette, 245

Yancy, George, 172, 173
Yuval-Davis, Nira, 62, 63

Zambrana, Ruth, 67
ZIP codes, 68

www.ingramcontent.com/pod-product-compliance
Lightning Source LLC
Chambersburg PA
CBHW020357080526
44584CB00014B/1060